DISCARDED

D0945177

The Portable Theater

STEINWAY
HALL.

THE PORTABLE THEATER

American Literature & the Nineteenth-Century Stage

Alan L. Ackerman Jr.

The Johns Hopkins University Press
BALTIMORE & LONDON

Printed in the United States of America on acid-free paper
9 8 7 6 5 4 3 2 1

The Johns Hopkins University Press
2715 North Charles Street
Baltimore, Maryland 21218-4363
www.press.jhu.edu

Library of Congress Cataloging-in-Publication Data
will be found at the end of this book.
A catalog record for this book is available from the British Library.

ISBN 0-8018-6161-6

FRONTISPIECE: Edwin Forrest's last appearance
in New York, Steinway Hall, 1872.

FOR MY PARENTS

Alan Louis Ackerman &

Barbara Berkman Ackerman

O! who'd believe where yet is heard
The screaming of the frightened bird, . . .
Yes—now where late the forest stood,
In Nature's wildest solitude,
Where all was but a Prairie sod
Which human foot but seldom trod—
We hail the Drama's spotless page
And breathe its pathos from the stage.

—from an address, written by Judge Thomson, spoken by Mr. Forbes, on the opening of the New Theatre, Market Square, Texas and Texas Register, *27 February 1839*

We are continually acting a part in
a more interesting drama than any written.

—HENRY DAVID THOREAU
A Week on the Concord and Merrimack Rivers

Contents

Preface

THEATER, Tocqueville laments in 1840, is inherently democratic. The spectator at the theater has no time to consult his memory or the judgment of his betters. Moreover, the spectator's betters sit above him or even beside him, equally "surprised" by the impression conveyed by the performance. Thus, "at the theatre men of cultivation and literary attainments have always had more difficulty than elsewhere in making their taste prevail over that of the people and in preventing themselves from being carried away by the latter. The pit has frequently made laws for the boxes" (1990, 79–80). Spectators at the theater, according to Tocqueville, do not seek the pleasures of the mind but the keen emotions of the heart; they do not want to be educated but to hear something that concerns themselves. For this reason in particular, "no portion of literature is connected by closer or more numerous ties with the present condition of society than the drama" (83). The drama may be a kind of literature, but, in the unruly space of the theater, subjected and responsible to the immediate reactions of a social body, the drama cannot be "literary."

Theatergoing Americans, Tocqueville then argues, tend to manifest the propensities that he has described, but, he cautions, as of the 1830s, there is yet curiously little evidence of a thriving theater in America. Americans, from his limited range of reference, seem to indulge in theatrical entertainments only with the greatest reserve, a fact Tocqueville attributes both to the influence of Puritan ancestors and to his sense that there are "no dramatic subjects in a country which has witnessed no great political catastrophe and in which love invariably leads by a straight and easy road to matrimony." Americans seem concerned primarily with making money and going to church on Sunday. While there is a deep element of truth in Tocqueville's claims about theater and democracy, his sense that theater did not, and could not, thrive in the United States is a function of both narrowness of scope and his bias against a cultural form so immediately susceptible to popular demands. Theater was not institutionalized or publicly subsidized in America, as it was in France, where, most notably in the Théâtre Français, dramatic standards were developed and practiced rigorously. Tocqueville complains that the number of authors, spectators, and theatrical representations in a democracy will be composed of "elements so different and scattered in so many different places" that they will not "acknowledge the same rules or submit to the same laws." Yet he is unable to follow the implications of this insight.

Theater in mid-nineteenth-century America was, in fact, a pervasive form of popular culture and an important forum for public life. Historians stress the congregation and interaction of diverse social classes particularly in the antebellum theater.[1] American theater, they argue, was a barometer of the culture's concerns and a microcosm of American democracy. In *The Guide to the Stage,* a handbook for would-be actors first published in 1827, Leman T. Rede lists well over eighty permanent theaters scattered across America. "Wherever emigration builds up a town or city," Rede concludes, "there rises up a Temple of the Drama, to hold the mirror up to nature" (17). Crews of strolling actors followed or, more aptly, shared the westward trails of the pioneers. One company bought a broadhorn and floated down the Allegheny River playing songs from *The Beggar's Opera* at solitary cabins. As Constance Rourke has argued in *American Humor: A Study of the National Character* (1931), "Americans had . . . emerged as a theatrical race" (106–10). But Rourke makes a clear distinction between the "theatrical" and that which constitutes the "drama." And in *American Drama: The Bastard Art* (1997) Susan Harris Smith has documented the way in which "American drama historically has been the most devalued and overlooked area in American literary studies" (10). Most literary critics persist either in following Tocqueville's lead and disparaging theater for being unliterary and anti-intellectual or ignoring its cultural significance altogether.[2]

In this book I consider the relationship between theater and literature in nineteenth-century America. I have chosen five authors who represent important aspects of theater in diverse genres and in different generations. Other major figures in American literature could well be included, but Walt Whitman, Herman Melville, William Dean Howells, Louisa May Alcott, and Henry James most clearly exemplify the range of ways in which American theater has been *displaced.* In a society in which "legitimate" theater is a weak institution, various genre distinctions may be blurred, and theater may still play an important role in intellectual life and literary production. Theater in America represented an important point of intersection for various cultural forms, including not only oratory and opera but also novels, poems, and essays. Therefore, key changes within American culture in general and in American literature in particular can better be appreciated by attending to changes in theater, both in dramatic theory and in theatrical practice.

Theater in nineteenth-century America played a crucial role in the process by which men and women imagined their relations as individual subjects to a public, "objective" reality. Unlike other modern cultural forms with literary content, such as novels, poems, or essays, theater *only* happens in the presence of other people. A theatrical event, therefore, is necessarily social, but the form of the social experience in different kinds of theater may range widely, from a feeling of community to a sense of isolation, from antagonism to complacency. For this reason theater, studied in its relation to literary history, can foreground questions about the public or private nature of literature. Although dramas tend to be consumed in different ways than novels or poems, their performance and mode of consumption are commonly represented in other kinds of literature. The significance of these representations may be both thematic and formal, both aesthetic and ethical. In all of these ways, from the poetry of Whitman to the fiction of James, theater has conferred its benefits on genres other than drama.

In the following chapters I describe how two distinctive dramaturgies both pervade thinking about theater and shape notions of social life from roughly 1830 to 1900. The first of these is melodrama, an artistic mode and worldview in which the individual is understood to be the locus of a play of cosmic forces, particularly moral forces, that are transindividual. Melodrama, as a result, is highly ostentatious, gesturing through various media, including verbal language and the material body, at truths beyond the immediate context of either language or the body. In being gestural and transindividual, melodrama is inherently public. In the second half of the nineteenth century notions of dramatic realism developed which relocated dramatic interest in interior states of consciousness and processes of individual psychology. Action in the realist theater shifted to domestic situations and became self-consciously private. In the exceptionally theatrical culture of nineteenth-century America, theater raises questions about the parameters of selfhood, origins and authenticity of character, and the concern of many to designate space for moral action, especially in regard to the responsibilities of audience.

The relationship of theater to ethical questions, as well as evidence of theater's widespread popularity, is clearly manifested in the intensity of contemporary debates about it, debates that also indicate the privileged status of theater as a cultural form. In *Acting Naturally: Mark Twain in the Culture of Performance* (1995) Randall Knoper vividly describes the immediacy of theatrical performances in the world of Mark Twain, in which "the oppositions between staging and realization, posing and expression, broke down" (2). Twain himself emphatically defended the theater's capacity for combining amusement with instruction. Writing for the *Galaxy* in 1871, for example, Twain spends his fury on a minister who refused to bury an actor: "This minister's legitimate, recognized and acceptable business is to *tell* people calmly, coldly, and in stiff, written sentences, from the pulpit, to go and do right, be just, be merciful, be charitable. And his congregation forgets it all between church and home. But for fifty years it was George Holland's business, on the stage, to *make* his audience go and do right, and be just, merciful, and charitable—because by his living, breathing, feeling pictures he showed them what it *was* to do these things, and *how* to do them" (128). The theater's moral power, in this portrait, resides in the fact that it not only represents but *presents* reality. Whether antagonist or advocate, all seemed to agree that the theater presented a reality that was somehow more real than real life, a curious deviation from the Platonic tradition of antitheatricalism.[3] Moncure D. Conway, an early go-between of Emerson and Whitman and, in 1857, a Unitarian minister in Cincinnati, claims that, though the clergy anticipated the theater's "entire destruction . . . yet God does not side with them, but rather it would seem with the theatre."[4]

Theater was understood less as a particular space than as a set of conditions. Plays were staged in churches and museums and on steamboats, but there was also a strong sense that even the wharves and the streets themselves could function as a kind of theater.[5] For example, when Dion Boucicault arrived in New York in 1853, he found that "it was not a city. It was a theatre. It was a huge fair. Bunting of all nationalities and of no nationality was flaunting over the streets" (Fawkes 78). As the period's leading playwright, Boucicault's use of theater as a metaphor may be unsurprising. There is an appropriateness in describing New York and America itself as a theater, rather than merely "theatrical." Theater, and particularly *the* theater, implies a certain type of designated and delimited social space. American public life, however, is remarkable for its continual deconstruction of the notion that that (or any) space is limited. Of course, this reappraisal of theatrical space is in part a function of the fact that America itself was a space not thought to be delimited. "The world is a fit theatre to-day," writes Thoreau in 1840, "in which any part may be acted" (*Journal* 1:129).

But what are the defining characteristics of this theater, and precisely *where* is theater if it is not in *the* theater? Recent work in American theater history, as in the burgeoning field of "performance studies," has increasingly focused on patterns of behavior and modes of human action outside of playhouses and of the arts in general. The application of the metaphor of theatricality to forms of social experience that appear highly self-conscious, imitative, or self-reflexive has been characteristic of widely ranging critical studies in the humanities and social sciences for the past fifty years. In *A Grammar of Motives* (1945) Kenneth Burke coined the term *dramatism* to describe his study of human motives: "Being developed from the analysis of drama, [the dramatistic method] treats language and thought primarily as modes of action" (xxii). More recently, theater historians, like theorists of "performativity," speak of "performing" gender, race, and class.[6] In *Theatre Culture in America, 1825–1869* (1997) Rosemarie K. Bank explains, "Theatre culture displays historical spaces of production, consumption, change and appropriation, but also insists upon class as a performance, ideology as a creation, and the 'authentic' as the most compelling deception of all" (8). As richly illuminating as such studies often are, they tend to confront two principal problems: first, though the subject matter may be historical, the historicity of the scholar's terminology is often neglected; second, since there is no space outside the operation of theatricality or performance, the status of theatrical art is either diminished or unaccounted for.

The present study seeks to adhere rigorously to historically contingent theatrical idioms, that is, to a language derived from the actual theaters of nineteenth-century America and employed recognizably by the authors who enjoyed performances there. In this regard I am deeply indebted to Stephen Greenblatt's notion of a "poetics of culture." In *Renaissance Self-Fashioning* (1980) Greenblatt reads literature as functioning within a concrete historical situation in three interlocking ways: "as a manifestation of the concrete behavior of its particular author, as itself the expression of the codes by which behavior is shaped, and as a reflection upon those codes" (4). I also investigate five aspects or constitutive features through which American theater manifests itself: (1) the forms taken by the drama (the written play-text), (2) the human voice or "utterance," (3) the gestural body, (4) mise-en-scène, and (5) audience (understood broadly as a set of economic, social, and artistic relationships). This book thus departs from previous studies, such as Richard Poirier's *The Performing Self* (1970) or Joseph Litvack's *Caught in the Act: Theatricality in the Nineteenth-Century English Novel* (1992), which are less concerned with historical specificity and which seem only tangentially interested in actual theater. As the extraordinary Russian playwright, scientist, and man of letters Nicolas Evreinoff wrote in *The Theatre in Life* (1927), "Each epoch has its own theatrical characteristics, its own wardrobe and scenery, its own 'mask'" (100).[7]

The following chapters interrogate a dynamic relationship of reciprocal exchange, transference, and, often, identification between the theater of nineteenth-century American life, the theater of staged play-texts, and the self-conscious use of dramaturgical idioms and strategies in the project of literature. Fundamental changes in the structures of thought in late-nineteenth-century America are indicated by changes in the theater and the drama. Tocqueville remarks that "the drama of one period can never be suited to the following age if in the interval an important revolution has affected the manners and laws of the nation" (83). Judging by substantially altered theaters, a revolution in manners did occur in nineteenth-century America. Thus, in considering the theatrical, I return continually to the theaters themselves and, specifically, to the theaters frequented by the authors who are the subjects of this study.

Acknowledgments

VERSIONS of chapters 4 and 5 have appeared previously, and I gratefully acknowledge permission to use them here: first, to *American Literary Realism* for permission to reprint "The Right to Privacy: William Dean Howells and the Rise of Dramatic Realism"; and, second, to Manchester University Press, which published "Theatre and the Private Sphere in the Fiction of Louisa May Alcott," in *Reading Nineteenth-Century Domestic Space* (1999), ed. Inga Bryden and Janet Floyd. I am generally indebted to the faculty of the Harvard English Department, where I wrote most of this study. And I greatly appreciate a Mellon Grant received in 1995 and Connaught Grants in 1998 and 1999. I thank the staff at the Harvard Theatre Collection for their assistance in procuring many of the illustrations for this volume; the illustrations are reprinted here courtesy of the Harvard Theatre Collection, the Houghton Library. And I gratefully acknowledge the material support of the English Department and the Drama Program of the University of Toronto, which have contributed to the completion of this book.

Many people at Johns Hopkins have contributed to the appearance of the manuscript in book form. Doug Armato, Linda Tripp, Kim Johnson, and Elizabeth Gratch have fostered the publication of this work and contributed to its final shape. I have also been ably assisted by Ian Carpenter, Bob Land, and Alexa Selph.

It is a great pleasure for me to acknowledge many of those without whom the writing of this book would not have been possible. To Elaine Scarry, whose brilliance as a reader is unsurpassed, I owe a primary debt. I am deeply grateful to Lawrence Buell, who has had a shaping influence on this work. Anthony Kubiak profoundly influenced the direction of this book in its formative stages through his intellectual generosity and warm friendship. Among those who have contributed to various aspects of the book by reading chapters and through conversations on relevant topics, I am especially grateful to Douglas Stewart. Philip Fisher, Michael T. Gilmore, Stephen Greenblatt, and Werner Sollors have also read chapters and provided much helpful commentary. And I have richly benefited from many conversations with Kirk Williams on the subjects of theater and history.

My greatest debts are to those whose gifts are too large to be defined. To Alan Ackerman Sr. and Barbara Ackerman, this book is dedicated. I can only begin to acknowledge the sustaining influence of Peter Ackerman and Elizabeth Kaiden. And, finally, last but certainly not least, I thank Andrea Most, for her critical insights, unflagging support, patience, and love.

Abbreviations

AR	*American Realism and American Drama*
CP	*The Complete Plays of W. D. Howells*
CPJ	*The Complete Plays of Henry James*
CW	*Walt Whitman and the Civil War*
GF	*The Gathering of the Forces*
GSW	*Great Short Works of Herman Melville*
GTD	*The Origin of German Tragic Drama*
Letters	*The Letters of Henry James*
LLJ	*Louisa May Alcott: Her Life, Letters, and Journals*
MF	*Melodramatic Formations*
ML	*The Melville Log*
P&P	*Complete Poetry and Collected Prose* (of Walt Whitman)
Prose	*The Complete Writings* (of Walt Whitman)
RT	*A Realist in the American Theatre*
SA	*The Scenic Art: Notes on Acting and the Drama*
SW	*Antonin Artaud: Selected Works*
SDC	*Selected Drama Criticism*
TWC	*Theatre for Working-Class Audiences in the United States*
T&D	*The Theater and Its Double*
UPP	*The Uncollected Poetry and Prose of Walt Whitman*
Workshop	*Walt Whitman's Workshop*

The Portable Theater

ONE

SETTING THE STAGE

Representing Nineteenth-Century American Theater

If you would judge beforehand of the literature of a people that is lapsing into democracy, study its dramatic productions.

ALEXIS DE TOCQUEVILLE, *Democracy in America*

"I may have been meant for the Drama—God Knows!" writes Henry James, "but I certainly wasn't meant for the Theatre" (*Letters* 1:226). The purity of the drama, as James imagines it, and the aesthetic it involves cannot escape the contamination of a medium so gross and palpable as the theater. The distinction that he stresses here, between the drama and the theater, comes at the end of a century in American letters for which this distinction is a truism, and James's failure represents a peculiar culmination of the divorce. In fact, there is a sense in the nineteenth century that drama can be, and is, displaced from theater. William Dean Howells laments:

> The real drama is in our novels mostly. It is they chiefly which approach our actual life, and interpret so far as it has yet been represented to the vast majority of our intelligent public . . . The theatre is the amusement of the city, of people whose lives are crowded with pleasures and distractions. And if the drama, with all our lavish love of the theatre, cannot hold its own there, and prosper and advance, as the novel has prospered and advanced, in spite of the unfriendly literary conditions, it simply proves that the drama is an outworn literary

> form. It cannot be willed back to life by criticism, censured back, or coaxed back. It must take its chances; it must make them. (SDC 29–30)

The meaning of *the drama* is unstable in this passage, for the term is used both metaphorically and literally. But Howells strongly conveys his sense that drama is a kind of migrant worker, homeless and bereft. The drama need not prosper in the existing theaters of New York or Boston, but it does not seem to be at home in the novel. Theater is another one of (or set of) those unfriendly literary conditions which makes the lives of contemporary novelists and poets such rough going.

The drama is the literary form predicated, if only in imagination, upon the theatrical structure of performance and audience. Through the drama theater maintains its claim to being, if not literature, literary. Keir Elam defines *drama* as "that mode of fiction designed for stage representation and constructed according to particular ('dramatic') conventions" (2). Proceeding further than Elam, Richard Schechner shows how modern drama has privileged verbal language as a central feature of the theatrical experience. He calls drama "a written text, score, scenario, instruction, plan, or map. The drama can be taken from place to place or time to time independent of the person or people who carry it" (72). Schechner argues that, while "patterns of doing" have always prefigured performance events, it is only recently in the West (concomitant with the rise of literacy) that the active sense of a basic code of the events has been replaced by drama. Thus, the doings of a particular production have become, in mainstream theater, the way to present drama in a new way. Language has been privileged, and "communication [has] replaced manifestation" (71).

The importance assigned to the literary text in mid-nineteenth-century American theater ranges from virtually none, as in the spectacular pantomimes performed at Niblo's Garden and the Bowery, to primary importance, as in Fanny Kemble's drawing-room readings of Shakespeare (see fig. 1). Theater texts of the period established a relation to the literary tradition ranging from parodies of Shakespearean language to the adaptation of contemporary novels. Dion Boucicault, one of the most prolific playwrights of his generation, had the greatest confidence in his own ability to "hold my audience with my pen," but he relied heavily on contemporary novelists. In fact, he was not unlike the literary gentleman in *Nicholas Nickleby* "who had dramatized in his time two hundred and forty-seven novels as fast as they

FIG. 1. Engraving of one of Fanny Kemble's famous readings of Shakespeare. The extra-large volume and book stand are compelling props.

had come out—some of them faster than they had come out—and *was* a literary gentleman in consequence" (726).[1] One scholar notes of Boucicault: "He took a lease of Scott and Dumas père . . . He treated these authors precisely as people treat a house they rent furnished" (Felheim 82). To many Americans Boucicault's name became synonymous with plagiarism. The intensifying debate over plagiarism later in the century indicates the heightened tension between a "literary" view of the drama and a view of drama shaped by the exigencies of producing theater (see figs. 2 and 3).

American theater borrowed much from theaters across the Atlantic as well. American borrowing from the French in particular illustrates how little emphasis was placed on the originality of the play-text in the overall production process. A manager could go to Paris, see a first-rate comedy, and be relatively assured of its success if, for a minimal sum, he could find a translator of the barest proficiency. An original piece by an American, on the other hand, would cost him at least ten times the price of a transla-

FIG. 2. Dion Boucicault: sharpening his quill and spinning off scripts as crowds in the background applaud.

tion. The logic of the situation did not bode well for playwrights of original scripts, and as a result many, like Boucicault, turned their hands to translations of French or German texts. William Dunlap (1766–1839), the "Father of American Drama," wrote fifty-six plays, twenty-seven of which were adaptations from French or German sources.[2] Of those who did manage to produce some original work, virtually none garnered critical as well as popular acclaim for their work in the theater. Emerson's call for the Ameri-

FIG. 3. Dion Boucicault, who had the greatest confidence in holding his audience with his pen, depicted in 1877 in *The Playwrights' Derby.*

can poet was anticipated by actress Fanny Kemble on her first American tour: "Where are the poets of this land?"[3]

The genesis of drama in America involved a reassessment of literary form and an attempt to integrate various paradigms. Shakespeare, of course, cast a shadow over the entire literary landscape, and many pseudo-Elizabethan verse dramas were produced. Certain genres, such as the romantic play in verse, developed in mid-century, principally to be read. Unfortunately, notes Arthur Hobson Quinn, these plays suffer from "the canon of dramatic art that demands national themes, a canon that has never been applied except to America." Longfellow, for example, began *The Spanish Student* with the hope that it would be produced on the stage, but, finding little encouragement, he ended by publishing it in book form (Quinn 1:266–67). In an extensive essay dealing both with *The Spanish Student* and American drama in general, Edgar Allan Poe criticizes Longfellow for "a very obvious vein of *imitation*." As a consequence of Longfellow's "grossly unoriginal" handling of dramatic material, Poe goes on to claim, "whatever may be its merits in a merely poetical view, 'The Spanish Student' could not be endured upon the stage."[4] Many of the verse dramas set in other countries, however, are concerned indirectly with American problems, such as the relationship between the bourgeoisie and an oppressive, Old World ruling class. Some of these plays, such as *The Broker of Bogota* (1834) by Robert Montgomery Bird and *Francesca da Rimini* (1855) by George Henry Boker, achieved substantial success on stage as well as being significant artistic achievements. The period's greatest financial success, however, was not a romantic drama set in a foreign land at all but George Aiken's adaptation of *Uncle Tom's Cabin. Uncle Tom* has been called the *first* American play to be produced with no ballet or between-act diversions, a claim that, though apocryphal, indicates the profound political and social importance of this play. The fact that it was one of the rare plays to be produced without diversions suggests that contemporaries were concerned with the issues raised by the play itself.

In general, most writing for the theater until 1870, from romantic "tragedy" to nationalistic comedy, manifested some aspects of melodrama. Aspects of melodramatic dramaturgy which appear in these texts include plot devices such as unexpected or fortuitous peripeteias, stories about lost-and-found parents and children, and a self-consciousness about acting and theatricality which is represented thematically in the use of masked or mistaken identities and stylistically in notoriously bombastic rhetoric and hyperbolic language. In melodramatic theater actors do not identify psychologically with the roles they play, and this distance is represented in the texts. There is little suggestion of character depth or complexity, and, when the substratum of character does become relevant in these plays, invariably it is radically problematic. *Francesca da Rimini,* for example, is fundamentally concerned with the failure of the visible world to reflect a predictable and stable "reality." The plot is broadly generated by each character's helpless frustration when confronted with the epistemological uncertainties that pervade his or her world. "Perhaps I lie—perhaps I speak the truth," says Francesca's waiting maid. While the play draws heavily upon Shakespeare's characters and plots, especially *Richard III* and *Othello,* Boker introduces significant variations. Unlike Richard, the hunchback in this play does not have a mind, or moral organ, which corresponds to his outward deformity. And the fool, whose overt resemblance to King Lear's companion superficially suggests a kind of innocence, has more in common with Iago. The problem of trust or the ability to know others, which resonates throughout Boker's play, finds its fullest expression, two years later, in 1857, in Melville's novel *The Confidence-Man: His Masquerade.* Like Boker, Melville manipulates Shakespeare to represent the dramaturgical assumptions of his age. Jacques's famous seven-ages-of-man speech, in *As You Like It,* for example, is abbreviated to articulate the epistemological problems of the placeless, "melodramatic" theater:

> All the world's a stage,
> And all the men and women merely players,
> Who have their exits and their entrances,
> And one man in his time plays many parts.
> (Melville 298)

Unlike realist theater, which seeks to maintain the integrity of its illusion and the coherence of its characters, the melodramatic stage commonly employs a metatheatrical rhetoric to indicate both the limits and, implicitly, the power of its own signifying apparatus.

Insofar as characters can be known in melodrama, they are known not psychologically but morally. The melodrama is essentially Manichaean, staging simple, intersubjective systems of belief, good versus evil. The plots tend to be tremendously complex, but the moral issues at stake are relatively simple. The action of Bird's play *The Broker of Bogota,* like that of *Francesca da Rimini,* is motivated by deceptions and misunderstandings. The phrase *true friend* reverberates throughout the play, and the villain Caberero resembles the stereotypical con man preying on misguided youth. Caberero is evil, a fact represented not only indirectly, in the action of the play, but in direct and repeated nominations: "Oh, thou bold bad man," "O grasping villain," "dangerous companion," and "devil-born destroyer of men's sons."[5] To live up to these names, Caberero drinks, gambles, thieves, cheats, and connives. The play's good characters, on the other hand, are named in equally straightforward fashion. One of the two virgins, for example, is named by her lover: "O thou simple sweet." There is, in other words, a moral straightforwardness in the very language of the text. Ultimately, though good men lose their lives, the play does not propose a *tragic* vision. There is no sense of blind necessity, and characters do not find themselves in an irrational or incomprehensible universe. On the contrary, insofar as human forces compete toward a just resolution, this vision is essentially democratic: the common man has control over his fate. The moral of the play is to be found in its emphasis on personal responsibility and self-reliance: "When one grief springs from ill fate, twenty come from our own faults. I have never known a young man sink in the world, without finding he had overburdened himself with follies" (I.i.).

Despite the simplicity of the moral vision, however, the text strains to express these truths. The moral of the story may be simply put, but the cosmic nature of the basic problem, goodness wronged, leads to the kind of high emotionalism and ostentation that verges on the inarticulate. At one climactic moment, when Ramon could save his father's reputation simply by speaking out, he is so overcome with emotion that he passes out: "Ramon, endeavoring to speak, falls into a swoon." The title character himself most significantly represents the crucial limitations of the melodramatic text. His mistakes of judgment lead to absolute abasement and humiliation, while his love for his children, at times almost sickeningly sweet, verges toward the sublime. The hyperbolic rhetoric of melodrama indicates not only the tenuous relationship between appearances and reality but also, of course, the inadequacy of language itself to express emotional or moral truths. John Augustus Stone's play *Metamora; or, The Last of the Wampanoags* (1829), for example, repeatedly seeks to establish the sublimity of the title character's resoundingly metaphorical speech ("The Great Spirit hears me and pours forth his mighty voice with mine!" cries the Wampanoag chief in one of his many monologues.) And yet the epilogue of the play indicates language's ultimate insufficiency:

> See that fair maid, the tear still in her eye,
> And hark! hear not you now that gentle sigh?

Ah! these speak more than language could relate;
The woe-fraught heart o'er Nahmeokee's fate.

A similar assumption about the spoken word is evident in Boker's play *Francesca da Rimini.* Speaking of her inner struggles, Francesca cries: "Can I say more? My blushes speak for me."[6] This lack of confidence in language is one reason that melodrama privileges stage effect and scenic display over text and, consequently, over the psychological coherence of character. As David Grimsted notes, melodrama "made light of rationality" and replaced it with "a concept of feeling or intuition" (20). The effectiveness of the representation of such states of feeling is beyond the *reader's* scope to judge, for those effects are beyond the immediate context of the drama.

The second-class status of playwrights and the drama in America gradually began to change in the third quarter of the nineteenth century. Innovations by European dramatists, such as Ibsen and Strindberg, were soon recognized by a few people of the theater in America; in 1882 Ibsen's *Ghosts* received its world premiere in Chicago.[7] Fundamentally, the raising up of the drama was a product of changing notions about the nature of dramatic language. For the realists concern with character, with psychology, with situations, ultimately boiled down to concern with dialogue and the act of writing. Language would be the life raft on which to save the drama. The privileging of language, however, fundamentally reshapes intersubjective experience. As Peter Szondi suggests, dialogue, which previously represented "the common space in which the interiority of the dramatis personae is objectified," is in the modern drama "alienated from the subject and appears as an independent entity. Dialogue becomes conversation" (53). In short, the nature of dialogue is altered in the modern drama when the "objectivity" of shared experience is thrown into question. Consequently, language (i.e., conversation) is privileged at the expense of "action."

One result of the new importance of conversation is that the experience of audience members will be less visual and less visceral; they will have to listen and, therefore, make less noise. Moreover, insofar as the play is constituted by language, the production of the play itself is seen less as a group effort and more as the work of a single artist. "It is the subordinate affair of the actor to adapt himself to the poet's conception," writes William Dean Howells at the century's end (RT 118). And, therefore, there is an evolving sense that reading and going to the theater are, or ought to be, essentially equivalent experiences. The framing of the equation, however, often seems to praise the novel at the theater's expense. Thus, Howells writes:

> The novelist sets up his stage here or there, and then plays the whole piece through before the reader, taking the part now of one character and now of another in the dramatic moments, and now of the chorus in the narrative and comment . . . and the audience of the portable theatre enjoys privileges impossible in the stationary theatre. The witness of the dramatic action of the novel may go away and return when he likes . . . he can retrace his steps in it for a verification of his impressions, or advance with it to the end at such a pace as he pleases.[8]

Howells's "passion for reading plays" and his recommendation that those who object to the high price of theater tickets should read novels instead belie his enjoyment of theatricality and good acting. Yet his idea of the "portable theatre" is premised on the notion that drama is not enhanced but degraded by spectacle. All of these factors engender a theatrical experience that is less publicly oriented. Dramatic realists reasserted in a fundamental way the notion that drama was a literary genre. In fact, so important was the idea of literary quality that the realist attitude might be paraphrased by saying that going to the theater ought to be more like reading a book. As a consequence, the trope of reading assumed a new importance in realist plays, signifying not only the privacy of characters' experiences but also the mediation of those experiences by print. For example, Charles Hawtrey's *Private Secretary* (1883), William Gillette's *All the Comforts of Home* (1890), and Bronson Howard's *Old Love Letters* (1897) all open with the act of reading personal letters. And, although men of the theater continued to assert that the work of the dramatist is unlike that of the novelist or poet, the language and form of their assertions commonly undermined that sense of difference, as in Bronson Howard's peculiarly titled lecture *The Autobiography of a Play* (1914).

In addition to the new stress on conversation over "action," there is also a structural difference between melodramas and realist dramas. Realist dramas manifest a shift in emphasis from plot to character, one that also leads to a less "public" kind of theater. As Ian Watt has persuasively shown, modern literary realism begins with the privileging of character over plot. Watt argues that characterization is so important in the rise of the English novel that Defoe's "total subordination of the plot to the pattern of the autobiographical memoir is as defiant an assertion of the primacy of individual experience in the novel as Descartes's *cogito ergo sum* was in philosophy" (15). This emphasis on the individual poses a problem for theater, however, which is essentially social. Drama, unlike the novel, necessarily portrays individuals in relation to other individuals. All of the devices of the melodramatic theater become helpless in the face of interior "truth," now understood not in moral but in psychological and intellectual terms. It is remarkable, therefore, that within a hundred years both the worldview and the formal innovations that gave rise to the novel began to make their way into plays and playwriting, and the notion that the representation of character was the drama's first concern did, in fact, seem to be a major turning point to American authors. In his editorial for *Harper's Monthly* (July 1889) Howells wrote a piece called "The New American Drama" in which he claimed that, "because the drama has been in times past and in other conditions the creature, the prisoner, of plot, it by no means follows that it must continue so; on the contrary, it seems to us that its liberation follows; and of this we see signs in the very home of the highly intrigued drama, where construction has been carried to the last point, and where it appears to have broken down at last under its own inflexibility" (RT 34).

Howells preferred "a series of sketches" or situations to the "neat carpentry" of the well-made play imported from France. By focusing on character, he insisted, the drama would come to resemble the novel. Action becomes "an affair of being, rather than doing"; it becomes, in other words, intellectual and psychological. There will be no more heroic deeds, but character will be expressed unceremoniously in the course "of dinner or of death."[9] Plot in realist drama loses the value it had in the melodrama or the well-made play because facile endings would not reflect "reality." The focus of the drama shifts from the relatively simple relations *between* characters to the *internal* complexities *of* characters. As the drama gains prestige, therefore, the theatrical experience becomes more readerly, and, in both language and dramatic structure, the realist plays increasingly represent the realities of private life. The value of these plays, therefore, is largely contingent upon the resonance of a particular scene and the quality of the conversation. The quality of the melodramatic plays, on the other hand, can *only* be evaluated with reference to other aspects of the productions, such as the quality of the acting, costuming, or spectacular effects.[10]

The increasingly readerly theater that Howells envisioned for realist drama necessarily entailed a muting of one of the melodramatic stage's most important expressive registers, that of the voice, commonly referred to in the mid-nineteenth century as "vocalism," or the "utterance." Whether bellowed or businesslike, however, the human voice is implicit in every dramatic text, and different dramaturgical assumptions about it indicate crucial differences in both social conditions and dramatic or literary aims. "Written words," says Walter Ong, "are isolated from the fuller context in which spoken words come into being. The word in its natural, oral habitat is part of a real, existential present" (101). In the early days of the American theater the voice was particularly emphasized. The utterance in the first half of the nineteenth century achieved a mythical status. For example, James Rees tells how one audience member was affected when the great Shakespearean actor, Edwin Forrest, as King Lear, cursed Goneril in a particularly inspired performance in New Orleans. "During the utterance of the curse," Rees remarks, "we heard a strange sound proceeding from a gentleman sitting beside us—a sound so strange and unnatural, which induced us to turn suddenly round. The fearful words of the curse were ringing in our ears as uttered by the only living actor capable of giving it with that fierceness and rapid vehemence so essential to render it effective." Rees and his friends are startled and then horrified to discover the man behind them sitting rigid, with his mouth hanging open, his eyes fixed, hands clenched, and a "death-like paleness" spreading over his face. The friends catch him by the shoulders and give him a hearty shake, whereupon the poor man comes to with a gasp and gazes around. "The awful curse," Rees concludes, "so fearfully uttered, was still ringing in his ears. It had taken away the man's breath, and my shaking him caused him to recover" (173–74).

The etymological root of *melodrama,* of course, is in music ("song drama"), and the origins of melodrama coincide roughly with the origins of opera in the late sixteenth century. One of the aims of incorporating the musical element in the drama is to relay through the voice what is otherwise inarticulate, and for this reason the antebellum drama has a close affinity with opera. In fact, Leman Rede remarks, opera had become so popular so quickly in antebellum America "that almost all members of a theatre are called into action in this department" (19). Some sense of the impact of the operatic voice on an American audience is conveyed in a letter Whitman wrote after seeing a performance of *Lucrezia Borgia* at the New York Academy of Music in 1863 in which he responds with unbridled enthusiasm to the dramatic power of the voice in action. One scene in particular seemed to him "as good a piece of performance as any I ever saw in my life":

> The lady as soon as she saw that her husband was really gone . . . sprang to her lover, clutched him by the arm, and poured out the greatest singing you ever heard—it poured like a raging river more than anything else I could compare it to—she tells him he is poisoned—he tries to inquire &c and hardly knows what to make of it—she breaks in trying to pacify him, and explain &c—all this goes on very rapid indeed . . . she quickly draws out from her bosom a little vial, to neutralize the poison, then the young man in his desperation abuses her and tells her perhaps it is to poison him still more as she has already poisoned him once—this puts her in such agony, she begs and pleads with him to take the antidote at once before it is too late—her voice is so wild and high it goes through one like a knife, yet it is delicious. (Qtd. in Traubel 3:103–4)

This passage indicates the importance of the voice both as a physical event and as a signifier of otherwise inarticulable meanings, specifically at climactic moments. The voice, in this sense, achieves regions of significance which are well beyond those that the written word can attain.

The tension between writing and speech emerges with a high degree of self-consciousness in all literary and quasi-literary genres of the period, not only in performance genres. For example, this feature of theater is thematically foregrounded in many novels, from *Wieland,* by Charles Brockden Brown (1798) to *The Bostonians,* by Henry James (1886), in which the heroine, Verena Tarrant, "spins vocal sounds to a silver thread" (228).[11] The narrator of Edgar Allan Poe's story "The Spectacles" first sees the woman he wants to marry in a theater; later, when he attends a soiree where he thinks he hears her singing, "the impression she produced upon the company seemed electrical." And "her utterance" continues to ring in his memory, for he has been overcome by her "miracles of vocal execution" (340–41). In Hawthorne's *Scarlet Letter* the Reverend Arthur Dimmesdale, that "pious minister of the Word" (207), has a notably peculiar voice. His "vocal organ was in itself a rich endowment; insomuch that a listener, comprehending nothing of the language in which the preacher spoke, might still have been swayed to and fro by the mere tone and cadence" (208).[12] And in *The Blithedale Romance* Hawthorne writes that, "with the living voice, alone," Zenobia compels "the world to recognize the light of her intellect and the depth of her heart!" (120).

In nineteenth-century American schools and colleges Shakespeare was taught not as literature, to be read silently, but as declamation or rhetoric (Levine 37). Fanny Kemble, both a leading actress and the author of several plays of her own, managed to make a living for twenty years by giving readings of Shakespeare's plays in England and the United States. In a memorial piece written after her death Henry James remembered being taken to a Kemble reading as a boy, vividly recalling "every detail of the picture and every tone of her voice" (*Temple Bar* 508). Oratory contributed significantly to Shakespeare's widespread popularity. Lawrence Levine argues, moreover, that the waning popularity of oratory at the end of the century contributed to the fact that Shakespeare also ceased to be regarded as a playwright of the people.[13]

Oratory had an important family relationship to theater, a relationship of ancient standing, recognized by most contemporaries.[14] It is notable, for example, that the title character of Brown's novel *Wieland,* who "never tired of conning and rehearsing" Cicero and "embellishing his rhetoric with all the proprieties of gesticulation and utterance," is also descended from the "founder of the German Theatre."[15] The relationship between theater and oratory can be seen further in the period's most prominent speakers. In comparing Abraham Lincoln and Edward Everett at Gettysburg, for example, Garry Wills reminds us "that Lincoln was himself an actor, an expert raconteur and mimic, and one who spent hours reading out speeches of Shakespeare to any willing (and some unwilling) audiences. He knew a good deal about rhythmic delivery and meaningful inflections. John Hay, who had submitted to many of those Shakespearean readings, gave high marks to his boss's performance at Gettysburg" (36). Still, for a devoted theatergoer such as Whitman, theater, as opposed to drawing room or pulpit or lecture platform, was the place to experience the dramatic rendering of the spoken word in its fullest glory. Although in his memoirs he lumps together actors, singers, orators, and preachers, ultimately, in Whitman's view, it is the actor Junius Booth who achieves "the charm of unswervingly perfect vocalization" (P&P 1192).

The decline of oratory as a popular form coincided with the shift in theater from melodramatic to realist modes of representation. A fundamental, in fact existential, premise of the realist theater is the idea that the play is not heard but overheard. As a situation unfolds, characters should not appear conscious of projecting their voices for the benefit of the audience but merely speaking to one another in a casual and ordinary way. Perhaps no author who was also intimately concerned with theater manifested more ambivalence or inconsistent thinking about the theatrical utterance than Henry James. In an article on the American actor George Rignold, in 1875, James writes, "When you have Shakespeare's speeches to utter, your reality must be a sort of imaginative compromise; you must wind up your whole conception to a certain exalted pitch, and there, at that impressive altitude, you may keep among the levels" (SA 34). James is vague about the "imaginative compromise," which implies that an exalted pitch of utterance can represent only a certain kind of reality and, certainly, an incomplete identification between the actor and his role. We might also recall that in *The Bostonians* Verena Tarrant's gift of utterance is both a blessing and a curse, for the recognition of her beautiful voice by others leads her into terrible confusion about the relative merits of public and private life.

In his remarks on the new generation of actors James also demonstrates his ambivalence about the utterance. For example, while he praises the young English actor Henry Irving for his intelligence and seriousness and a certain meditative quality, he also complains, "In declamation he is decidedly flat; his voice is without charm, and his utterance without subtlety" (SA 36). James did not recognize the inconsistencies of his own dramaturgical assumptions, for they are inconsistencies informed by mixed, and not always conscious, allegiances. James's nostalgic memories of the theater of his youth, in New York around 1850, were qualified by what he learned at the Théâtre Français and by what he appreciated in late-nineteenth-century realist theater. Howells, on the other hand, is more consistent in his realist orthodoxy, and, as a consequence, he expresses more clearly than James what he perceives as the problems of a theater in transition. Commenting, in 1891, on a production of Clyde Fitch's *Beau Brummel* starring the Irvingesque Richard Mansfield, Howells complains of the melodramatic aspects of the production but praises a Mansfield performance that imparts a new tone to the theater.[16] Despite the maudlin feeling and hackneyed art, Howells writes, "the play has a great and saving virtue: it has quiet. This quiet is the one true touch in it; and it is so true that it imparts a color of veracity to the whole . . . It teaches in unanswerable terms that the strongest emotions may be expressed with the least noise, and that the lover of the drama may be made to understand the purport of a play without being hit on the head" (RT 52).

Howells's preference for quiet and a refinement of the utterance is also reflected in William Winter's praise for a more intellectual style of acting. In his 1893 monograph on Edwin Booth, Winter describes Booth's Hamlet in terms that can be understood only as a reaction against the romantic stage of Forrest and Booth's own father, Junius: "The text was spoken with ample vocal power and fine flexibility. The illustrative 'business' was strictly accordant with the wonderful dignity and high intellectual worth of Shakespeare's creation."[17] In place of the language with which James Rees and Walt Whitman praised their favorite performers (*awful, raging, wild*), Winter's language is tempered with the qualities he ascribes to Booth, "dignity" and intellectuality, a "power" that is not overwhelming but "ample" and a "fine flexibility." *Adequate* becomes a term of praise, for the emphasis is no longer on "expression" but on intellect: "[Booth's] figure stood forth, distinct and stately, in a clear light. The attitudes, movements, gestures, and facial play combined in a symmetry and always adequate expression" (Winter 250). Implicit in new attitudes toward vocalism, therefore, are assumptions about physical performance as a whole. As realists minimized the importance of the utterance, so too did they reject previous assumptions about the body in performance.

The mid-nineteenth century was the age of the actor, and those who were physically commanding were most celebrated. One factor promoting bold physical performances was the architecture of New York theaters in the early and mid-nineteenth century. The Bowery Theatre, for example, opened in 1826 with a seating capacity of three thousand. After the last of four fires and subsequent renovations, the theater was able, in 1845, to seat four thousand. According to the manager, the stage was "126 feet in depth, with corresponding width—the largest, perhaps, in the world."[18] Such a stage required especially dynamic performers. For Walt Whitman, looking back in *November Boughs* (P&P 1186–88), Junius Booth and Edwin Forrest were foremost among the "dramatic artists" who performed there. Of Junius Booth, Asia Booth Clarke writes, "There was inspiration in his embodiment of Shakespearean characters, and even when the words were lost to the hearing the eye needed no vocal interpreter, for Booth, more than any other actor we have ever seen, possessed the power of combining meaning in every gesture, and a silent glance was equivalent to a delivered sentence" (65). The "physical" style of acting, however, was epitomized by Edwin Forrest. Seeing Forrest perform led Fanny Kemble to exclaim, "What a mountain of a man!"[19] Forrest's sheer size, his "herculean" proportions, and his physical strength were among his most important theatrical attributes, and he made the most of his body on stage, observing a "rigid physical-culture program to keep his biceps bulging for heroic roles" (Perry 11; see fig. 4).

Like the melodramatic voice, gesture bore the burden of the verbally inexpressible, states of feeling either so extreme that the character was rendered speechless or so basic that speech was rendered unnecessary. In the melodramatic theater the reduction of states of feeling (anger, distress, grief) or of moral states (innocence, duplicity, courage) to a register of simple, physical signs invited audience members to respond unanimously, to celebrate virtue or to be outraged by hypocrisy, to sympathize but not to empathize. The public nature of this dramaturgy is reflected in Emerson's use of theater as a metaphor in "Self-Reliance." Emerson imagines the affirmation of publicly formed ethical standards in terms of a "melodramatic" theater: "The nonchalance of boys who are sure of a dinner . . . is the healthy attitude of human nature. A boy is in the parlor what the pit is in the playhouse; independent, irresponsible, looking out from his corner on such people and facts as pass by, he tries and sentences them on their merits, in the swift, summary way of boys, as good, bad, interesting, silly, eloquent, troublesome" (261). The boys in the parlor or the pit in the playhouse are interested only in that which is exteriorized and immediately legible, not in the complexities of the interior life. Their evaluations are "swift and summary."

Dramaturgical assumptions about the body on stage are reflected, moreover, in the importance of gesture in oratory. Orators were instructed in countless manuals on precise movements of arms, hands, head, and expressions of the face. Gesture is defined by one handbook as "a suitable conformity of the motions of the countenance, and several parts of the body in speaking, to the subject matter of the discourse." And, while there was substantial debate about the relative influence of voice or body on an audience, the author of *The Columbian Orator* concludes that gesture has the advantage because it affects us by the eye and so conveys the impression more speedily to the mind. Sight, he reasons, is the quickest of the senses (Bingham 19).[20]

FIG. 4. Forrest in a forceful pose as the intensely muscular Gladiator.

The "advantage" of what Whitman later calls "elliptical" expression, however, was considered by many critics of the "democratic" stage to be a fundamental problem of the theater. Impressions conveyed by the performing body allow no time for reflection or critical thought. As Tocqueville remarks, dramatic performances "lay hold on you in the midst of your prejudices and your ignorance" (79).

The New York theater between 1840 and 1870 provides numerous illustrations of the power of physical performance to obviate more considered interpretations of the dramatic text. Physical humor was a crucial aspect of the mid-century theater. Even in melodramas with a serious social message, such as Aiken's *Uncle Tom,* physical humor and stage business could take over. For example, after Ophelia declares that she will marry Deacon Perry, "Cute makes a dash at Deacon, who gets behind Ophelia. Topsy enters with a broom and beats Cute around stage. Ophelia faints in Deacon's arms. Cute falls, and Topsy butts him. Quick drop" (94). This sort of emphasis on the performing body is epitomized by the great comic actor and pantomimist George Lafayette Fox. Fox took stage business to a new height in an age when it already occupied a central position, and his performances were considered to be among the greatest of his time. Unlike the performances of Booth or Forrest, however, Fox's performances generally were not interpretations of scripts.

Earlier in the nineteenth century theaters had featured spectacular pantomimes and acrobatics generally as afterpieces to more serious productions. In the 1830s, however, the Ravels, a highly acclaimed troupe of pantomimists, arrived from France to revolutionize pantomime in America, transforming it into an extremely popular form of entertainment in its own right. Fox, whose early roles included phrenological lecturer, hypnotist, and a proliferation of comic Irishmen, derived much from the Ravels. In 1850 he made his way to the Bowery theaters, which were gradually becoming more proletarian as the Broadway venues were becoming increasingly upscale.[21] It was there that Fox became the century's premier pantomime clown, raising pantomime to new heights as a theatrical form in its own right. His greatest success and most lasting fame came as Humpty Dumpty (see fig. 5). Fox's great range of facial expressions epitomized the "plastic figurability of emotion" characteristic of the melodramatic stage.[22] And Fox's extremely violent physical humor consolidated and re-presented the brutal street life of the Bowery, or what the *New York Herald* disparaged as "the coarseness of the east-side." Humpty's slapstick, claimed one witness, "was all action—action—action" (qtd. in Senelick 142). Because of the immediacy of these representations, Fox's *Humpty Dumpty* was said to be "thoroughly American. There was nothing foreign in anything he did" (154).[23]

The importance and familiarity of pantomime performances (which often

FIG. 5. George L. Fox as Humpty Dumpty. The scene is replete with local references to a dry goods store and to Broadway itself. As the low-class clown Humpty Dumpty, Fox is boorishly greeting a milliner's manikin.

included some dialogue) and of the melodramatic dramaturgy that privileges the human body as a medium of primary (and cosmic) significance can be seen in the way it is co-opted and re-presented in more self-reflexive literature. For example, Poe's poem "The Conquerer Worm" inverts the notion that a man's body can be heroic, suggesting, on the contrary, that the true hero in the drama of life is the body-destroying Worm. The mimes become "mere puppets," shuffling beneath vast scenery. The poem typifies

Poe's technique of the "grotesque" while also reinforcing the melodramatic dramaturgy from which the basic concepts are drawn.

Sit in a theatre, to see
  A play of hopes and fears,
While the orchestra breaths fitfully
  The music of the spheres.

Mimes, in the form of God on high,
  Mutter and mumble low,
And hither and thither fly—
  Mere puppets they, who come and go
At bidding of vast formless things
  That shift the scenery to and fro,
Flapping from out their Condor wings
  Invisible Woe!

. . . . . .

But see, amid the mimic rout,
  A crawling shape intrude!
A blood-red thing that writhes from out
  The scenic solitude!
It writhes!—It writhers!—with mortal pangs
  The mimes become its food,
And seraphs sob at vermin fangs
  In human gore imbued.

Out—out are the lights—out all!
  And over each quivering form,
The curtain, a funeral pall,
  Comes down with the rush of a storm,
And the angels, all pallid and wan,
  Uprising, unveiling, affirm
That the play is the tragedy "Man,"
  And its hero the Conquerer Worm.

Poe understands the nature of the symbolic transvaluation of the body in melodrama and brings attention to bear on it with a rush that is at once both sickening and strangely comic. His unrelenting insistence on the writhing worm and the quivering form of the mime inverts melodramatic assumptions while retaining the language of that dramaturgy.

In the 1870s, as the careers of clowns like Fox and heroic actors like Forrest waned, a new breed of actors began to emerge who were defined by a new set of terms representing aspects of an interior life: culture, refinement, and quiet. Edwin Booth's Hamlet, for example, in the definitive 1870 production at Booth's Theatre, seemed unaware that there was an audience in the house. Unlike Forrest's active and even violent Hamlet, Booth's "sad, slight Prince" seemed inspired by the art of sculpture; Booth was, in fact, occasionally criticized for posing (see fig. 6). Unlike the muscular Forrest or even his own short but flamboyant father, Junius, Edwin Booth used his "small lithe form" for a new kind of gentle acting, exploiting "the mobility and intellectual sadness of his face, and his large melancholy eyes." George William Curtis, editor of *Harper's* noted in April 1865 that Booth's Hamlet had the subtlety of a portrait by Titian or Vandyck; the essence of the character is not conveyed in any particular scene but in "the consistency of every part with every other, their pervasive sense of a true gentleman sadly strained and jarred" (30:674).[24]

In 1881 an American scholar named Edward Vining argued in *The Mystery of Hamlet* that Shakespeare imagined *Hamlet* as the story of a woman in disguise, not unlike the stories of Viola, Rosalind, and Portia. Although Hamlet talks rather than acts, dallies with opportunity rather than seizing it, Vining reasons, he remains an exemplary character because the charms of his mind are essentially feminine in nature. Hamlet is the counterpart of the masculine Lady Macbeth, each "gifted with a mind naturally noble, but misplaced in the body through which it acts." This peculiar idea is most significant because Booth found Vining's book true to his own conception of the character. In particular, Booth was excited by the large number of details of Hamlet's "womanliness," which Vining enlisted to support his argument. "I have always endeavored," Booth wrote, "to make prominent the femininity of Hamlet's character and therein lies the secret of my success—I think. I doubt if ever a robust and masculine treatment of the character will be accepted so generally as the more womanly and refined interpretation. I know that frequently I fall into effeminacy, but we can't always hit the proper keynote" (qtd. in Shattuck 64). Booth, whose extraordinary good looks made him extremely popular with women both on and off the stage, never liked

FIG. 6. Edwin Booth posing as the meditative and melancholy Hamlet.

playing lovers' roles. Although young women and girls were immensely attracted to his youthful Romeo, after 1869 and many hostile reviews, he dropped it from his repertory. Nearly all critics agreed, moreover, that muscular roles, such as Macbeth or Othello, were beyond his range, physically and artistically. He would not compete head-to-head with the older generation of actors. While Booth paid close attention to gesture and posture, his style anticipates realist acting in its lack of violence, its emphasis on the intellectual life of the character, and the actor's profound identification with the role.

Booth's "feminized" Hamlet is, in fact, hardly idiosyncratic; rather, it marks a trend that may be said to culminate with Sarah Bernhardt's portrayal of that role at the end of the century. Reviews of Bernhardt's Hamlet show how dramatically the aesthetic of the body had changed in American theater since the days of Forrest. Her diminutive body is directly associated with the contemplative nature of the character. One reviewer for the *New York Times* wrote, "This new Prince of Denmark, so low of stature, so wonderfully graceful in every motion and gesture, so agile, and so restless most of the time, but so incomparably effective in repose; this Hamlet of the short tunic and the daintily molded limbs . . . will please the few, the art-loving, the appreciative, if not the multitude" (26 December 1900).[25] And Bernhardt herself explained her attraction to the "subtle" and "torturous" character of Hamlet, by remarking, "It is not male parts, but male brains that I prefer."[26]

The new stress on character through a more delicate and subtle physical performance was another feature of the increasingly intellectual experience that, realists hoped, would resemble reading a novel. In general, theorists of dramatic realism discuss the body remarkably little, a significant departure from the previous generation. What the realist theorists do discuss is the progress of a character through successive states of mind. James, for example, speaks of the great French actor Coquelin, whose "progress through this long and elaborate part, all of fine shades and pointed particulars . . . resembles the method of the 'psychological' novelist" (qtd. in Murphy 34).[27] James Herne relates his own acting to his reading of Dickens: "Dickens seemed real to me. I knew the people in his books . . . Dickens made me an actor." In 1896 the *Boston Sunday Post* noted of Herne's play *Shore Acres,* "Those familiar with the writing of Charles Dickens cannot but notice a similarity between his character sketches and those of Mr. Herne" (qtd. in Perry 18, 19). Howells also favored character actors who focused on developing the characterological intricacies of individual roles, actors who conveyed effects by "suggestion" rather than "imitation." This style was cultivated by Howells's favorite actor, Joseph Jefferson, who made a career out of playing Rip Van Winkle, and whose art Howells described as "dignified and refined to an ideal delicacy and a beautiful reality never surpassed, to our thinking."[28] In Albert Smith's play *The Cricket on the Hearth* (1895), as Howells saw it, Jefferson's "rarer gift was to make you forget the piece altogether from time to time. The wretched mechanism all fell away from him" (RT 65). Unlike melodrama, therefore, in which the actor's performance contributes to a larger feast of sights and sounds, the realist theater calls not only for a more refined performance by the actor but also for a less spectacular dramaturgy in the theater as a whole.

"The stage," writes Antonin Artaud, "is a concrete physical place which asks to be filled, and to be given its own language to speak" (T&D 37). As Artaud himself acknowledged, his advocacy of a "concrete language, intended for the senses and independent of speech," which he calls mise-en-scène, harks back to the voluptuous visuality of the melodramatic stage of the nineteenth century.[29] Despite the limited physical resources of many American theaters, audiences hungered for spectacular stagings and cataclysmic effects. In 1846 Charles Kean brought his visually elaborate, historically "accurate" *King John, Henry VIII,* and *Richard III* to New York. *King John* alone cost an extraordinary $12,000 to stage, and, "for magnificence in every detail," Kean's production set a new standard for spectacular stagings in America (Odell 5:252). His Shakespearean productions were not universally appreciated, however, and *King John* also led the *Spirit of the Times* to complain, "It is an era not in the history of the legitimate drama, but in that of pageantry and spectacle" (qtd. in Grimsted 87).

Although spectacle often served as pure visual excitement, it also represented the moral assumptions of the melodrama. In *Pocahontas; or, The Settlers of Virginia* (1830), by George Washington Parke Custis, the virtuous heroine, having warned John Smith of an impending Indian attack, confronts the roaring wind and heaving surf: "I must launch my little barque, and as it tosses amid the foam and fury of the waves, feel sure that good and guardian Spirit, which urg'd me to the rescue of my fellow creatures, will not forsake me amid the dangers of the storm. (Pocahontas *re-embarks, and is seen at first struggling with the waves.—Exit.*)" (III.i.).[30]

In a similar spirit Eliza's intrepid flight across the ice blocks was a climactic moment of the dramatized *Uncle Tom's Cabin.* Henry James later remembered the scene in *A Small Boy and Others:* "The rocking of the ice-floes of the Ohio, with the desperate Eliza, infant in arms, balancing for a leap from one to the other, had here [the National Theatre] less of the audible creak of carpentry, emulated a trifle more, to my perception, the real water of Mr. Crummles's pump. They can't, even at that, have emulated it much, and one almost envies (quite making up one's mind not to denounce) the simple faith of an age beguiled by arts so rude" (162). The humorous, indulgent tone of James and other literary men commenting on the scenic effects of the mid-century theater belies both their genuine enjoyment and, arguably, some less obvious displacements. In the equestrian drama *Mazeppa* the beautiful Adah Isaacs Menken, dressed only in a flesh-colored body suit, was tied to the back of the wild horse of Tartary and carried to the peak of a papier-mâché mountain. Mark Twain, a young newspaper reporter in the audience at one of these performances, later wrote in the *Californian:* "A magnificent spectacle dazzled my vision—the whole constellation of the Great Menken came flaming out of the heavens like a vast spray of gas-jets, and shed a glory abroad over the universe as it fell."[31] On more than one occasion Twain's reviews mildly burlesqued the spectacles in which Menken appeared, discounting her performances in favor of other aspects of theatricality. Randall Knoper suggestively attributes Twain's spectatorial displacement to a profound ambivalence about the performing woman. Menken, in the role of the prince Ivan Mazeppa, was, ironically, cross-dressed in order to display her own female body. As a woman, the supposed epitome of domesticity and decorum, Menken is caught up in an explicitly masculine spectacle (Knoper 49–53). The contradictions inherent in feminine expressivity in the nineteenth century are, in this view, subsumed in a humorous celebration of spectacle itself.

Nineteenth-century American theater, in general, placed great and sometimes primary importance on set design and special effects, including panoramas, dioramas, and cycloramas. William Dunlap, for example, was not only one of the first playwrights and historians of the American stage but also one of its most important painters and set designers. For *A Trip to Niagara; Or, Travelers in America* Dunlap designed a moving diorama requiring twenty-five thousand square feet of canvas which depicted landscapes from the harbor of New York to Niagara Falls. "The main intention," Dunlap plainly admitted of this play, "was to display scenery."[32] Panoramas, too, perfected by theatrical scene painters and showmen such as John Banvard, became so popular in America that the craze became known as "panoramania." Banvard promoted his "Three-Mile" Mississippi panorama in Barnumlike fashion as family entertainment (Hanners 35–53). In the history of American art the panorama phenomenon may be said to culminate with the century's unique way of presenting paintings, such as the "Great Pictures" of Albert Bierstadt. Yet critics expressed dismay at what they felt was a devaluing, and hence discouragement, of native "legitimate drama" because of a fascination with spectacle.

American theatrical spectacles quickly incorporated contemporary developments in technology. Augustin Daly, for example, used the new railroad to turn a profit in *Under the Gaslight* by staging the first rescue of an innocent victim from the railroad tracks, a stunt that has become a theatrical cliché. The success of the stunt resulted almost immediately in imitations that soon led to a complex and lengthy lawsuit over rights to the stage effect.[33] George L. Fox staged a burlesque version, with a miniature railroad, which could not escape Daly's litigious reach. The relatively recent invention of the camera found its way into Boucicault's popular melodrama of 1859, *The Octoroon,* in which, by virtue of miraculous timing, it proves to be the only witness to a murder. Boucicault's simple melodrama *The Poor of New York* achieved phenomenal success because, in the last scene, the house where the repentant villain lived was set on fire, a real fire engine arrived on stage, the fire was extinguished, and the villain emerged from the smoking ruin (Fawkes 95).[34]

Current events, such as local construction, were depicted immediately on the stage. Local color could be as important as spectacle in attracting the masses, for the lives of working folk could be idealized while still providing the pleasure of recognition in the reality of presentation. "The pieces are local" was a common theatrical advertisement (Covares 52). George L. Fox's staging of *Humpty Dumpty* at the Olympic Theatre in 1867 especially excited its audience by its rich and immediate representation of New York and of the Bowery in particular. The familiarity of scenes, which took place in locales ranging from a typical German billiard saloon to Walstein's Optician Stores on Broadway and which included a view of the Olympic Theatre itself by night, "bestowed a sense of participation on the audience" (Senelick 141). Theater not only helped to make tolerable the social system or situation as it was, but it also kept the society's citizens in a more flexible state with respect to that system and with respect to possible change.[35] The images and symbols with which the society expressed itself are sectioned off and framed in order to be scrutinized and, often, celebrated and reinforced.

A variety of symbolic spectacles in nineteenth-century America can be better appreciated if they are understood now, as they were then, as having a family relationship with the theater of that time. "Our broad areas," writes

Whitman, "are even now the busy theatre of plots, passions, interests, and suspended problems . . . And on these areas of ours, as on a stage, sooner or later, something like an *éclaircissement* of all the past civilization of Europe and Asia is probably to be evolved" (*Complete Prose* 2:187). Mary Ryan argues that Americans, between 1825 and 1880, invented the modern parade. Between these years the parade in America signified much about American democracy, documenting "the development of such concepts as class, ethnicity, and gender" (151). Ryan notes, "The disorder and cacophony that reigned most of the year was ordered into reassuring, visually and audibly pleasing patterns" (152). Yet, while the parade is ordered, it is important to consider its fluidity, its movement through the streets, and its sheer magnitude, for parades of this period could involve a sizable proportion of the urban population. "The dense built environment," writes Ryan, "provided few open spaces large enough for the entire population to enact their communal dramas. A swift march through the public arteries would seem to be the ceremonial path of least resistance, for social as well as spatial reasons" (137). From civic spectacles to the privately run theaters to the entrepreneurial inspiration of artists such as Banvard and Bierstadt, Americans almost obsessively staged themselves for themselves.

Between 1870 and 1900, moreover, enormous advances were made in technologies of an already highly sophisticated stagecraft. In 1879 Steele Mackaye opened a refurbished Madison Square Theatre with a new "elevator stage" and a two-level set that allowed for scene changes in forty seconds. A new generation of theatrical innovators, such as Mackaye and David Belasco, were wizards at special effects and, in the tradition of Charles Kean, aimed to present highly realistic scenes on stage. Belasco even tried to create natural effects like "real" rain and a "California" sunset. As Brenda Murphy remarks, however, while developing remarkable innovations, Mackaye and Belasco did not contribute to changing notions of theatrical illusion. They were romantics: "They aimed to heighten the sensational, the exotic, and the unusual in their productions rather than to create the recognizable illusion of everyday life that the realists were seeking. What's more, they used their talents to create reflexive effects, which were antirealistic because they were meant to call attention to themselves as artistic or technical feats" (20). Yet, although the technical virtuosity of Belasco and Mackaye enhanced the audience members' sense of the theatrical event, not, as realists desired, their immersion in the scene on stage, the technological innovations of the 1870s were crucial in the development of dramatic realism. Increasing sophistication in stagecraft pointed the way to a more complete illusion of a staged reality. Technologies pioneered by Belasco and Mackaye were ultimately incorporated into a new vision of experience in the theater.

Fundamental to notions of dramatic realism which began to gain attention around this time is the integrity of the illusion. To maintain an illusion, a muting, rather than a heightening, of spectacle is required. Audience members ought to feel as if they were sitting in place of a fourth wall of a room enclosing a private scene. The shift away from the spectacular in the realist theater is nowhere more evident than in James A. Herne's play *Margaret Fleming* (1890). Howells called the piece "an epoch-making play." Receiving critical acclaim but only minimal popular support, it marks a crucial turning point in the history of American drama. For the first performance Herne had tried unsuccessfully to hire theaters in New York and then in Boston. He eventually rented Chickering Hall, a small Boston auditorium, seating about five hundred. Still, being unable even to fill this small theater for more than a short run, the play faced an uphill battle. It was first produced on 4 May 1891 and ran for only two weeks. For a small circle, however, including Howells and Hamlin Garland, it was a revelation. And the fact that the play was staged in a relatively little theater contributed to the sense of domestic realism. The first performance, according to Arthur Hobson Quinn, "became a confession of faith of the realistic movement in America" (2:140). And Herne later came to be called the "American Ibsen."[36]

To begin with, *Margaret Fleming* focuses on the private sphere. And the thematic concern with private life is symbolized in the spatial trajectory of the action, which moves from Philip Fleming's office at the mill to "Margaret's home." The basic problem is a husband's infidelity, and the action consists of interpreting and discussing the event. The play does not present a conflict between right and wrong or even a clear indication of what is right or wrong. Philip Fleming, the husband who has caused the problem, bitterly exclaims: "I did not consider whether it was right or wrong. I did not know the meaning of those words. I never have."[37] This man is not a villain but a friendly, hardworking bourgeois, and his predicament is presented in such a way as to provoke sympathy and contemplation, not outrage and emotionalism.

Most important in the play's symbolic position as a turning point in American theater is its twist on the ancient theatrical trope of blindness, which was also being reimagined around this time in Europe by Ibsen in *The Wild Duck* (1884). Both of these realist dramas represent a pronouncedly unspectacular dramaturgy in the relationship between blindness and vision. Margaret, the title character of Herne's play, goes blind. The play de-emphasizes the visual in order to stress interior life, and it struggles with the question of whether language, or its counterpart, silence, is a medium adequate to the expression of that life. Thus, Margaret learns of her husband's infidelity when a letter meant for Philip from his dead mistress is intercepted and read aloud; then Margaret "is lost in spiritual contemplation of the torment she is suffering"; "she stares into space and a blank look comes into her face as though she were gazing at things beyond her comprehension"; "she drifts away into that inner consciousness where she evidently finds peace" (540). The symbolic repression of the specular is related to a general muting of all expressive registers. There is no wailing and gnashing of teeth, no bloodshed. As Howells wrote after seeing it, "It was common; it was pitilessly plain; it was ugly; but it was true, and it was irresistible" (RT 54). Ultimately, the worst retribution that Margaret and Philip can expect from their society, when they decide to stay together as a couple after the scandal, is a lot of talk. Margaret says, "Of course, there will be a lot of talk—mean talk—but they will get tired of that in the end" (544). The play ends as it began, with each individual going to his or her respective sphere and "getting to work." The dramatic space is unspectacular; the simplicity of the home is a backdrop for the characters' development and their intimacy with each other. In the end the picture on stage emphasizes the basic structure of the home, as Margaret sits at the table with her work and Philip steps through the door into the garden. Spectacle has made way for the simplicity of domestic order.

Insofar as *Margaret Fleming* dramatizes the contingency of social and market considerations in all questions of value, a contingency it represents not only thematically and formally but also in its production history, the play indicates an important aspect of the modern theater. And yet socioeconomic features of theater in mid-nineteenth-century America had been far more overt and volatile than they were at the century's end, with the mid-century theater situated in a broad context both of entrepreneurial display and of cross-class relationships. The economics of American theater were manifested not only in the profit motive, which lured entrepreneurs such as

P. T. Barnum and Augustin Daly, but also in a complex and dynamic interrelationship between the language of the marketplace and the language of theater. Deeply related to the economics of production, moreover, was the phenomenon of reception, which entails questions about the social class of those attending and the nature of audience participation in the "popular" American theater before the rise of dramatic realism. By the time of *Margaret Fleming* a structural transformation of both theater and "normative" social experience had been accomplished.

The profit motive that turned artists such as Albert Bierstadt into showmen was so pervasive that in 1890 we find Henry James dreaming, in a letter to his sister, that, if only his newly dramatized version of *The American* can "keep the stage," it "would mean profit indeed, and an income to my descendents" (*Letters* 1:167). James's dream, of course, was never realized. But entrepreneurs such as Boucicault, Barnum, and Daly quickly made and lost bundles of money through theatrical speculations. Daly, who was fundamentally a producer, was frequently in court fighting for his "rights." Still, he could declare righteously, "the standard of the best management is high except where theatres are managed purely as commercial speculations" (qtd. in Felheim 39). For P. T. Barnum, who exploited Gypsies, dwarfs, rope dancers, puppets, and "industrious fleas," it was all show business, with the emphasis on *business*. "Little did the public see the hand that indirectly pulled at their heart-strings, preparatory to a relaxation of their purse-strings," grins Barnum (197), and the huckster, or con man, so pervasive in the mythology of the nineteenth century, found his proper milieu in the theater. Nowhere is this relationship of commerce, confidence, and theatricality more evident than in Herman Melville's novel *The Confidence-Man: His Masquerade*. As Jean-Christophe Agnew notes, in that novel "every character, every relation, and every form of discourse eventually succumbs to the moral and epistemological ambiguities of a permanent theater and a placeless market. Theatricality and commerciality are so deeply interwoven as to confer on all forms of exchange . . . a problematic and deeply disquieting character" (196).

The stage itself epitomized the language of the marketplace and the commodification of culture. The central chapters of *Huckleberry Finn,* which involve the duke and the king, reflect two important and related notions of theater in the nineteenth century. First, theater is understood essentially as a commercial venture. And, second, as con men/actors, the duke and king represent the kind of dishonesty spawned by an unregulated market economy. Theater represents not only deception but also commercial speculation. When the two rascals who call themselves the duke and the king come aboard Huck and Jim's raft, they decide, amazingly, that the best way to raise money in the tiny towns spotting the banks of the Mississippi will be to stage performances of scenes from Shakespeare's *Richard III, Romeo and Juliet,* and *Hamlet.* The notion that the "presentation of Shakespeare in small Mississippi river towns could be conceived of as potentially lucrative," notes Lawrence Levine, "tells us much about the position of Shakespeare in the nineteenth century" (13). This scene conveys a sense of Shakespeare's popularity throughout the young nation, but, more important, since the version that these rogues produce is a carnivalization of the language of the original, it represents a deflation of the literary/theatrical object from the sphere of "art" by, and to, the sphere of the marketplace:

> To be, or not to be; that is the bare bodkin
> That makes calamity of so long life;
> For who would fardels bear, till Birnam Wood do come
> to Dunsinane.
> (*Huck Finn* 150)

The duke's past career includes a variety of professions: "a little in patent medicines; theater actor—tragedy, you know; take a turn at mesmerism and phrenology when there's a chance; teach singing-geography school for a change; sling a lecture sometimes" (134). These characters are clowns, but they have an important symbolic function. They deflate a foreign ideal (the notion of nobility of birth) to an American ideal (self-reliance), while at the same time they represent a historical reality (hucksterism and a kind of life on the Mississippi). Here the carnivalesque, which is a liminal mode in the Europe they parody, becomes the normative mode in American society. Not only did relatively diverse audiences attend the mid-nineteenth-century American theater, but there had been an important sense that theater (including Shakespeare) must represent a particularly "American" experience.

America is a society that combines play and the marketplace in ordinary experience. On a Saturday afternoon after the ironworks let out, for example, downtown Pittsburgh became what one observer described as "a decent carnival" (Covares 49). The pervasiveness and popularity of theater in America, moreover, indicates the importance of theater in the process of defining both what *America* means and what it means to be an American. Ironically, however, the economics of the American theater may have militated against the development of an American drama. In general, despite popular nationalism, manifested most violently in riots against English actors (e.g., against Edmund Kean in 1825 and William Charles Macready in 1849), the transatlantic theater trade flourished, a fact that may have significantly weakened the chances for the development of a native theater. The lucrative nature of American theater was such that a "star system" developed which drew great actors from England including Edmund and Charles Kean, Charles and Fanny Kemble, as well as William Charles Macready. Barnum made a fortune in 1850, managing the great Swedish opera singer Jenny Lind.[38] But the star system had its drawbacks from an artistic point of view. For one thing it resulted in a fierce bidding war between the managers of theaters. Moreover, as Quinn notes, the stars "contributed almost nothing to our drama. It was not that they were hostile to it, they were simply indifferent. They had their own plays and they saw no reason to adopt new and untried parts." As long as the star's drawing power lasted, there was no need for managers to take risks on untried plays. Thus, Quinn concludes, "Full houses do not always mean prosperity to the native playwright, while theatrical failure sometimes spells success for him" (1:203). In fact, the stars created major obstacles for native playwrights. Edwin Forrest, for example, prohibited publication of the plays he controlled, so that they would not be acted by others. Robert Montgomery Bird, one of the period's most talented and respected playwrights, wrote for Forrest such plays as *The Broker of Bogota,* a romantic verse tragedy that Forrest made a fortune acting for thirty years. But Forrest's tight-fistedness effectively drove Bird from the theater in the long run. "It is often asked," wrote one playwright frustrated at the sight of theatrical managers stuffing their pockets, "why there is no Standard American Drama. One of the best answers is, nobody will pay for it" (qtd. in Quinn, vol. 1 n. 299).

Audiences, which, as Lawrence Levine shows, had not yet separated into the "highbrow" and the "lowbrow," may not have subsidized many budding playwrights, but they did exercise a considerable amount of control over the nature of the theatrical event from night to night. American theater retained its popular character roughly until the time of the Civil War. Many observers, from that time, particularly the Jacksonian era, and our own, have noted what Francis Covares refers to as "the overwhelmingly plebeian and masculine" character of the working-class theater. Whitman characteristically recalls "any good night at the old Bowery, pack'd from ceiling to pit with its audiences mainly of alert, well-dress'd, full-blooded young and middle aged men": "the best average of American born mechanics—the emotional nature of the whole mass, arous'd by the power and magnetism of as mighty mimes as ever trod the stage—the whole crowded auditorium, and what seeth'd in it, and flush'd from its faces and eyes, to me as much a part of the show as any" (P&P 1188).

Audience lights were often left undimmed, partly to increase the visibility of the stage but largely to allow the audience members to see one another (MF 14). In fact, even a playwright complained that one theater allowed "too much light on stage, and too little in the boxes" so it became difficult to "recognize a friend across the house" (qtd. in Grimsted 58). At times the surveying of the audience was motivated by attention to difference: "Watching Indians watch a play . . . was as good sport as seeing them do a war dance on stage" (61). But, more often, it was a unifying force. As Rosemarie Bank shows in her vivid description of Lafayette's 1824–25 travels in America, when the general was entertained in countless theaters across the nation, "visiting theatres in order to display oneself to the public, to receive acclamations, or to address the people was a common use of these places of assembly in the nineteenth century" (12). An evening at the theater was social in a sense that disappeared by the end of the century, and it allowed for the illusion at least of a kind of union or community but also of a sense in the theater (and not just on the stage) of the potential for public action. As numerous theater riots in the first half of the nineteenth century attest, audiences felt licensed to give or withhold consent to a performance. Between those who produced the play and those who watched it, there was a dynamic of continual negotiation.[39]

No single event reflected more deeply the complexity of the American public's relationship to its theater and the volatility of its ideological structure than the Astor Place Riot in 1849, an event that took place on the eve of the flowering of American literature in the "American Renaissance." The Astor Place Riot, which tore up a theater and left more than twenty people dead and more than one hundred and fifty injured, was, as Joel Porte notes, essentially about dramatic interpretation.[40] But contributing to that interpretation was also a combination of intense nationalist feeling, anti-intellectualism, and a profound class antagonism. Rival productions of *Macbeth* were being staged, one at the Astor Place Opera House featuring the Englishman William Charles Macready, known for his cerebral acting style, aristocratic demeanor, and allegedly anti-American comments, and one at the Broadway Theatre, featuring America's own flamboyantly patriotic Edwin Forrest. Macready's second performance at the Astor Place Opera House (the first had been abortive) was disrupted by a large crowd of blue-collar workingmen, many allegedly supporters of Forrest. The day after the riot an article appeared in the *New York Tribune* in which the writer claimed, "Great cities have ever been and probably ever will be . . . the theater of the mob" (TWC 17). The metaphor highlights a relationship between theater and mob which had become a widespread cause of concern. Bruce McConachie goes so far as to claim, "Apocalyptic melodramas flourishing on the stages of working-class theatres in New York between 1835 and 1850 helped to legitimate many of the preindustrial riots in the city involving working-class mobs during the same period," specifically because of their "shared symbolic universe" (TWC 18–19). McConachie simplifies the relationship, but the crowd did indeed exercise a peculiar and important power both over what was presented on stage and how it was presented. And, as McConachie notes, the ability to applaud at any time, to holler, and to throw fruits, nuts, and other aerodynamic missiles was regarded as a *right* not to be infringed. Thus, the stage and the mob were mutually engaged in a process of "self-fashioning" which, in this period, gave release to the most radical "democratic" and nationalistic impulses. In the volatile relations *between* the conceptual, imaginative, and social realities, relations mediated or represented by the theatrical event, American self-consciousness was shaped.

The reciprocal creativity of mid-nineteenth-century audiences and performers indicates the underlying popular assumption that self-fashioning is a public phenomenon to which any person present is equally able to contribute. This kind of public creativity was spontaneous and improvisatory. On the one hand, it was commonly recognized that improvisations were always taking place on stage: actors forgot or made up lines; props fell apart or caught on fire. And audiences, on their side, could drown out speeches or compel multiple renditions of a favored scene. Significantly, American audiences of this period have been noted for a remarkable tendency to mistake plays for reality, often interrupting a performance in process. There are many wonderful stories of this sort. For example, Levine recounts an 1832 production of *Richard III* starring Junius Brutus Booth at the Bowery Theatre in New York in which the audience "mingled with the soldiers during the battle of Bosworth Field and responded to the roll of drums and blasts of trumpets by racing across the stage. When Richard and Richmond began their fight, the audience 'made a ring round the combatants to see fair play' " (29). Grimsted tells of the New Orleans boatman's suggestion to Othello, grieving over the loss of the handkerchief, "Why don't you blow your nose with your fingers and let the play go on" (60). And Lawrence Buell recalls Nathaniel Deering, attorney and writer, of Portland, Maine, who became so excited by a performance of *Uncle Tom's Cabin* that he reportedly sprang onto the stage to outbid the cruel master during a slave auction scene, crying "Six thousand!" (1986, n. 435).

If audiences of this period felt particularly licensed to express themselves to the characters in the stories before them, however, it is naive to suggest that they were somehow more susceptible to mistaking fiction for reality than audiences of the realist theater. Few people would have gone to the theater had they not felt that they would be able to participate in some way in the process of performance and, therefore, in a sense, in the process of creation. In effect, this form of social participation in the theatrical event represents the invasion of the secular consciousness into the previously sacred space of ritual enactment. "History," writes Walter Benjamin, "merges into the setting" (92). The stage, in the mid-nineteenth century, was not supposed to be the ontological integer that it has become, and the flow of the drama occurred within an expanded, or at least a different, set of parameters. (In fact, absolute silence probably would have been more disruptive in those theaters than screaming from the galleries.)[41] "The acting on stage was good," reported a St. Louis newspaper in 1844, "and the cavorting in pit, boxes, and galleries was extremely interesting" (qtd. in Grimsted 61). Ultimately, theater and normative social experience generated a codeterminate and codependent language. The notion of a permanent, placeless theater representing the liberal, market-oriented culture of America provided writers and intellectuals like Melville and Twain with a rich fund of metaphors for understanding and developing ideas about society and, in particular, the elusive idea of America.[42] Nearly fifty years after *The Confidence-Man,* when Henry James sets out to explore his native land and himself, he too describes "a world created, a stage set." In *The*

American Scene James imagines his return to his native land as a "drama . . . The very *donnée* of the piece could be given, the subject formulated: the great adventure of a society reaching out into the apparent void for the amenities, the consummations" (12).

America in 1904, however, as James quickly discovered, was radically different from the place of his birth sixty years earlier. The "crudity of wealth," the rapidly growing immigrant population, and James's own general "consciousness of quantity . . . as opposed to quality," all contributed to an adventure "embalmed . . . [in] odd sharp notes." Theater, too, had changed. In New York City, for example, James visited the Bowery Theatre, where "a young actor in whom I was interested had found for the moment a fine melodramatic opportunity." Yet, despite great anticipation, he is disillusioned to find in "that vast dingy edifice" a striking contrast with an "image antediluvian . . . *the* Bowery Theatre . . . contemporary with my more or less gaping youth." It is not only the bewildering array of "foreigners" whom he observes from the curtained corner of a private box but also their relation to the action on stage which disappoints him: "The old signs would have been those of some 'historic' community, so to speak, between the play and the public, between those opposed reciprocal quantities: such a consciousness of the same general terms of intercourse for instance, as I seemed to have seen prevail, long years ago, under the great dim, bleak, sonorous dome of the old Bowery" (AS 195). Henry James had not been among the "b'hoys" who followed George L. Fox or rioted in the streets. Indeed, he had censured the less seemly side of the "democratic" theater. The Astor Place Riot, for example, he had considered an example of the "instinctive hostility of barbarism to culture" (qtd. in Levine 225). Nonetheless, his memory of a "community" in the theater characterized by a vital interaction across the footlights is essentially accurate, and his disillusionment reflects an important change that occurred in the American theater within his lifetime.

The Astor Place Riot had been a watershed event in the life of the American theater. It was the culmination of the theater's volatility, of anti-intellectualism, and of audience participation. Never again in America would the theater be such an overtly dangerous (or democratic) place. In fact, by 1897 *Harper's Weekly* could complain: "American audiences are only too indulgent. We could save ourselves much poorish and worse musical art were our audiences more disposed to use time-honored 'privileges.' How much we endure unprotesting!"[43] As the notion of audience rights and, indeed, the notion of what constituted an acceptable community in the theater changed, a corresponding change occurred in the drama performed on stage.

The evolution of dramatic realism in America corresponds to the development of an increasingly rigid cultural hierarchy. In the latter half of the nineteenth century experience both on the stage and in the audience began to change. In particular, metatheatrical pleasure metamorphosed from visceral excitement (or excitation) to a more serene, self-congratulatory pleasure of the mind. Eugene O'Neill, leader of the parade of new dramatists in the next century, in both his work and his life, illustrates an oedipal relationship to his forebears in this particular sense. Many critics note what Robert Brustein calls O'Neill's "rebellion against the mindless nineteenth-century stage," on which his father, James, was so prominent an actor. O'Neill himself once said, "As a boy I saw so much of the old, ranting, artificial romantic stuff that I always had a sort of contempt for the theater" (qtd. in Brustein 334).[44] O'Neill's hierarchicalism, which is implicit in Brustein as well, is most clearly articulated in playwright Bronson Howard's 1914 lecture to students and faculty of the Shakspere Club at Harvard University: "Let me say here, to the students of Harvard . . . it is to you and to others who enjoy the high privileges of liberal education that the American stage ought to look for honest and good dramatic work in the future" (Howard 13). Howard envisages a theater for a polite and well-educated social class, one far from the Bowery of the 1850s, where obstreperous b'hoys had wildly applauded George L. Fox's *Humpty Dumpty* or cheered lustily for Edwin Forrest in *The Gladiator.* "I thank the gods that I am a barbarian!" Forrest had exclaimed as Spartacus, one of his most famous roles. It was a claim, many felt, that applied not only to the Roman slave but also to the actor himself. That democratic impulse, however, expressed so extravagantly in Forrest's melodramas, was explicitly to be excluded from the realist theater.

Theater informs nineteenth-century American literature in basic ways. The literature between 1830 and 1900 reveals a remarkably fruitful proliferation of theatrical metaphors, not simply of the "all the world's a stage" variety but also more obliquely in the self-referentiality of theatrical voices, theatrical bodies, and the stages or platforms upon which fictional and real characters "perform." Moreover, formal aspects of theater are reimagined in nineteenth-century America as being themselves representable in prose and poetry. Consequently, the theater comes to have diverse consequences for literary form. In "The Philosophy of Composition" Poe imagines the writer's craft and the process of composition as that of an actor or stage manager, made up of wheels and pinions, tackle for scene-shifting, cock's feathers, red paint, and black patches. Whitman's notion of "indirect expression" is also explicitly theatrical, as are Ahab's speeches on the deck of the *Pequod* and, to some degree, the novels James structures in scenes or acts. The lack of a standardized, "legitimate" theater did not betoken a society without theater, but, on the contrary, it enabled a theater that, like a living organism, spread into new forms in order to survive.

The pervasiveness of basic dramaturgical assumptions, whether of melodrama or of realism, indicate how deeply theater was registered in the imaginations of nineteenth-century American authors. The existential and ethical problems raised by theater—the expressive potential of the voice or body, the difficulty of knowing a character when confronted with an actor playing roles, the need to visualize, to plot, and to make order out of seemingly chaotic urban life, and the desire for a social form of amusement—are all engaged by "nontheatrical" genres. Dramatic realism represents an attempt to reimagine the drama and to redraw the parameters of theater, but it also represents an attempt to renegotiate the relationship between theater and literature. Dramatic realists not only seek to imagine dramatic novels and novelistic plays but also to reimagine the literary/dramatic work in a way that privileges a certain kind of experience, a private over a public experience. While "melodramatic prose," such as certain passages in Melville's work, for example, may seek to incorporate public features of the theater into the act of reading, realist dramas assume that a private, readerly experience has a higher artistic value than theatrical experience, even in the theater. Dramatic realism represents a perceived and, for that reason alone, a real decline of American public life. As the focus of dramatic interest shifts from simple relations between characters to complexities within them, the sense of ambiguity, incompleteness, even danger, shifts from the space of the theater to the less stable structure of the drama.

Developments in the history of American theater have traditionally been understood in Darwinian terms. Howells, for example, refers to the theater's "evolution": "For a while yet we must have the romantic and the realistic mixed in the theater. That is quite inevitable; and it is strictly in accordance with the law of evolution. The stage, in working free of romanticism, must carry some rags and tags of it forward in the true way; that has been the case always in the rise from the higher to a lower form; the man on a trapeze recalls the ancestral monkey who swung by his tail from the forest tree; and the realist cannot all at once forget the romanticist" (RT 53). But, of course, it is not clear exactly what makes the "true way" true. Instead of considering the early American theater in the light of standards to which it cannot conform, we can derive new insights from understanding the theater of mid-nineteenth-century America as an important social phenomenon and cultural form in which most major writers had an important stake. Edgar Allan Poe, whose parents were actors,[45] wrote theater reviews, had a story ("The Gold-Bug") adapted to the stage, and refers to himself in "The Philosophy of Composition" as a "literary *histrio.*" Many American writers—including Washington Irving, Longfellow, Whitman, Twain, Bret Harte, Louisa May Alcott, Howells, and James—were at some point professional drama critics and/or playwrights. And many more, including Cooper and Melville, were avid theatergoers with friendships among actors and playwrights. Even Harriet Beecher Stowe made a significant, if inadvertent, contribution to American theater in providing the story for the most successful melodrama of the nineteenth century.[46] Of course, like James and Whitman, there were many important figures in this history whose lives spanned several generations and who, therefore, experienced opposed, even contradictory, dramaturgical systems. James A. Herne began his acting career in *Uncle Tom's Cabin* and ended as the American Ibsen.

Rip Van Winkle is a fitting emblem for this re-presentation of American theater history. For one thing this play indicates a relation between American literature and theater. Published in 1819, Irving's story was first produced as a play in 1829 in Albany, New York. The play was staged in different forms over the next twenty years throughout America and in London. And in 1865 Joseph Jefferson asked Dion Boucicault to revise the play, which Boucicault did for a production that year in London. Thus, the play brought together key figures of both American literature and American theater. Yet the content of *Rip Van Winkle* is also relevant here, for it is concerned with both the act of remembering and the problem of communicating between dissimilar cultures.

The play itself teaches an important history lesson. Rip's old village of Falling Water is the image of temporality and fluidity, and the play, in structure, tone, and theme, indicates the need for flexibility. The action of the play, in moving from the village to the Kaatskill Mountains, correspondingly changes tone, moving between registers of the colloquial and the lyrical. After Rip meets the elves, in act 3, Jefferson notes in his introduction, "the play drifts from realism to idealism" (402). The plot, as is well-known, is generated centrally by problems of communication and language. (Rip's first language in this dramatic version is German.) When he returns from the hills, he and the English-speaking villagers regard one another with confusion. The villagers go so far as to say that the old man is crazy, and the problem of identity seems almost impossible to solve. The play is resolved with an act of nomination when Rip's own daughter, Meenie, now grown, is forced to acknowledge her parent with a climactic "Father!" "One by one," she says, "your features come back to my memory." So, in the pages to come, features of a theater long forgotten will be remembered in literary genres that seem to have little relation to theater. Ultimately, a recognition of that deep and abiding family relationship enables a greater comprehension not only of the ethical and artistic significance of nineteenth-century American letters but also of the rich complexities of particular American lives.

TWO

CHARACTER ON STAGE

Walt Whitman and American Theater

Now I stand here in the Universe, a personality perfect and sound; all things and all other beings as an audience at the play-house perpetually and perpetually calling me out from behind my curtain.

WALT WHITMAN, Manuscript Notebook

In "Memoranda," written toward the end of his life, Whitman imagines himself as an actor making his way to the flies, or exit door, of the "earth's stage" and nostalgically recalls his life "out in the brilliancy of the footlights—filling the attention of perhaps a crowded audience, and making many a breath and pulse swell and rise" (P&P 1293). It is one of many references Whitman makes in prose and poetry to the *theatrum mundi.* Theater, he notes elsewhere, has informed his worldview fundamentally: "Seems to me, I ought to acknowledge my debt to actors, singers, public speakers, conventions, and the Stage in New York, my youthful days, from 1835 onward . . . and to plays and operas generally. (Which nudges a pretty big disquisition: of course it should be all elaborated and penetrated more deeply . . .) For theatricals in literature and doubtless upon me personally, including opera, have been of course serious factors" (P&P 1289).

The sense that Whitman's life and work have a "theatrical" or "dramatic" quality, moreover, is not confined to Whitman himself. Whitman criticism is pervaded by these terms.[1] Paul Zweig, in *Walt Whitman: The Making of the Poet* (1984), suggests that theater may be viewed as an analogy or model not only for the immediacy of Whitman's voice in *Leaves of Grass* but also for "a whole aspect of Whitman's behavior as a public figure": "His poems are, in some sense, a script brought to life by the voice and physical presence of the player, who speaks beguilingly to an audience of rapt souls . . . Theater is, after all, the art of which it is undeniably true that perfection of the life is perfection of the work" (11). What such statements lack, however, is an adequate appreciation of the historical resonance of the theatrical terms or models they employ, the culturally specific *theater* that may have rendered Whitman's work or his personality *theatrical.* There is, as Whitman himself is highly aware, a particular kind of theater, the stage from 1835 onward, with a specific dramaturgy that underlies, informs, and is reworked in his imagination.

"I have always had a good deal to do with actors," Whitman told Horace Traubel in 1889. "They are gassy . . . but after that is said, there is more, and more important [*sic*] to their credit" (qtd. in Traubel 3:519). Whitman's substantial body of work as a drama critic for the Brooklyn *Daily Eagle* in the 1840s shares deep connections with his work as a poet. The connections are apparent especially in a certain theatrical mode of presenting the self. In "Crossing Brooklyn Ferry" Whitman demands: "Live, old life! play the part that looks back on the actor or actress!"[2] Here and in writings such as *Specimen Days, November Boughs,* and *Democratic Vistas* theater provides a particular terminology for both national and personal identity. The dramaturgy of melodrama, which underlies these terms, describes epistemological boundaries within which self or nation acquires specific powers to signify. The melodramatic theater represents both a particular kind of space and a mode of moral action. As Robert Heilman suggests, "The issue [in melodrama] is not the reordering of the self, but the reordering of one's relations with others" (86).

The melodramatic theater was explicitly conceived both as a space of influence (of actor upon audience) and of an empathic wholeness of feeling (of audience for actor) which Heilman calls "monopathy." In antebellum America, however, theatrical space also often became a space of contention, a space of reciprocal engagement, sometimes harmonious but often agonistic. The realm of moral action may be the space in which Whitman's complexity as a dramatic theorist is most pronounced. On the one hand, he enjoys the sense of radical immersion that comes with a deep experience of theatrical illusion and a sense of oneness with the audience. But he also insists that an audience must be critical and must challenge the performer. As a drama critic in 1846, he claims that "the drama of this country *can* be the mouth-piece of freedom, refinement, liberal philanthropy, beautiful love for all our brethren, polished manners and an elevated good taste. It can wield potent sway to destroy any attempt at despotism" (GF 314–15). This statement conveys a notion of theater as a moral and fundamentally public institution as well as some sense of the relation, in Whitman's mind, between theater and personal responsibility. The theater also gave Whitman a vocabulary to express disillusionment with the public sphere in the 1870s in *Democratic Vistas.* Traubel tells us that even in 1889, two years before his death, "The Stage" was part of Whitman's regular Sunday reading (3:568).[3]

While Whitman kept abreast of changes in theater throughout his life, it was the theater of the 1830s and 1840s that most deeply conditioned his thinking, and it was that theater to which, he insisted, he felt the most profound allegiance. Although the older Whitman appreciated young actors such as Henry Irving, they could never hold a candle in his imagination to Junius Booth or Charlotte Cushman. "I have heard, read, much, thought a good deal, about [Irving]," Whitman told Traubel in 1889, "[yet] my impression is that he would not satisfy me—would not fill me—would not fit the bill. All my ideals have been made up by long study of the elder Booth—Edwin's father" (3:519–20). In 1884 Whitman requested and received from Edwin Booth a picture of his father, when the younger actor sent the poet a copy of Asia Booth Clarke's 1882 biography, *The Elder and the Younger Booth* (see fig. 7). "I am sorry that I can find none better than these reproductions," wrote the younger Booth. "They give [Junius Booth's] face before and after the nose was broken, but are badly printed. I trust they will be of service to you" (qtd. in Traubel 1:46). In his old age Whitman's most cherished theatrical memories were of his trips to the theater in New York, when Booth was in his prime: "The Park [Theatre] held a large part of my boyhood and young manhood's life" (P&P 1186). Not only the acting but also the spectacle and oratory of productions in the 1830s and 1840s deeply affected Whitman—so much so, in fact, that a particularly extravagant production of *King John* by Charles Kean rendered that play one of Whitman's enduring favorites by Shakespeare. In the reminiscences of his old age Whitman continually returns to the romantic theater of his youth. He even recalls "a small but well-appointed amateur-theatre up Broadway" in which he was a member "and acted in it several times . . . Perhaps it too was a lesson . . . at any rate it was full of fun and enjoyment" (1293).

Whitman's world was saturated with the pleasures of theater. Americans

FIG. 7. Junius Booth. Frontispiece from Asia Booth Clarke's 1882 biography, *The Elder and the Younger Booth.*

in the 1830s and 1840s saw, among many popular forms, vernacular dramatizations of the Bible as well as major innovations in the style of popular sermons, the most famous of which were the dramatic and imagistic sermons of Father Edward Thomson Taylor in the 1830s, the model for Melville's Father Mapple and a preacher whom Emerson called "the Shakespeare of the sailor & the poor." This new urban evangelism was based "as much on pulpit showmanship and verbal pyrotechnics as on otherworldly message" and competed openly for its audiences with staged melodramas and reform movements in the popular press (Reynolds 1989, 24). In general, as David Reynolds notes, there was a widespread shift in the style of popular religious discourse from the doctrinal to the imaginative.[4] The history of American adaptations of French plays in the first half of the century also is characterized by an amplification of moral absolutes in order to awaken audience sympathies.[5]

In short, the stage of Whitman's youth featured self-consciously potent vocalizations, embodiments, and characterizations. The highly expressive voice is endowed with extraordinary, sometimes otherworldly, significance in this theater, in part because dramas share the cultural stage with opera and oratory, genres in which the voice becomes preeminent. This notion of voice has a deep relation with music. The voice is also understood on a continuum with bodily enactments, which similarly tend toward the highly expressive. In the era of Poe's "man of the crowd" extravagance of expression, unusual appearance, or even "an air of excessive frankness" is looked upon with suspicion in nearly every space of public concourse except the theater (Poe 53). In fact, the crowd into which Poe's man blends is an audience leaving the theater. Inside the theater, however, performers are not only licensed but required, through gesture and appearance, to convey character as strongly as possible. In the theater the body becomes a crucial signifier of an ethical self. Both the nature of the ethical self and the relationship between body and self, however, become serious subjects of debate and subjects to which Whitman makes a significant, if unrecognized, contribution. Character in this theater is morally mutable but psychologically simple. The 1830s and 1840s do not witness great character studies on the stage but elaborately contrived plots in which characters embody specific moral principles (courage, faith, innocence, malice). There is little concern with the life of the mind or the psyche, the interior life, but much concern with the seduction of the innocent or redemption of the fallen. Whitman makes deep and explicit use of this theatrical idiom of character. For the theater of Whitman's youth and young adulthood is a public and inherently moral space. It can be a kind of school for morals, but that is only the most simple articulation of theater's value in a democratic society, as Whitman understands it. The issue of theater as a public and moral space is related to a long debate about Whitman as public poet or "imperial self." And, as with the other aspects of theater represented significantly in his work, my aim, in discussing Whitman's interest in theater as a moral institution, is to broaden the context for critical debates about the poet. Certainly, the function of theater in Whitman's thinking is not unidimensional or even always well thought out. But theater does inform his imagination deeply, as it does that of many of his contemporaries.

THE MELODRAMATIC VOICE

In the summer of 1846, after more than a year of performing in London, American actress Charlotte Cushman drew from the London press the extravagant compliment of being ranked as a "second Siddons." Whitman, who loved Cushman above any other actor of their day, was not satisfied with this tribute. "Charlotte Cushman is *no* 'second Siddons!' " he exclaims. "She is *herself,* and that is far, far better!" (see fig. 8). Cushman stands above the greatest actors of her day because, according to Whitman,

> she seems to identify herself so completely with the character she is playing . . . Who has seen her Evadne, in "The Bridal," but acknowledged the simple grandeur of her genius! In the simple utterance of her shrieking "yes! yes! yes!" as she swings down to her brother's feet, was one of the greatest triumphs of the histrionic art, ever achieved! In the twinkling of an eye—in the utterance of a word—was developed the total revolution of a mighty and guilty mind—from pride, defiance, anger, and rioting guilt, to an utterly crushed state of fear, remorse, and conscious vileness! (GF 325–26)

Utterance is a pervasive word in Whitman's writings. The 1872 preface to *Leaves of Grass* begins: "The impetus and ideas urging me, for some years past, to an utterance, or attempt at utterance, of New World songs, and an epic of Democracy . . ." (*Prose* 2:185). The fact that in the passage on Cushman's Evadne *the simple utterance of a word* becomes the refrain, and indeed the one concrete example of how a character is formed, indicates the profound significance of the voice in Whitman's thinking. It also indicates the crucial role of the voice in establishing the monopathic connection between the actor and her audience. As a boy, Whitman did not simply go to *see* the great actors of his day perform; he went to "the Bowery Theatre, where Booth and Forrest were frequently to be *heard*" (P&P 1187; my emph.). Of Booth he said, "I never heard from any other the charm of unswervingly

FIG. 8. Charlotte Cushman as Lady Macbeth.

perfect vocalization without trenching at all on mere melody, the province of music" (1192).

Whitman himself was well-known for developing his own voice through meditating on the art of the actor, stressing in particular the highly emotional and expressive. One ferry hand recalled Whitman declaiming on the Brooklyn Ferry: "In my judgement few could excel his reading of stirring poems and brilliant Shakespearian passages. These things he vented evidently for his own practice and amusement. I have heard him proceed to a length of some soliloquy . . . and when he had stopped suddenly and said with intense dissatisfaction, 'No! no! no! that's the way the bad actors would do it,' he would start again and recite the part most impressively" (qtd. in *Workshop* 210). Voice represented for Whitman a crucial feature of the deep affinity he felt between himself and actors. He once told Traubel, for example: "These actor people always make themselves at home with me and always make me feel at home with them. I feel rather close to them—almost like one of their kind." The reason for this feeling of kinship, Whitman explains, is that, as a young man, thinking that he had something to say but afraid that he might not have a chance to speak through books, he aimed to be an orator: "I think I had a good voice: I think I was never afraid—I had no stage reticences (I tried the thing often enough to see that). For awhile I speechified in politics, but that of course did not satisfy me . . . what I really had to give out was something more serious, more off from politics and towards the general life" (qtd. in Traubel 1:5–6).

Whitman's view of artistic expression (and I include the various modes of public address under this designation) is, at least superficially, Hegelian: the mission of art, in general, is to bring before sensuous contemplation the truth as it is in the spirit. Poetry somehow "wins out" because it is the richest and most unrestricted of the arts. Poetry is the "total art" because it repeats in its own field the "modes of presentation characteristic of the other arts" (Hegel 2:627).[6] In a discussion of American culture between 1830 and 1850 the conflation of theater and other modes of public address or performance is, at times, inescapable, though I am not trying to claim that either theater or oratory or opera directly influenced Whitman's poetry or that there is a simple causal relationship.

My reading is partly a response to F. O. Matthiessen's discussion of oratory and opera in *American Renaissance* (1941). Matthiessen, who is interested primarily in Whitman's linguistic experiments and literary form, argues for the importance of Whitman's purposeful stress on oratory and opera as major analogies for his poems. In other words, he attempts to show certain kinds of influence. Although he does acknowledge that "it is often impossible to tell whether passages of loosely rhythmical prose were originally conceived for a speech or as a draft towards a poem," he actually thinks in terms of more specific, causal relationships: "As a result of going over these notes and arranging them for publication, Bucke believed it certain that Whitman's first intention, some years before *Leaves of Grass* had been thought of, was to publish his ideas by lectures" (550). For Whitman the different forms do not exist in isolation, a fact that can be seen in Whitman's easy conflation of "all art-utterance." Oratory and opera, like theater proper, should be understood not as analogies for Whitman's poems but as cultural forms that interact in a larger, and more fluid, discourse about the voice as art-utterance.[7] Whitman did not hesitate to lump together, as "possessing this wonderful vocal power," performers as diverse as Fanny Kemble, "the old actor" Junius Booth, the contralto Alboni, the tenor Bettini, the Quaker demagogue Elias Hicks, and the seaman/preacher Father Taylor. In short, Whitman reimagines the poetic voice in the crucible of genres and media which existed in mid-century America: "New politics, new literatures and religions, new inventions and arts. / These my *voice* announcing" ("Starting from Paumanok"; my emph.). Nonetheless, I privilege theater in this discussion for two reasons. First, theater is the cultural form in which dramaturgical assumptions (of speaking voice, of gesturing body, of role-playing, of actor-audience relation, etc.), manifested elsewhere in isolation, are all necessarily involved, and Whitman clearly attributed importance to the theater for this reason. Junius Booth, for example, provided a "lesson in artistic expression." "To me," Whitman writes, "Booth stands for much else besides theatricals" (P&P 1192). And, second, the qualities that we may call "melodramatic" derive from a tradition of melodrama in theater, a kinship acknowledged in nineteenth-century America by orators, clergy, and opera enthusiasts alike.

The staged melodramas of the 1830s represented the voice as a more or less stable signifier and celebrated its power. In the melodramatic theater there are many references to or verbal re-presentations of the voice. At the end of Nathaniel Parker Willis's blank verse tragedy, *Bianca Visconti; or The Heart Overtasked* (1837), Bianca, whose actions have led indirectly to the death of her brother, begins, in a protracted death scene, to lose her mind. She hears the voice of her poor little brother Giulio:

> Hark! I hear
> His voice now! Do the walls of Paradise
> Jut over hell? I hear his voice, I say!
> [*Strikes off* Sforza, *who approaches her.*]
> Unhand me, devil! You've the shape of one
> Who upon earth had no heart! Can you take
> No shape but that? Can you not look like Giulio?
> [Sforza *falls back, struck with remorse.*]
> Hark! 'tis his low, imploring voice again . . .
> Pray on, my brother! Pray on, Giulio!
> I come! [*Falls on her face.*]

Not only does the imagined voice of Giulio evoke thoughts of heaven and hell, good and evil, but the voice is paratactically related to the body of Sforza, her *present* husband, whom she must strike off to listen. The imagined voice, the utterance (a prayer but for the audience, and perhaps for Bianca too, a wordless prayer), provokes a physical action on the stage. The voice draws Bianca forward; it literally topples her. The voice both represents moral truth (Giulio's goodness and the sin of his murder) and generates an actual spatial relationship.

As Tenney Nathanson observes, "Voice is a crucial mediating trope in Whitman's work: defining the figure of the poet, it melds presence and language, body and name" (8). The melding of presence and language, the aura that surrounds both the speaker and the audience and that defies the reifying tendency of the written word, was referred to by Whitman and his contemporaries by a variety of terms but most commonly as "electricity" or "influence." Influence, writes Karen Halttunen, was "the power by which any person's character affected the characters of others, for good as well as for evil . . . As a force for good, influence was spoken of as a moral gravitation, a personal electricity, a cosmic vibration" (1982, 4). Charles Durang, a friend of the actor Edwin Forrest, describes a Forrest entrance that "made a *tout-ensemble* that at once struck like an electrical chord of harmony from the actor to the audience" (qtd. in Shattuck 1976, 65). Similarly, the influence of public speakers vis-à-vis the voice was imagined as a visceral, as well as an intellectual, relationship with their audience: "The orator's province is not barely to apply to the mind, but likewise to the passions; which require a great variety of the voice, high or low, vehement or languid, according to the nature of the passions he designs to affect" (Bingham 16). Whitman, in his notes for lectures, advocates an "electrical spirit" that vibrates "energies from soul to soul" (*Workshop* 38). And even toward the end of his life he comments on his own continuing responsiveness to speakers of great vocal range. "I am particularly susceptible to voices," he remarks to Horace Trauble, "voices of range, magnetism: mellow, persuading voices" (1:103).

The brilliant performances of the period's most charismatic speakers endowed Whitman, from an early age, with a deep sense of the connection between the spoken word, the aura of the speaker, and higher truth. These features seemed to make oratory "the rarest and most profound of humanity's arts" (P&P 1143). In 1829, at the age of ten, Whitman had gone with his parents to the ballroom of Morrison's Hotel on Brooklyn Heights to hear the charismatic and unorthodox Quaker Elias Hicks. Hicks, Whitman remarks in a long essay in *November Boughs,* would preach anywhere, "no respect to buildings—private or public houses, school-rooms, barns, even theatres." As a child, Whitman was unable to follow the discourse, but Hicks's performance remained vividly with him, "a magnetic stream of natural eloquence, before which all minds and natures, all emotions high and low, gentle or simple, yielded entirely without exception. Many, very many were in tears" (1234). The language with which Whitman describes the rapport between Hicks and his listeners recurs frequently in Whitman's writing about the performer-audience dynamic. Justin Kaplan remarks that "in the making of a poet's vision of reality and identity Hicks preceded Emerson and outlasted him" (69).

Whitman's favorite orator, Father Taylor, preached primarily to sailors in a theatrical shiplike church that resembles the one that Melville describes in *Moby-Dick.*[8] In Melville's novel Father Taylor becomes the famous New Bedford whaleman/preacher, Father Mapple. Melville describes the setting, in which Father Mapple enters up a rope ladder to the pulpit: "The wall which formed [the pulpit's] back was adorned with a large painting representing a gallant ship beating against a terrible storm off a lee coast of black rocks and snowy breakers . . . Nor was the pulpit itself without a trace of the same sea-taste that had achieved the ladder and the picture. Its panelled front was in the likeness of a ship's bluff bows, and the Holy Bible rested on a projecting piece of scroll work, fashioned after a ship's fiddle-headed beak." Yet, Melville notes somewhat disingenuously, "Father Mapple enjoyed such a wide reputation for sincerity and sanctity, that I could not suspect him of courting notoriety by any mere tricks of the stage" (43).

Like the Whaleman's Chapel, Father Taylor's New York church also featured a pulpit backed by a mural, which, as Whitman notes, was meant less for art critics than for "its effect upon the congregation." When attending services there, as in the theater, Whitman paid close attention to the audience, "their physiognomies, form, dress, gait," and the effect upon them of the occasion and atmosphere. But, as soon as Father Taylor opened his mouth, the pictures, the church, the audience, drifted away as "a far more potent charm entirely sway'd me." Taylor did not speak from notes, as he paced back and forth. He reminded Whitman "of old Booth, the great actor, and my favorite of those and preceding days," as well as of Hicks; like those performers, Taylor managed to blend passion with tenderness: "such human-harassing reproach (like Hamlet to his mother, in the closet)." He, too, invariably affected Whitman to tears. Above all, it was Taylor's vocal quality that worked upon his audience: "The mere words, (which usually play such a big part) seem'd altogether to disappear, and the *live feeling* advanced upon you and seiz'd you with a power before unknown" (P&P 1144). This quality of voice resulted in a "personal electricity" that, along with "the whole scene there," leads Whitman to reflect on impressions he experienced while seeing Booth and other actors perform at the Park and the Bowery.

The power of the theater, writes Tocqueville in 1840, is its ability to "lay hold on you in the midst of your prejudices and your ignorance" (79). There is no space for rationality or logic, no time for serious consideration. This instantaneous and overwhelming power, celebrated by Whitman, was for many of his contemporaries a source of grave anxiety. One of the most important textbooks on oratory, reprinted throughout the nineteenth century, Caleb Bingham's *Columbian Orator* (1797), manifests many of the tensions that result from a sense that the voice is a powerful medium, connecting body and soul, and an instrument of extraordinary influence. The relationship of the physiological voice to truth is not always clear, and, in countless advice manuals for young men, oratorical textbooks, and antitheatrical tracts, that indeterminacy was imagined to have dangerous consequences. Bingham's textbook manifests ample (though reluctant) recognition that the dramaturgy that conditions its most basic assumptions, its system of expression, persuasion, and audience psychology, is shared with the theater. More than twenty of the exercises for public speaking in this practical guide are taken from plays (e.g., "Slaves in Barbary, a Drama in two Acts," "Scene from the Drama of 'Moses in the Bulrushes,'" "Scene from the Tragedy of Cato," and "Scene from the Tragedy of Tamerlane"). Yet theater, and specifically the art of the actor, is continually disparaged for being "wholly counterfeit," unlike oratory, which is founded on truth and in which, therefore, art and nature coincide. The most disturbing problem in the theater for Bingham is the concept of character and its role in the "art of persuasion." Bingham asserts that there is a crucial connection between voice and character; fine speakers, it seems, are those of fine character:

> "It is not of so much moment what our compositions are, as how they are pronounced; since it is the manner of the delivery, by which the audience is moved." The truth of this sentiment . . . might be proved from many instances . . . [Hortensius] was highly applauded for his action [i.e., pronunciation]. But his orations after his death, as Quintilian tells us, did not appear answerable to his character; from whence he justly concludes, there must have been something pleasing when he spoke, by which he gained his character, which was lost in reading them. (9)

Yet, in what seems like an open contradiction, Bingham also claims that voice is such a powerful force that bad characters can abuse it. Therefore, the orator *must* be a good man whose message is known to be "true" if oratory is to work for the social good.

In the theater, writes Bingham, "though we are sensible that every thing we see and hear is counterfeit; yet such is the power of action [i.e., pronunciation], that we are oftentimes affected by it in the same manner as if it were all reality" (10). Simply to be *affected* by a representation that is "counterfeit" is to be immoral. Bingham, who continually disparages the relatedness of oratory and theater, becomes particularly heated when it comes to the mutability of character and its possible effects upon a susceptible public. This excitement derives from an anxiety about the power of the human voice to persuade. As Lawrence Buell argues, "The myth of oratorical power . . . reflected both a greater aesthetic susceptibility to eloquence than obtains today and also a not entirely groundless hope, or fear, that a single individual might be able to engineer a major social change through sheer rhetorical force" (1986, 142). It is the nature of the "aesthetic susceptibility" with which we are concerned, for Americans between 1830 and 1850 were highly aware of the danger of being "taken in" and vehemently opposed to such deceptions, while, at the same time, they seemed to find the theatricalized voice wonderfully compelling and seductive. The voice, like the theater as a whole, had a sexual element that Victorians treated with profound ambivalence, if not hypocrisy, a combination of desire and moralistic repugnance.

The seductive power of the voice in this kind of theater derives, in part, from a belief that even the most banal and ordinary of utterances may be charged with the sacred. In melodrama "everything should be sublime, including the style of the simpleton" (*Traité du mélodrame;* qtd. in Brooks 40). Whitman's "kosmos" is made present in the utterance of the individual. One crucial consequence of a rhetoric characterized by hyperbole, antithesis, and oxymoron, however, is a refusal of nuance (Brooks 40). The catachrestic voice is, paradoxically, meaningful yet inarticulate. The poet's persona in "Song of Myself," for example, is a medium for "dumb voices." Thus, both the plays of Nathaniel Willis and the poems of Walt Whitman explicitly announce that there is always an element of Truth which remains ineffable no matter how subtle or sweet or powerful the voice.

> Speech is the twin of my vision, it is unequal to measure itself,
> It provokes me forever, it says sarcastically,
> *Walt you contain enough, why don't you let it out then?*

In both Whitman and Willis the trope of the *musical* voice in particular conveys the tension (often with strong sexual overtones) implicit in the meaning-full but inarticulate utterance: "A tenor large and fresh as the creation fills me, / The orbic flex of his mouth is pouring and filling me full." The melodramatic voice signifies an emotional excess that cannot be verbalized. In Willis's romantic verse comedy *Tortesa the Usurer* (1839) the heroine Isabella speaks in these terms of the voice of her lover:

> There was a spirit echo in his voice—
> A sound of thought—of under-playing music
> As if, before it ceased in human ears,
> The echo was caught up in fairy land!

In general, Willis's characters are so self-conscious about conventions of the musical voice that they can treat it playfully as a theatrical cliché, referring to it ironically, as when the maid Zippa tells Tortesa, a Shylock type, "Your voice is uncommon musical." He replies, "Nay, *there,* I think you may be honest!" More often than not, however, the musical voice is treated with high seriousness. Returning to the subject of her lover's voice, Isabella suggests that only certain people of a highly sensitive nature can even begin to be aware of the special qualities of Angelo's voice, for it escapes mere words:

Hast never heard him speak
With voice unlike his own—so melancholy,
And yet so sweet a voice, that, were it only
The inarticulate moaning of a bird,
The very tone had made you weep?

Like Willis's play, Whitman's "Out of the Cradle Endlessly Rocking" makes use of the singing bird as a vital metaphor. Indeed, in Whitman's piece the song of the bird is the origin of all reflections and the central subject of the poem. Whitman "listen'd to keep, to sing, now translating notes," creating out of the melodramatic voice, in his mockingbird, an even more powerful version of the melancholy lover, in a he-bird singing for his mate, a "lone singer wonderful causing tears." The emotional power of the singing bird is evoked by the scene and the place of the voice in the scene, not by a particular verbalized message. The bird, after all, is inarticulate, singing not words but notes. "Come now," writes the poet in "Song of Myself," "you conceive too much of articulation."

Melodrama, as a distinct genre in theater, is fundamentally linked to its use of music. Music marks entrances, announcing by its theme what character will appear on stage and the emotional tone he or she will bring. It is also used at climactic moments or to underscore mute action or, in general, whenever the playwright wants to strike an emotional chord. These features are still evident in movies and television. Music is, as Peter Brooks notes, a desemanticized language that both provides an additional legibility and simultaneously evokes the ineffable (14, 48–49). Sung language, in Whitman's view, has a special status among art-utterances because the music, which is included in the way of uttering the words, may have little or no observable relationship to the meanings of the words themselves. Moreover, the effect upon the hearers of words and music uttered simultaneously may be quite different. "Great is the power of music over a people!" writes Whitman. "The subtlest spirit of a nation is expressed through its music—and the music acts reciprocally upon the nation's very soul" (GF 345). Whitman favored opera, the lyric stage, above all other forms of music. The most important opera houses of the 1840s and 1850s in New York, from Niblo's Garden to the Park Theatre and the Astor Place, housed a large variety of theatrical acts and plays, which were produced not only on alternate nights but usually in conjunction with the opera: "The old Park theatre—what names, reminiscences, the words bring back! . . . singers, tragedians, comedians. What perfect acting!" (P&P 703). Whitman was particularly enthralled with the Italian operas of Rossini, Donizetti, Bellini, and Verdi, all of which tended to take the dramatic form of a play. If opera is understood as a musical form of drama, "a play, all in music and singing," as Whitman called it, the function of the music in the drama is to define the response of characters to situations or developments in plot (Kerman 13).

In particular, the Italian opera of the nineteenth century emphasized singing and the voice through a technique known as *parlante,* which overcame, to some degree, the old dichotomy between aria and recitative. *Parlante,* expressed essentially through declamatory vocal lines, could slip easily between the two modes, while the opera retained the beautiful melodies of the aria. The rich, often florid arias, which singers in the past had generally decorated with their own improvisations, became more essential to the drama. Rossini, in particular, began to pay much greater attention to these passages and their specific dramatic significance. Interpreted through a style of singing known as *bel canto,* the arias added to the characterization of the part while also giving the singer opportunities to display the resources of his voice (Kerman 134–37; Faner 30).

Whitman's delight in the dramatic action of the Italian operas focused primarily upon such vocal illuminations of character. In a letter from Brooklyn to his friends in Washington, for example, Whitman writes of a performance of *Lucrezia Borgia* at the New York Academy of Music in 1863. Ecstatically, he recalls the whole scene in every detail, nearly overwhelmed by the intensity of the relationships of husband, wife, and lover. Telling her lover that he is poisoned, at the climax of the opera, the heroine "poured out the greatest singing you ever heard." Only through her voice is Lucrezia able to represent the scope of her love and anguish: "Her voice is so wild and high it goes through one like a knife, yet it is delicious" (Whitman, qtd. in Traubel 3:103–4). These passions are intense but uncomplicated; the passions are not diluted by misgivings or indecisiveness. Passions are not discussed but expressed. Whitman's notion of voice involves the sense that it conveys some quality of character which is sublime, or "true." Indeed, in some fragmentary notes Whitman planned his own operas: "Songs (with notes—written for the voice) with dramatic activity as for instance a song describing the cutting down of the tree by wood-cutters in the west—the pleasures of a wood-life, etc." (*Prose* 7:25).

Ultimately, Whitman carries this program for the voice not into making operas but into making poems, perhaps most brilliantly in the construction of "Out of the Cradle." This poem is created out of memories, both of the "bird that chanted to me" and memories of the bird itself of its lost mate. All memories are associated with the voice heard by the boy and now sung again in "fitful risings and fallings." It is the voice of the he-bird which resonates in this "scene revisited." The narrative sections, *parlante,* merge seamlessly into the arias of the bird, in which Whitman portrays a birdlike voice with repetitions, such as "*Shine! shine! shine!*" or "*Blow! blow! blow!*" or the refrain "*with love, with love.*" These condensed, desemanticized reiterations ("Blow! Blow! Blow" or "Shine! Shine! Shine!") may call to mind the "Yes! Yes! Yes!" of Charlotte Cushman, an emotional utterance expressed similarly at a defining, or climactic, moment. In both cases it is the voice, the pattern of language and tone of utterance, which carries the drama. In "Out of the Cradle" the voice establishes the relation of boy to bird to nature as well as a sense of continuity between the temporal and the spiritual. The arias merge into the *parlante* sections: "The aria sinking, / All else continuing, the stars shining." While Whitman appreciated great technical virtuosity in a singer, his favorite opera stars were those who most effectively portrayed the drama of the piece. Perhaps this preference for a sense of drama led him in *Specimen Days* to emphasize his love of theater over that of opera. "This musical passion," he notes, "follow'd my theatrical one" (P&P 704).

In the dramas of Whitman's youth the sense of the charged, or overcharged, significance of the voice was most explicit in self-consciously excessive vocalizations at moments of dramatic climax. And no actor was more famous for representing the highest, most violent passions in his voice than Edwin Forrest. Forrest was especially famous for his performances of Shakespearean heroes. The following passage is an extract from an article written by James Rees following a Forrest performance of *King Lear.* This segment is typical of the elaborate representations of performances by contemporaries in this period which, in their hyperbole, are not only themselves "dramatic" but mirror the dramaturgy they describe. They are attempts, in other words, to capture that which is "beyond the power of pen to describe":

> Mr. Forrest's starting point in Lear, is where he *utters* the curse on Goneril, Act I. Let any one not a theatre-goer, read this awful malediction, and then imagine what an effect it would have on an audience when given by Mr. Forrest. It is sublime even in the terror it creates. Mr. Forrest's *utterance* of this passage is, perhaps, the most startling and thrilling that was ever heard upon the stage; there is no dramatic preparation for its coming . . . The house was hushed into silence, the audience seemed to feel the oppression, for the very air was stilled; and the sense of some powerful influence pervading, held the breath as it were in abeyance. As he progressed in its *utterance,* he arose in grandeur, awful in his terrible sublimity; and when he reached its climax, and exclaimed, 'Away! Away!' the audience awoke as from a fearful spell, and sound again broke upon the awful stillness which its delivery caused. (Rees 172; my emph.)

The hyperbolic quality of the dramaturgy, evoking tempests, whirlwinds, and infinite depths of pathos, has infected even the discourse of the critic. The excessive expressions of the actor have been transferred into normative vocabularies, outside the dramatic world of the play itself. Thus, in *Leaves of Grass* Whitman's poetic chants "shoot in pulses of fire ceaseless to vivify all," his shouts "soar above everything," "my own voice resonant," he even "howls" (like Lear?). Significantly, in Rees's representations, as in Whitman's, the starting point is the utterance.

Whitman, however, unlike Rees, was not a simple Forrest devotee. In the *Daily Eagle* he criticizes the actor's style largely, it seems, because Forrest's vocal powers were exerted almost exclusively in scenes of high drama, such as the bursts of passion Rees describes. "In candor," wrote Whitman the drama critic in 1846, "all persons of thought will confess to no great fondness for acting which particularly seeks to 'tickle the ears of the groundlings.' We allude to the loud mouthed ranting style—the tearing of everything to shivers—which is so much the ambition of some of our players, particularly the younger ones. It does in such cases truly seem as if some of Nature's journeymen had made men, and not made them well—they imitate humanity so abominably" (GF 332). Mr. Forrest, Whitman allows, is a "deserved favorite with the public," but there is a danger in identifying him with an American style of acting, as so many of Forrest's imitators and followers did. According to his vision of a truly democratic theater, Whitman is interested in a somewhat broader range of vocal characterizations, a style that is more "natural." Whitman is not interested only in moments of high drama or grandiloquence. As in his poetry, Whitman desires a "voice neither high nor low."

Whitman stresses the importance of the relationship between the physical voice and a particular personality: "Are you full-lung'd and limber-lipp'd from long trial? from vigorous practice? from physique?" ("Vocalism"). On the one hand, voice makes character distinctive, and, on the other, character makes voice meaningful. The experience of Junius Booth's "electrical personal idiosyncrasy" led Whitman to comment, "As in all art-utterance it was the subtle and powerful *something special in the individual* that really conquer'd" (P&P 1192). Whitman also aims to enfranchise those who have been deprived of character by giving them a voice, resurrecting something special, if unseemly, in each figure through a distinctive voice:

> Through me forbidden voices,
> Voices of sexes and lusts, voices veil'd and I remove the veil,
> Voices indecent by me clarified and transfigured.
> ("Song of Myself")

Character originates in the utterance: "The actor must go direct to nature and his own heart for the tones and action by which he is to move his audience; these the author cannot give him, and in creating these, if he be a great actor, his art may be supremely great" (qtd. in Stovall 77).

In likening himself to the actor or the singer, performers who make use of the living voice, Whitman was, in a sense, distancing himself from conventional notions of the author as writer. One crucial lesson of Booth or Forrest was the ability to invest the moment of performance with emotional power through the unique expression of a particular character. As in drama, in the province of music it was character that inspired Whitman. He praises "negro minstrels" for their fine voices but particularly for a genre he dubs "character songs." Character, he says, is "a feature far above style or polish—a feature not absent at any time, but now first brought to the fore." Though never absent in art, character will give a predominant stamp to the "advancing poetry" and "its born sister, music." This type of music, specifically the opera of Wagner, Gounod, and Verdi, like the new poetry, demands "poetic emotion" and, with it, "vocalism" (*Prose* 2:216–17).

THE BODY AS SIGNIFIER

In 1871 the fame of French acting coach François Delsarte (1811–71), which had long since spread throughout Europe, was published in the United States in the *Atlantic Monthly.* "I believe," writes Francis Durivage, "that whoever makes the external interpretation of the sentiments of the human soul his business and profession, whether painter, sculptor, orator, or actor, that all men of taste . . . will applaud this attempt to create the science of *expressive* man." Delsarte had, indeed, invested the study of performance with not only the rigor but also the methods of contemporary scientific discourse. He had begun his career as an opera singer in 1830, but (like Charlotte Cushman) his career in opera was curtailed when inept coaching resulted in the failure of his voice. That failure, however, seems to have spurred his interest in discovering a more scientific basis for performance. Delsarte devoted the next five years to the study of anatomy and physiology, "to obtain a perfect knowledge of all the muscles, their uses and capabilities."

Delsarte spent years accumulating data on how human beings of all ages, social strata, and temperaments react to emotional stimuli. He went to medical school, dissected corpses, and studied the insane. Through dismembering the body, Delsarte conceived of three principal agents of expression in the body (head, torso, and limbs) which "perform each a distinct part in the economy of a character" (Durivage 618). Similarly, Delsarte's studies of physiognomy led him to isolate a separate function for every part of the face. Wrath, for example, is expressed not in the eyes but in the mouth, and this fact can be discovered simply by covering first the upper and then the lower part of the face while trying to express that emotion. He studied declamation not on the stage but, as his contemporaries remarked, in *real life*. Delsarte, in other words, "substituted law for empiricism in the domain of the most potential of the fine arts" (613). He called this law the "Law of Correspondence": "To each grand function of the body corresponds a spiritual act" (qtd. in Shawn 22).

Delsarte's own lectures and performances were reported to have immense power. Durivage praises not only Delsarte's voice but also a specimen of his pantomimic powers: "He depicted the various passions and emotions of the human soul, by means of expression and gesture only, without uttering a single syllable; moving the spectators to tears, exciting them to enthusiasm or thrilling them with terror at his will; in a word, completely magnetizing them. Not a discord in his diatonic scale. You were forced to admit that every gesture, every movement of a facial muscle, had a true purpose,—a *raison d'etre.* It was a triumphant demonstration" (614). Gesture, claimed Delsarte, "is the direct agent of the heart. It is the fit manifestation of feeling . . . It is the elliptical expression of language" (qtd. in Shawn 25). Gesture conveys sentiment most compellingly because it bypasses, or omits, language, the vehicle of reason, or "making sense." Language can only *translate* feeling for the mind. Gesture is transparent. Through gesture the actor speaks to the audience members as physical entities themselves.

At first glance Whitman seems to share much with Delsarte. He is ambitious to "develop language anew, make it not literal . . . but elliptical & idiomatic" (*Workshop* 35). His interests in phrenology, physiognomy, and various cults of physical health indicate similar preoccupations with the body as signifier. Phrenology provided one solution to the problem of character. For a culture anxious about the insubstantiality of character—that is, the absence of any concrete referent for character—phrenology suggested a way of locating intellectual faculties in folds and fissures of the brain.[9] In fact, phrenologists provided "character-charts," to give their clients a true account of their "real characters." Phrenologists "are not poets," said Whitman, "but they are the lawgivers of poets." And Justin Kaplan suggests that phrenology supplied Whitman with "the underpinnings of a personal mythology" (151–52). It is easy, however, to be misled by Whitman's avowed interest in phrenology and similar "sciences" to form an overly simple view of his notion of character, where it is located, and how it is presented. There are important differences between Whitman's theories of acting and Delsarte's. Primarily, Whitman's stress on identification of the actor with the role differs from Delsarte's emphasis on technique.[10]

In particular, if we consider Whitman's philosophy of acting as it is articulated in his drama criticism, we discover a different and far more subtle notion of the relationship between character and the body than the one propounded by phrenologists. It is worth quoting at length from an article for the *Daily Eagle* (1846) called "Dramatics and the True Secret of Acting." "The philosophy of acting resides entirely in the feelings and passions," writes Whitman, "to touch them, wake them, and calm them":

> Now there are two ways of exercising such a sway over the passions of an audience—the usual way, which is boisterous, stormy, physical, and repugnant to truth and taste; and another way, that actors rarely condescend to take, which consists in an invariable adherence to Nature, and is entirely mental, and works from within to the outward, instead of being altogether outward. The mental style was [William Charles] Macready's in his best days; he touched the heart, the soul, the feelings, the inner blood and nerves of his audience. The ordinary actor struts and rants away, and his furious declamation begets a kind of reciprocal excitement among those who hear him, it is true—but there is as much difference between it and the result produced by the true actor, as between mind and body . . . The best way in the world to represent grief, remorse, love, or any given passion, is to feel them at the time, and throw the feeling as far as possible into word and act . . . The strange and subtle sympathy which runs like an electrical charge through human hearts collected together, responds only to the touch of the true fire. We have known the time when an actual awe and dread crept over a large body assembled in the theatre, when Macready merely appeared, walking down the stage, a king. He was a king—not because he had a tinsel-gilded crown, and the counterfeit robe, but because he then dilated his heart with the attributes of majesty, and they looked forth from his eyes, and appeared in his walk . . . Throw into your identity . . . the character you are to represent. This, under the guidance of discretion and good taste, is all that is necessary to make the best of performers. Discard the assistance of *mere* physical applications. You have hammered away long enough at the ear—condescend, at last, to affect the heart. (GF 321–25)

There are two important ideas in this passage which make "technical" theories of the body in Whitman difficult to accept without qualification. First is the notion of influence, that vague but powerful force that a performer exerts upon an audience. Whitman speaks of "the strange and subtle sympathy which runs like an electrical charge through human hearts collected together." And second is a theory of identification: "Throw into your identity . . . the character you are to represent." These two points, moreover, are closely related to each other. Influence may be achieved precisely by throwing one's identity into a given character. These points also epitomize crucial elements of the melodramatic dramaturgy. On the one hand, character is understood as ultimately whole, not divided or indecisive, as in tragedy; there are no psychic or physical fumblings to complicate a strong impression of character. Idiosyncrasies are turned into strengths. And, as a result of this wholeness of character, the relationship between audience and actor is "monopathic," a unifying feeling that may come almost anywhere in the spectrum of emotional possibilities, a feeling that can be evoked in a drama of either triumph or of disaster (see Heilman 85).

Metaphors of electricity and magnetism, commonly used to describe the performer-audience dynamic, pervade various forms of artistic and scientific discourse popular in antebellum America. David Reynolds, for instance, has compellingly described Whitman's deep interest in mesmerism, a fad of the 1830s and 1840s which posited an electrical force linking all physical and spiritual phenomena (1995, 259–62). But Whitman's terminology is also clearly related to a theory of acting and of science already current in the late eighteenth century. In fact, Whitman had studied the great English actor David Garrick and felt a particular affinity for Garrick's mode of performance. "Garrick was the first to break through the old bonds," Whitman remarked in 1888 (qtd. in Traubel 3:431). Joseph Roach has eloquently described the innovative quality of Garrick's acting as a form of "vitalism."[11] That body of theory attempted to account for theatrical spontaneity without recourse to a transcendental soul; in short, there is a vital force within the body itself. In a letter of 1769, for instance, Garrick had contemplated "that Life blood, that keen sensibility, that bursts at once from Genius, and like *Electrical fire* shoots through the Veins, Marrow, Bones and all, of every Spectator" (2:635; my emph.). The spirit emanates from a peculiar organization of matter (Roach 96). Thus, like Whitman, Garrick is simultaneously an artist of the soul and an artist of the body.

In Whitman's remarks on acting the body serves as both concrete object and abstract idea. In general "Dramatics and the True Secret of Acting" is a critique of any attempt to locate character solely in an actual, physical body. That which is merely physical is "repugnant to truth and taste."[12] For Whitman the seat of feeling in the audience, the identity of the audience, which is touched only by the mental style, is found in "the heart, the soul, the feelings, the *inner* blood and nerves" (GF 321; my emph.). In Whitman's view theater is a social and political model, and as such it must be grounded in a notion of freedom, not in a strict law of correspondence. Delsarte, on the other hand, imagines a physiological connection between physical actors and physical audience members, a kind of objective correlative.[13] Delsarte's "objective" view limits the free play of character by insisting upon a straightforward interpretability of each aspect of character in isolation. This view of character is ideologically alien to Whitman's, whose emphasis is upon potentiality and possibility. "I, now, for one, promulge [*sic*], announcing a native expression-spirit, getting into form, adult, and through mentality, for these States, self-contain'd, different from others, more expansive, more rich and free," Whitman writes in *Democratic Vistas* (P&P 977). The "native expression-spirit" is expansive and free, searching, presumably, for new and as yet unimagined manifestations.

To be sure, Whitman did appreciate the importance of the "real" body in the execution of the "mental" style of acting. Each physical detail was, in his view, crucial in the overall conception of character. "Mrs Siddons, in characters where a moving passion was maternal grief, wept hot, scalding, real tears!" (GF 326). The "real tears" are subsumed, however, into a larger conception of character. Tears correspond not just to grief but to a particular maternal grief that is comprehensible only by understanding the character of that mother. Whitman implies that one ought not to be excited, as Durivage seems to be at the performance of Delsarte, by isolated expressions and gestures, no matter how brilliantly executed. "I am less the reminder of property or qualities, and more the reminder of life" ("Song of Myself" 1855). Like the great poet, Whitman believed, the great actor had an appreciation for the details of experience and could give to the mundane the status of the remarkable. Whitman was impressed with the way a great actor could take a mistake or personal defect and turn it into a compelling character trait in order to generate a more "natural" character and, thus, a more complete stage illusion: "Not an inch nor a particle of an inch is vile" ("Song of Myself"). He tells Traubel of one case when

> [E. A.] Sothern was coming on the stage one night from the wings: tripped: almost fell: caught himself: passed off the incident in a sort of lisp or whatever. Sothern, then, had caught on himself, or some bright girl did (the girls are always up to that) and, from time to time, Sothern adopting this fugitive mannerism, this accidental idiosyncrasy, was successful in creating a stage illusion. I don't know that the story is literally true, but it illustrates how such a little turn is often the making of a man's life. (Qtd. in Traubel 3:519)

Of course, in the theater of this period blunders of all sorts, from missed cues to the collapse of stage equipment, were not uncommon, and clearly Whitman finds the fall itself unremarkable. It is the use made of the fall, and the lisp, their integration into the concept of a character, which is the lesson. When a fully formed character does appear, he or she will inevitably have a powerful influence upon the house: "We have known the time, when an actual awe and dread crept over a large body assembled in the theatre, when Macready merely appeared, walking down the stage, a king" (GF 322–23).

Influence is achieved *indirectly,* for it involves a working out of psychological and emotional motivations that affect an audience through a *process* of empathy. For example, Whitman was deeply affected by the appearance of Abraham Lincoln, whom, he claimed in 1863, he saw nearly every day. On one occasion Lincoln "bow'd and smiled, but far beneath his smile I noticed well the expression I have alluded to. None of the artists or pictures has caught the deep, though subtle and indirect expression of this man's face" (qtd. in Porte 233).[14] Indirect expression, an elliptical mode, is the only way, in Whitman's view, of arousing sympathy ("Logic and sermons never convince."). This form of communication expresses the private self through the public, revealing the "within" where character is concealed: "From my breast, from within where I was conceal'd, press forth red drops, confession drops" (*Calamus*). As Joel Porte argues: "*Expression* here must be taken in a double sense, not simply alluding to what the paradigmatic poet, Whitman himself, says, but to what his body expresses (as in the frontispiece [of *Leaves of Grass*]): the innerness of being, the essential privacy without which a public figure is simply a hollow shell. The *expression* of each of these men [Whitman and Lincoln] betokens not only a capacity for human engagement but also a fund of human meaning not yet articulated" (234).

In his lecture notes Whitman develops a theory of "interior gesture, which is perhaps better than exterior gesture" (*Workshop* 37). Whitman equates interior gesture with a "flowing forth of power." His definition implies that where character is concerned the whole is greater than the sum of the parts. While Whitman acknowledges and advocates a rigorous training of the body, he finds that there is still a quality that remains undefined: "That subtle something equivalent to gesture and life plays continuously out of every feature of the face and every limb and joint of the body whether active or still" (38). Whitman's notion of "interior gesture" is partly a response to texts such as *The Columbian Orator* which provide comprehensive discussions of outward gesture, gesture as objective correlative. The lifting of the head signifies arrogance or pride, and eyes turned down show modesty. Interior gesture, on the other hand, corresponds to the ineffable qualities that go into the making of a character: "Your very flesh shall be a great poem and have the richest fluency not only in its words but in the silent lines of its lips and face and between the lashes of your eyes and in every motion and joint of your body" (preface to *Leaves of Grass,* P&P 11). If, in Delsarte, features of the body function metaphorically, each gesture referring to a particular emotion, in Whitman they function synecdochically; the part stands for the whole.

The actor and acting style that most profoundly influenced Whitman's worldview were Junius Brutus Booth (1796–1852) and the "romantic" style. In Whitman's eyes the performing body was epitomized by the "singularly spontaneous and fluctuating" Booth, "whose instant and tremendous concentration of his passion in his delineations overwhelm'd his audience." Booth had been taken in his youth for the double of Edmund Kean. He resembled Kean physically (at five foot three inches in height, he was one inch shorter), and early in his career in London he was accused of a certain plagiarism of style. But Booth developed the romantic style of Kean, particularly in the completeness of his character conceptions. One American fan said: "Booth was Kean, *plus* the higher imagination . . . To see Booth in his best mood was *not* 'like reading Shakespeare by flashes of lightening,' in which the blinding glare alternates with the fearful suspense of darkness; but rather like reading him by the sunlight of a summer's day, a light which casts deep shadows, gives play to glorious harmonies of color and shows all objects in vivid life and true relation" (qtd. in Shattuck 1976, 44).

In general, Booth was celebrated because each character he projected was a unique and perfectly realized individual. Even in the same role, notes

FIG. 9. Junius Booth as Richard III.

Whitman, "each rendering differ'd from any and all others. He had no stereotyped positions" (P&P 1188). Whitman saw Booth in his prime in the late 1830s, and Whitman's deep appreciation of theater is, perhaps, captured nowhere as well as in his enraptured recollection in *November Boughs* of Booth as Richard III, his most famous role (see fig. 9). It is a passage so vivid that it can still cause shivers:

> I can, from my good seat in the pit, pretty well front, see again Booth's quiet entrance from the side, as, with head bent, he slowly and in silence, (amid the tempest of boisterous hand-clapping,) walks down the stage to the footlights with that peculiar and abstracted gesture, musingly kicking his sword, which he holds off from him by its sash. Though fifty years have pass'd since then, I can hear the clank, and feel the perfect following hush of perhaps three thousand people waiting. (I never saw an actor who could make more of the said hush or wait, and hold the audience in an indescribable, half-delicious, half-irritating suspense.) . . . The great spell cast upon the mass of hearers came from Booth. Especially was the dream scene very impressive. A shudder went through every nervous system in the audience; it certainly did through mine. (P&P 1191)

On seeing Booth perform, Whitman felt that he had experienced "inner spirit and form . . . crystallizing rapidly upon the English stage and literature . . . His genius was to me one of the grandest revelations of my life, a lesson of artistic expression" (1192). Whitman's theory of the performing body involves a quality that not only eludes particular gestures but also a quality that eludes language. In this sense the action of the face, the peculiar and abstracted gestures, resemble a space between the lines.[15] The performing body functions not only as a trope but also as a locus of something like "truth value" in Whitman's work. Performance has an essential link with knowledge, the emotional and psychic process whose reified manifestation is the phrenologist's chart of bumps. "What are verses," he asks in the first edition of *Leaves of Grass,* "beyond the flowing character you could have?"

The most vivid staging of the body in *Leaves of Grass* is the representation of a slave at auction in "I Sing the Body Electric." In this poem Whitman appropriates the selfless, characterless body in its most notorious manifestation. Here the human body is on stage, but because it lacks character it is completely unproductive of sympathy for the average spectator, certainly for the auctioneer. Whitman seizes upon the slave at auction as the negative example par excellence of his project of celebrating the body. The first line, "A *man's* body at auction," instantly identifies the culture's most profound inconsistency, the slave as non-man—body lacking self and, so, implicitly lacking personality or character (my emph.). Slavery is, as Philip Fisher writes, "the fundamental denial of transparency within American experience." This section of "I Sing the Body Electric" illustrates two crucial features of Whitman's idea of character. First, character is located in the living body, a physiology with all its mystery. If we, like the auctioneer, do not recognize character in the body, it is only because we, like him, are slovens who do not half-know our business. The immorality of treating the body irreligiously is akin to concealing the self within the body: "those who corrupt their own bodies conceal themselves." One regards the soul, implicitly, as one regards the body. This notion is at the core of Whitman's thought and is expressed in one of his most famous conjunctions:

> I am the poet of the body,
> And I am the poet of the soul.
> ("Song of Myself" 1855)

To celebrate the body is to celebrate the soul. And, second, in the "slave at auction" section the audience plays a crucial role in eliciting character from the body, in effect impelling the body into performance. The audience not only interprets the body but encourages it, excites it. In fact, Whitman seems to believe that it is the audience's responsibility to bring out the best—that is, character—in the performer. In Whitman's imagination spectator and performer are united by a mysterious bond, or, as he remarks of Booth, a "great spell [is] cast upon the mass of hearers."

CHARACTER FORMATION

In *Democratic Vistas* Whitman claims that the two main constituents for a truly great nationality are a "large variety of character" and "full play for human nature to expand itself in numberless and even conflicting directions." This claim is aimed at the heart of one of the most discussed issues of nineteenth-century American life, the stability and substantiality of character. In *The Use of the Body in Relation to the Mind* (1847) George Moore, M.D., argues:

> Every atom is proof of the divine presence, and every mind a response to God, for He constitutes the identity both of atoms and of minds, each in itself an unalterable unity, to be located and manifested in evidence of His own will, which alone is power. Molecules and minds

> have each their affinities because they have unchangeable natures. They may stand in new relations, but are themselves still the same in reality, for what they are, or are capable of, is the consequence of an eternal decision, the changeless mandate of the Almighty. (59)

Moore is arguing here against scientists who claim that it is possible to lose one's identity in passing from one state of consciousness to another, as may happen through using drugs or going mad. Moore insists, albeit without much scientific evidence, that even a person with multiple personalities retains his or her core identity.

Whitman's position, which incorporates and inverts Moore's vocabulary (e.g., "Every atom belonging to me as good belongs to you"), seems specifically aimed, at least in part, at the hugely popular genre of advice manuals for young men in the 1830s and 1840s, a genre whose very existence is premised on the problem of character formation. In the 1830s, when Whitman was a teenager typical of the audience at whom the conduct books were aimed, the discourse about character and public life was extraordinarily heated, aimed both at the chameleonlike character of individuals and the developing character of the young nation. In fact, during the winter of 1837–38 Whitman participated in a debate on the question: "Has Nature more influence than education in the formation of character?" He argued against nature and lost. "Character formation," writes Karen Halttunen, "was the nineteenth-century version of the Protestant work ethic" (1982, 28).

Against this background Whitman's poetry seems iconoclastic. Throughout his mature writings Whitman seems to celebrate the ability to play many diverse roles. The poet himself assumes different characters: "I am the actor, the actress, the voter, the politician, / The emigrant, and the exile" ("The Sleepers," P&P 544). This performativity is not only a matter of content but also of form. Often the passages in which such characters are allowed to develop are indicated by performative utterances, which are both statements and actions: "I become any presence or truth of humanity here." Truth of humanity is present in the process of becoming. In his 1855 preface to *Leaves of Grass* Whitman refers to the poet as a performer. "The touch of him," claims the poet, "tells in action." In general Whitman depicts a theatricality of character which would have been anathema to writers of conduct manuals for young men. William A. Alcott's *Young Man's Guide* (1833) was intended to "aid in forming the character of young men for time and for eternity." Authors like Alcott perceived theater not only as a den of vice in which young men might be susceptible to shady influences but also as an inherently dangerous space in its own right. Theater, in their view, taught the corruption of false appearances. Consequently, Alcott advised young men to practice total abstinence when it came to theater: "My own experience and observation had convinced me that it was a very dangerous place for young men to visit" (177). In his writing Whitman comprehends and eventually reimagines this anxiety about the theater's impact on young and malleable characters. He deeply registers the antitheatrical bias, representing it in some early work, seemingly uncritically, but transforming it later in his poetry and in his worldview generally.

Franklin Evans; or, The Inebriate, Whitman's temperance novel, first appeared in 1842. Four years later the novel was reprinted in the Brooklyn *Daily Eagle,* when Whitman became editor. This story, the author tells us, is unlike that of an ordinary novel: "It will not abound, either with profound reflections, or sentimental remarks. Yet its moral . . . will be taught in its own incidents, and the current of the narrative" (103–4).[16] It is, in a fundamental sense, a melodrama. The morally mutable yet psychologically unsophisticated hero of Whitman's tale represents a typical, if formulaic, characterological case study. And, though Whitman himself later dismissed the work as "rot of the worst sort" and claimed to have written it for cash in three days while simultaneously downing a bottle of port, the tale does provide insight into an important view of character formation in the 1830s and 1840s. The plot follows the classic antebellum tale of seduction, which inevitably drags the unwary youth into a gorgeous theater, the appropriate milieu of confidence men and seducers of all kinds; of course, such characters are themselves skilled actors (see Halttunnen 1982, 2). Whitman's story depends on the malleability of character. Franklin Evans, like many of his generation, comes for the first time to the big city: "A mere boy, friendless, unprotected, innocent of the ways of the world . . . I stood at the entrance of the mighty labyrinth, and with hardly any consciousness of the temptations, doubts, and dangers that awaited me" (125). Evans's experience of the theater in particular is characterized by the erosion of his ability to think critically, until the theater and the illusions housed in it become his greatest pleasures. But theater also functions, perhaps more significantly, in supplying a dramaturgy by which to judge the deterioration of the character of Franklin Evans himself. As the narrative progresses, dramaturgical assumptions of the melodramatic theater are increasingly applied to Evans's character. At one climax, late in the novel, the narrator remarks, "Like an actor who plays a part, I became warmed in the delineation, and the very passion I feigned came to imbue my soul with its genuine characteristics" (191).

The protagonist's enjoyment of theater functions as a barometer of his demise. Chapter 5 begins with the epigraph, "All is not gold that glitters," and it depicts the youth's second night out in New York City:

> Colby and myself, accompanied by a friend of my friend's, whom we met at the drinking-room, determined to go to the theatre that evening . . . The house was crowded. Beautiful women and elegant men . . . brilliant fashionables of all varieties, combined to render the scene exhilarating and splendid. And the music from the orchestra, now soft and subdued, now bursting out with notes of thunder—how delicious it glided into the ear! The curtain drew up and the play began. The plot was worse than meager—the truthfulness of the scene a gag, which ought not to have excited aught but ridicule—the most nauseous kind of mock aristocracy tinging the dialogue from beginning to end—yet it was received with applause, and at the conclusion, with vociferous and repeated cheers! The manager had printed upon his bills that London was pleased with it, and that one of the scenes represented life as in the private parlor of an English Duke . . . I blushed for the good sense of my countrymen.

The passage anticipates some of Whitman's most biting criticism of contemporary theater in his reviews for the *Daily Eagle*. Evans's own good sense, however, becomes increasingly impaired in this environment. Theater, combined with liquor, is a place of excitement and illusion which involves not only the play upon the boards but also the audience in the boxes.

Whitman stresses the intoxicating nature of the whole event; his protagonist becomes infatuated with both an actress in the farce and a "gentleman" in a stage box. The fine-looking gentleman, a "perfect pattern of perfection," turns out to be a waiter at the oyster bar across the street. And the "charmer hoyden in the farce," the beautiful actress, is discovered backstage to be a coarse, "masculine" woman with eyes made bleary by the constant glitter of strong light and an oily brown complexion, mottled with paint. The occurrences of the night, confesses Evans, "taught me to question the reality of many things I afterward saw; and reflect that, though to appearance they were showy, they might prove, upon trial, as coarse as the eating house waiter, or the blear-eyed actress." Yet this apparent realization is undermined, as the tale progresses, by the continual bleeding of theater into "normative" experience. He and his friends, Evans asserts, are "*naturally* fond of that species of amusement." Theater, like alcohol, is a kind of drug that the increasingly jaded companions realize provides only an artificial high, but, as they come more and more under its power, its artificiality becomes increasingly irrelevant. Despite the lesson of the first night, the theater soon becomes not only a regular part of Evans's experience but his favorite recreation. He neglects his work in order to hasten home to prepare himself for the theater, a problem that leads to his first major catastrophe, the loss of his job.

Melodramatic scenes literally surround theaters in the narrative. The juxtaposition of an evening at the theater and deeply dramatic experiences on the way home infuses even normative experience with elements of the melodramatic. For instance, after an evening of his favorite pastime, Evans is accosted by a pitiful boy begging for pennies in an alley. Following the "little wretch" home, he comes upon a death scene of a poor woman who has not only given her life to the bottle but who is all the more pathetic for the deeply maternal feelings she expresses to the children she is about to orphan. It is a moralistic set piece. The woman, the narrator asserts, had been as guilty as she is wretched. Soon, however, Evans is referring to his own life as a dramatic piece. When his first wife, Mary, dies of neglect, "the innocent victim of another's drunkenness," he describes the final death scene, in which, temporarily sober, he receives her forgiveness; it is "the closing scene of that act of the tragedy" (154). Theater becomes a structuring device and a unifying motif (e.g., "The course of my narrative needs now that another character be introduced upon the stage" [189]). Moreover, while each character has a part to play, certain actors, specifically those who consciously manipulate their roles for private ends, are far more despicable than the rest. In particular the young men who merely play at being gentlemen come in for the ultimate derision. Their behavior is compared to the staginess of melodrama: "Such fellows are as far removed from true gentlemen as the gilded sun, in stage melo-dramas, from the genuine source of light himself" (217).

In short both audience members in the theater and actors on the stage enact and manipulate notions of character. In Whitman's view *character* is both a moral and an aesthetic term, raising questions of citizenship and of artistic beauty. Therefore, although *Franklin Evans* seems to share in the cultural anxiety about the mutability of character, the problem posed elsewhere in Whitman's writing is how a notion of mutable character can be made to serve new, "American" moral/aesthetic ends, embracing principles of freedom, newness, and simplicity. In an article entitled "Why Do Theatres Languish? And How Shall the American Stage Be Resuscitated" (1847) Whitman suggests that the problem is not that imitation or role-playing is inherently bad but that Americans are playing the wrong roles, imitating the wrong characters, and he suggests "the noble scope of good of which the American drama might be made capable" (GF 314). There is, he argues, "a lurking propensity toward what is original, and has a stamped American character of its own" (316). Still dissatisfied in 1870, Whitman attacks American theater in *Democratic Vistas* for not promoting, among other things, a new vision of character: "America, betaking herself to formative action . . . must, for her purposes, cease to recognize a theory of character grown of feudal aristocracies, or form'd by merely literary standards" (P&P 974). Whitman's preference for well-executed characterizations is to be found throughout his writings. Much of the material he wrote for the *Daily Eagle* around the time of the second publication of *Franklin Evans* represents a rich appreciation of the possibilities available in the formation of character on stage. He criticizes a production of *The Barber of Seville* in 1847, for example, for the "inefficient manner in which some of the characters are sustained" (GF 349–50). The opera gave Whitman a concrete language with which to conduct his protest against the elaborately contrived, plot-driven melodramas of the nineteenth century and their counterparts in the other arts.

Yet Whitman's interest in character should not be confused with a realist notion of character. Unlike the dramatic realists, Whitman was not concerned with the complexities of psychology but with fundamental "inner truths" and how basic features of personality were to be revealed reliably in public. In this sense he retains a deep affinity with people like Moore, Alcott, and the phrenologists O. S. and L. N. Fowler. In some notes under the heading "American Opera" Whitman suggests that the plot should not be "complicated but simple—Always one leading idea—as Friendship, Courage, Gratitude, Love . . . the vocal performer to make far more of his song, or solo part, by by-play, attitudes, expression, movements, &c. than is at all made by the Italian opera singers—The American opera to be far more simple, and give far more scope to the persons enacting the characters" (*Workshop* 201–2).

Whitman insists in "A Backward Glance o'er Travel'd Roads" that his ambition in writing *Leaves of Grass* was to "articulate and faithfully express in literary or poetic form . . . my own physical, emotional, moral, intellectual, and aesthetic Personality" (P&P 658). Poetry, he writes elsewhere, is "like a grand personality" (1058). In his writings on actors and in his poetry Whitman indicates an ambiguous yet essential relationship between private and public character which becomes particularly important in the moment of performance. The moment of contact between performer and audience can be a kind of revelation. The lifting of a curtain, the removal of a veil or mask, therefore, become central images in his work:

> Out from behind this bending rough-cut mask,
> These lights and shades, this drama of the whole,
> This common curtain of the face contain'd in me for me, in
> you for you, in each for each,
> (Tragedies, sorrows, laughter, tears—O heaven!
> The passionate teeming plays this curtain hid!)
> . . . a look.

As Erving Goffman notes, the word *person,* in its first meaning, is a mask, and the use of the word represents a recognition that everyone is always and everywhere playing a role. Yet, Goffman goes on, "in so far as this mask represents the conception we have formed of ourselves—the rôle we are striving to live up to—this mask is our truer self, the self we would like to be . . . We come into this world as individuals, achieve character, and become persons" (19–20). For Whitman successful theater is achieved only through the imagined conjunction of voice, body, and character.

Both in his life and in his literature the character Walt Whitman evolved with the length of his beard. *Leaves of Grass,* Whitman explains in 1855, is an attempt "of a naive, masculine affectionate, contemplative, sensual, imperious person, to cast into literature not only his own grit and arrogance, but his own flesh and form."[17] The poet in 1855 is cast as the representative American: "Of pure American breed, large and lusty—age thirty-six years—never once using medicine—never dressed in black, always dressed freely and clean in strong clothes—neck and beard well mottled with white, hair like hay" (18). Of course, there have been critics who have complained that the self-styled carpenter-poet could not build houses or handle tools well enough to earn a living, that he was, in fact, something of an aesthete, that he never enjoyed the mythic health with which he endowed the mythic self in his poems.[18] But, again, in Whitman's view role-playing and self-making were positive and, indeed, vital actions, so long as the roles promoted what Whitman understood as American values. In 1865, following his wartime service, he begins to enter a new incarnation, benevolent and paternalistic, a role idealized in William Douglas O'Connor's quasi-hagiographic "vindication," *The Good Gray Poet* (1866). As the "wound dresser" in *Drum Taps,* Whitman imagines his persona: "An old man bending I come among new faces."

Throughout his career Whitman associated his book with himself. Fundamental to this association was an implicit division between public and private life, one that Whitman occasionally had to assert. In a letter to an infatuated reader Whitman once wrote tactfully: "My book is my best letter, my response, my truest explanation of all. In it I have put my body & spirit. You understand this better & fuller & clearer than any one else. And I too clearly and fully understand the loving & womanly letter it has evoked. Enough that there exists between us so beautiful & delicate a relation, accepted by both of us with joy" (qtd. in Kaplan 332). The simple word *enough* conveys the kind of distance essential to an appreciation of the poet's "true" self. "Playacting," writes Richard Sennett, "requires an audience of strangers to succeed, but is meaningless or even destructive among intimates. Playacting . . . is the very stuff out of which public relations derive their emotional meaning" (28–29).

In his own mind Whitman truly became the man of his poems in the Civil War, "the most profound lesson of my life," the experience without which, he claims, *Leaves of Grass* (1855) could not have been written. In the war, notes Zweig, "the theatre had come indoors into the long hospital sheds" (332). For more than three years during the war Whitman attended the hospitals nearly every day, making, by his estimation, over six hundred visits. To numberless young men Whitman was an angel of mercy, radiating health, good cheer, and a benevolent paternalism. The desire to perform public action and the quest for a space within which to act correspond to Whitman's crucial desire for *strangers* who will absorb him. It is Whitman's recognition of this quality of public life which allows him to come to us, "face to face," across the tides of years, furnishing parts toward eternity. Whitman loved the actors he knew and always felt a deep affinity with them. "Actors," Whitman once commented, "have always been more friendly to me than almost any other professional class" (qtd. in Traubel 1:6). Whitman explicitly recognizes the actor's craft as a model for his own. Across the apron of the stage the actor achieves his special electrical bond with his audience: "Out in the brilliancy of the footlights—filling the attention of perhaps a crowded audience, and making many a breath and pulse swell and rise—O so much passion and imparted life!" (P&P 1293).

PUBLIC SPACE

The idea of reading (and writing) poetry as theater indicates a deeply held belief that literature, including those genres that are held to be most private, is a social experience and a public act. In stressing Whitman's deep relationship to theater I am situating myself in relation to two conflicting visions of Whitman. The first is a school of Whitman criticism epitomized by Quentin Anderson's study *The Imperial Self* (1971). The "imperial" self, argues Anderson, attempts to affect a "revolution on the inner scene, not action on the outer one." Whitman's project in *Leaves of Grass* represents a kind of desocialization, absorbing or assimilating all other existences into himself. "In this world," writes Anderson, "the other is absent" (114). The world is merely an extension of Whitman's self. This kind of view has been powerfully articulated in different forms as early as D. H. Lawrence's *Studies in Classic American Literature* (1923): "I am everything and everything is me and so we're all One in One Identity, like the Mundane Egg, which has been addled quite a while" (173). Lawrence complains that "Walt becomes in his own person the whole world." More recently, in "Democratic Social Space: Whitman, Melville, and the Promise of American Transparency" (1988), Philip Fisher argues that Whitman epitomizes an American aesthetics that is "intrinsically an aesthetics of abstraction or, even more radically, an aesthetics of the subtraction of differences" (71). A crucial feature of democratic social space, in Fisher's view, is that it contains no oppositional positions.[19]

On the other hand, there are a number of critics who have understood Whitman as a public poet with a worldview that includes oppositional structures. E. Fred Carlisle, using Buber's *I-Thou* as a model, insists that in Whitman "meaning and identity emerge only in the lived moment through encounter" (8). The self, in this view, is neither centered in a subjective interiority nor grounded in an objective, external reality but, rather, emerges only in dialogue. In *Whitman's Drama of Consensus* (1988) Kerry Larson also argues that Whitman's aesthetic is "above all concerned to evoke a transactive process between the self and the multitude of persons, places, and things that course through it." Although Larson's notion of consensus has much in common with Fisher's idea of democratic social space, Larson emphasizes the movement, in Whitman, from "isolated individuality" to "affirmed unanimity," the process of working toward consent. Most recently, in *Walt Whitman and the Citizen's Eye* (1993) James Dougherty has insisted on understanding Whitman as a public poet addressing an American audience. Whitman's struggle, argues Dougherty, "is to align his inner vision with the outer world . . . He attempts that alignment in two reciprocal movements, corresponding to the One and the Many in the nation" (7).[20]

There is much evidence to support both sides of this argument. To a large degree Whitman projects an imperial, assimilating self. But the poet also represents a performer in an arena that is sometimes harmonious but often agonistic and oppositional. My aim here is to complicate the issue by enriching the context of the debate. In Whitman's diverse comments on theater, a complex and often contradictory "American" aesthetic emerges, one in which the competing claims for public and private experience are not entirely resolved and in which assimilation and opposition are often simultaneously articulated. On the one hand, in some comments on theater, especially recollections of boyhood experiences, Whitman clearly enjoys the sense of absorption into the theatrical illusion and the feeling of oneness with the audience, experiencing the whole event as a process of radical assimilation and, in fact, disliking anyone to distract him from it. On the other hand, in much of his work as a journalist in the 1840s he vituperates the uncritical mass and argues that American theater can fulfill its important role as a moral institution, that is, as a shaper of American character, if "intelligent writers for the press will only express their real opinions of the stage, and of players" (GF 318). A truly democratic theater, in this view, is premised on the oppositional structure in which the critic is the crucial figure. These two positions exist, fundamentally unreconciled though often side by side, throughout Whitman's work. *Democratic Vistas* is the prose work in which Whitman most explicitly acknowledges the two strains: "To democracy, the leveler, the unyielding principle of the average, is surely joined another principle, equally unyielding, closely tracking the first, indispensable to it, opposite . . . This second principle is individuality" (P&P 958). Significantly, theater becomes an important metaphor in this essay of political theory.

Although the two sides of the debate posit different views of Whitman's relationship to a public realm, underlying both is the understanding that Whitman is fundamentally concerned with some kind of relationship of the one to the many. Even Anderson acknowledges that what he calls Whitman's narcissism is far from a lapse into solipsism. The very act of Whitman's proclaiming his self-absorption, Anderson admits, "was carried out in the presence of the superego, was in its conception quasi-public already" (105). Thus, Whitman's worldview is fundamentally conditioned by the theater. Whitman enjoyed theater at an early age, and, from boyhood, life in America seemed somehow theatrical. As a boy, he went to see a well-loved actress "nearly every night she play'd at the old Park." And he had seen "quite all of Shakspere's acting dramas, play'd wonderfully well" (*Specimen Days,* P&P 704). But Whitman was drawn to political and religious rallies, to ferry boats with their "queer scenes," to the World's Fair, and even to the spectacle of the Civil War for many of the same reasons. "I could have watched for a week," he said of General Sheridan and his cavalry on parade in May 1865 (769). The sense that any public space could suddenly become a theater, or that the idea of theater was somehow related to any form of social experience, is an early feature of Whitman's understanding of his world. "Here's a good place at the corner," the poet writes, "I must stand and see the show" (*Leaves of Grass,* P&P 135).

In an article for the Brooklyn *Standard* Whitman reflects on twenty years of theater history in Brooklyn, beginning with the Brooklyn Theatre of 1828, which "was so arranged in its interior that it could be changed in a few moments from a theatrical stage into accommodations for a circus, or vice versa" (UPP 2:254). Much of the article is devoted to detailing what entertainments were available in the city before these "legitimate" theaters were established or at times when such theaters were shut down. Theater becomes the impetus for discussing, and literally remembering, various forms of public entertainment in American life. "There were the churches, especially the Methodist ones, with their frequent 'revivals' . . . Then we had various sorts of 'celebrations'—sometimes of the Sunday Schools, sometimes the regular educational establishments, sometimes of an anniversary of one kind or another. Of course we came out great on a Fourth of July celebration. This was always an affair to be carefully seen to and planned deliberately—and the 'oration' was something talked of both beforehand and long afterward" (2:255). Society is a "visible stage," a vast performance space, as Whitman notes in *Democratic Vistas*. And America, as a republic, "is, in performance, really enacting today the grandest arts, poems, &c." (*Democratic Vistas,* P&P 936). In an age when, as Paul Zweig notes, "Americans loved to be part of an audience," Whitman may be considered the period's most vital proponent of a kind of displaced theater, one that found its way into the marketplace, into politics, and ultimately into poetry (218).

Several features led to the pervasive climate of theatricality in America and, therefore, help to characterize American society of Whitman's youth during the 1830s. The beginning of mass migration to the cities corresponded to the breakdown of traditional social structures and hierarchies of authority in small communities, including traditional roles for church and family. The nature of politics was also changing. The earlier republican period, roughly between 1789 and 1830, had been characterized by a consensus tradition and local organization, that is, a politics focusing on well-known local leaders. The 1830s saw the emergence of mass political parties. The nationalization of public opinion, through press and speaker's platform, enabled a theatrical structure in which party men, individuals whose private characters were unknown to their audience, appealed directly to an emotionally susceptible people without deference to local authorities (Halttunen 1982, 16).

Whitman himself was an avid party member, representing the Democratic Party in the 1840s, both in the popular press and on the debater's platform. His support for the Democratic Party resulted in his being elected for a year or two to the position of secretary of the General Committee of Queens County (Allen 74). The change in political life also made the electorate a much more important part of the political process, for the people became a body that had to be won over. This structure has parallels in other social arenas, including religion as preached by the likes of Father Taylor and Elias Hicks, the hucksterism of P. T. Barnum, whom Whitman met and interviewed for the *Daily Eagle* in 1846, and the rise of a popular theater. Charismatic demagogues and performers known for personal magnetism were not confined to politics. These new features, among others, made American society theatrical in a way that it had not been before.

Whitman never shied away from the often highly antagonistic opposition between the performer and the audience, whether in the press or on the political stage. In his notes for lectures Whitman imagines the place occupied by the orator and his audience as "truly an agonistic arena." In that space the orator "wrestles and contends" with his hearers, suffering and sweating (*Workshop* 37). In *Leaves of Grass* he "*descends* into the arena" ("Starting from Paumanok"). Once an electrical harmony is achieved, however, the oppositional relationship is transformed: "The organs of the body attuned to the exertions of the mind, through the kindred organs of the hearers, instantaneously and as it were with an electrical spirit vibrate those energies from soul to soul" (*Workshop* 38). Whitman makes it clear that a true performance space is fluid and that a great performance can transform the character of the audience, not only in the theater but also in a more lasting way. There is, in this theater, an inexorable moral logic: good is meant to be emulated; wickedness is punished.

Fundamental to Whitman's conception of character on stage is the role of the audience. For Whitman, David Reynolds asserts, "by far the most important aspect of the theatre experience . . . was the interaction between the audience and performers" (1995, 157). American theater in Whitman's day was a space of interaction and communication between the audience and the stage and among audience members themselves. The audience is an existential prerequisite for the body electric: "I sing the body electric, / The armies of those I love engirth me and I engirth them." The very notion of electricity is premised upon a public space of action and interaction: "the whole crowded auditorium, and what seeth'd in it, and flush'd from its faces and eyes, to me as much a part of the show as any—bursting forth in one of those long kept up tempests of hand-clapping peculiar to the Bowery—no dainty kid-glove business, but electric force and muscle from perhaps 2000 full-sinew'd men" (*November Boughs,* P&P 1189). The freedom of members of the public to express themselves in the theater reflects, in Whitman's view, the general state of a democracy. This idea is central to *Democratic Vistas,* in which Whitman asks, "What is more dramatic than the spectacle we have seen repeated, and doubtless long shall see—the popular judgement taking the successful candidates on trial in the offices—standing off, as it were, and observing them and their doings for a while, and always giving, finally, the fit, exactly due reward?" (P&P 954). On stage the characters portrayed must be responsive to audience demands.

The ethical problem that arises, however, is how to retain the enthusiasm of a popular audience while ensuring that it will exercise its power intelligently and responsibly. As a theatergoer, in his younger days, Whitman enjoyed sitting in the pit, particularly the pit in the Bowery Theatre, which "always showed more democracy and better animal specimens than the Park Theatre (with which house I was perfectly familiar)" (CW 54). His neighbors there were: "alert, well-dress'd, full-blooded young and middle-aged men, the best average of American born mechanics." Most of Whitman's recollections of youthful days in the theater take place in the pit, where he "used to go and get a good seat." From his place among the folk Whitman, who "always scann'd an audience as rigidly as a play," could see the great men of his day seated above him, "the faces of the leading authors, poets, editors of those times, Fenimore Cooper, Bryant, Paulding, Irving . . . occasionally peering from the first tier of boxes; and even the great National Eminences, Presidents Adams, Jackson, Van Buren and Tyler, all made short visits there [the Old Bowery] on their Eastern tours" (P&P 1188). In Whitman's view the climax of an evening's entertainment in the theater involved a collective experience of the highest order, a kind of spiritual connection of the most diverse social and intellectual types, an electric union of minds from footlights to lobby doors, from the pit to the dome.

The spiritual connection, or union, which Whitman imagines also requires a certain critical intelligence. And, more often than not, as Whitman recognizes in his drama criticism, audiences did not maintain the clean-cut quality. Remarkably, however, even in the late 1840s, as audiences became more unruly and theaters began to change, Whitman was still optimistic that theater was "destined to take a new form and triple vigor, in this Republic" (GF 339). And, although Whitman heartily disapproved of unruly behavior in the theater as well as the mindless hurrahs of newsboys and apprentices, he believed strongly that audience members had certain, inalienable "rights." Whitman criticizes, for example, antidemocratic developments in the Cuban theater in which, he complains, members of the public "are prohibited from calling out any actor or actress, or for repetition of any piece, under penalties of fifteen days in prison" (343). Aware of the difficulty of establishing a contemporary drama that is also "among the first rank of intellectual entertainments," Whitman never fundamentally questions the validity or the importance of this mission, primarily because drama, as an inherently social form, appears to him preeminent among "those agents of refining public manners and doing good" (336).

The tension that is evident throughout Whitman's writing between critical detachment, the responsibility of the individual to make political and moral judgments, and a desire for complete, almost ecstatic, immersion in experience is particularly evident in his writings on the theater of his early youth. Whitman recalls how, as a "perpetual theatre-goer" between the ages of fourteen and eighteen, he enjoyed the complete immersion offered by perfect illusion in the theater: "At first, as I remember, I used to go with other boys, my pals; but afterwards I preferred to go alone, I was so absorbed in the performance, and disliked any one to distract my attention . . . Illusions of youth! Dreams of a child of the Bowery!" (CW 53–54). The pleasure of being "absorbed" in the performance is also recollected in memories of great lectures he attended, great operas, parades, and other stirring events of communal life.[21] Yet there is an important difference, Whitman remarks in an article for the *Eagle,* between the "reciprocal excitement" produced among audience members by an ordinary actor, who merely struts and rants, and the "strange and subtle sympathy which runs like an electrical charge through human hearts collected together" (GF 322). The difference is located in the word *sympathy.* "A man is only interested in anything when he identifies himself with it," says Whitman, suggesting not only the nature of the actor's investment in his role but also the proper mode of audience response. Identification is important for Whitman, as it had been a century earlier for Lessing, because only by stressing a notion of sympathy for our equals, over the blind and sudden irrationalism of terror, can theater become the "school of the moral world" (Lessing 8).

The theatrical audience in Whitman's prose is a metaphor for American democracy. Whitman imagines the relationship of the American people to the moral, aesthetic, and political phenomenon of America, as he does the relationship of the audience to the play, and vice versa. The audience, required for any performance, is necessarily present in the political and aesthetic action of the play. Junius Booth, "in his pride and prime," achieves a stunning success at the Old Bowery because "the audience was electric—just the kind to call out a great actor's best. He was well supported" (CW 55). Whitman's demand that the play not be adjusted to please the popular audience but that the audience of common folk be raised to appreciate a higher art resonates throughout his work. Yet, while the audience must be raised intellectually and morally, it must not lose the exuberance and assertiveness of the best audiences of the 1830s. Audience members ought not to observe passively but should actively participate.

The audience is not only a collective mass but a community of individuals and, therefore, becomes in Whitman's thinking a fit metaphor for the fundamental paradox of American life: individualism and union. In his 1855 preface to *Leaves of Grass* Whitman challenges the individual in the audience with an epistemology clearly influenced by Emerson's "Self-Reliance": "The most affluent man is he that *confronts* all shows he sees by equivalents out of the stronger wealth of himself" (P&P 15; my emph.). But theater, as Whitman recognizes, is social; it is produced only in community. Democracy is not made up by "that half only, individualism, which isolates. There is another half, which is adhesiveness or love, that fuses, ties and aggregates" (*Democratic Vistas,* P&P 949). Theater, like the United States, cannot be founded on self-reliance alone. *Democratic Vistas,* the culmination of Whitman's political writings and "observings," is itself a metaphor for his vision of the United States: a "collection of memoranda . . . harmoniously blended in my own realization and convictions" (930). Great literature, he argues, which is requisite for the survival of America, "shapes aggregates *and* individuals" (my emph.). Theater, both as empty spectacle and as profound, spiritual drama, becomes, in this long essay, a crucial metaphor: "Behind this fantastic farce, enacted on the visible stage of society, solid things and tremendous labors are to be discovered" (937).

The relationship between audience members and the stage has, in the 1870s, lost its agonistic energy; it has become dainty and even apathetic. Compared to this idealistic notion of a democratic theater, the drama of the 1870s, like the society, has become tainted by rank commercialism: "Of what is called the drama, or dramatic presentation in the United States, as now put forth at the theatres, I should say it deserves to be treated with the same gravity, and on a par with the questions of ornamental confectionery at public dinners, or the arrangement of curtains in a ball-room—nor more, nor less" (*Democratic Vistas,* P&P 979).[22] At the heart of true democratic theater, on the other hand, is that vital sense of "formative action." Such theater does not contain the flux and flow of American life but, rather, expresses it. The people, an "aggregate of living identities," Whitman imagines both individually and collectively not only as spectators but also as actors themselves upon one broad, "universal, common platform." Only then, he writes, will the history of democracy "be enacted" (960).[23] It is interesting to note that these concerns, both for the quality of individuals and the state of the union, are focused in *Democratic Vistas* by the "important question of character" and how it is to be expressed. It may be argued, Whitman remarks, that the republic is "in performance, really enacting today the grandest, arts, poems, &c.," but, without the moral and artistic purpose which fuses the States into the "only reliable identity," the material achievements remain hollow (936).

"To have great poets," Whitman says, "there must be great audiences, too" (P&P 1058). In part this statement can be read as an imperative of Whitman's poetic form, in which the "truest and greatest *Poetry*" is imagined, like the "greatest eloquence," to be produced in community ("New Poetry," P&P 1056). Kerry Larson articulates this view when he argues that "much of the revolutionary impact of *Leaves of Grass* entails breaking the mediations conventional to the fictional contract by devising a mode of address able to traverse the gap between intimate seductiveness and generic inclusiveness" (5). In Larson's view Whitman's poetry does not recommend a consensual framework so much as embody one.[24] Theater provides an important generic model for Whitman both because he aims to imagine a subject that is formed collectively and because he rebels against the idea of reading as a solitary act, a view supported in part by the poet's frequent use of the second-person voice. As Larson suggests, Whitman's poems "are vehicles for social cohesion" (xvi).

The poet is made present to the reader and expects to be held accountable. As Whitman claims in his early preface to *Leaves of Grass* (1855): "I will not have in my writing any elegance or effect or originality to hang in the way between me and the rest like curtains." Moreover, this presence in space and time is issued as a kind of challenge:

> I am a man who, sauntering along without fully stopping, turns a
>   casual look upon you and then averts his face,
> Leaving it to you to prove and define it,
> Expecting the main things from you.

The responsibility of the individual in a collective aesthetic/political experience is stressed repeatedly by Whitman. "You shall listen to all sides and filter them from your self," he writes in "Song of Myself." In *Leaves of Grass* the reader's ability to remain detached is continually put to the test.

In the seemingly contradictory roles of the public teacher/lecturer and the private seducer, Whitman engages his audience in what he calls "act-poems." For example, the poet "comes personally to you . . . / Enjoining you to acts, characters, spectacles, with me." Although challenged directly to "prove and define" the poet's look, as well as democracy itself, the reader is also continually excited by Dionysian exhortations:

> O something ecstatic and undemonstrable! O music wild!
> O now I triumph—and you shall also;
> O hand in hand—O wholesome pleasure—O one more
> desirer and lover!
> O to haste firm holding—to haste, haste on with me.

Whitman attempts to catch us off-guard, slipping almost imperceptibly between the reasonable and the passionate. The "strange and subtle sympathy," which is the pleasure of experience in the theater, is easily converted into an unreflective adherence to the group or a kind of hypnotism by the performer and an abandonment of the critical faculty. In his drama criticism Whitman demands more critics who will go to the theater and make their minds up for themselves, uninfluenced by the "general contagion." Critics must have the courage to form and then profess their own opinions. The intelligent critic at the theater, therefore, can be the model of the democratic citizen. "He is," Whitman reflects, "as much a part of the audience as any other one man, and he had far better be himself than anybody else, in making up his mind" (GF 319). This notion of responsible spectatorship is the challenge of *Leaves of Grass.*

Whitman is both the lover, in the flesh, attempting to seduce us, "out from behind this bending rough-cut mask," and the public figure, the melodramatic hero, whose every action signifies a great idea or moral truth. The poet's lifelong devotion to the theater should alert us that, if we are tender to the lover, we must also reckon with the public man. Like the character of Christopher Columbus, who appears as an actor in "Passage to India," one version of Walt Whitman aims to project himself across generations as the melodramatic hero. In that poem Columbus walks down the stage, a "type of courage, action, faith":

And who art thou sad shade?
Gigantic, visionary, thyself a visionary,
With majestic limbs and pious beaming eyes,
Spreading around with every look of thine a golden world,
Enhuing it with gorgeous hues.

As the chief histrion
Down to the footlights walks in some great scena [*sic*],
Dominating the rest I see the Admiral himself.

Whitman, like Columbus, stands "in time" before us. And, like the actor Macready, who "merely appeared, walking down the stage, a king," both Whitman and the admiral walk down to the footlights, dominating "the rest." Whitman's "dramatic, pictorial, plot-constructing, euphonius and other talents" ultimately found expression in his poems (P&P 987). And, if Whitman's dramatic theories have been largely unappreciated in the theater, they may nonetheless enhance our understanding of his monumental contribution to our notion of an American character and of the persona of Whitman himself. From the opening poems of *Leaves of Grass* he imagines us, even a century later, as an audience waiting for him to perform: "See projected through time / For me an audience interminable" ("Starting from Paumanok").

THREE

"ANOTHER VERSION OF THE WHALE-SHIP GLOBE"

Narrative and Drama in *Moby-Dick*

The papers were brought in, and we saw in the Berlin Gazette that whales had been introduced on the stage there.

HERMAN MELVILLE, *Moby-Dick*

"Obviously *Moby-Dick* is a novel and not a play," writes Charles Olson, though the influence of Elizabethan tragedy and Shakespeare in particular upon characterization, structure, language, stage directions, and soliloquies in *Moby-Dick* has been acknowledged with varying degrees of interest and intensity by critics since George Duyckinck (1851). The most famous reading of Shakespeare's influence in *Moby-Dick,* after Olson's, is F. O. Matthiessen's chapter in *American Renaissance* (1941), "The Revenger's Tragedy."[1] Yet both Olson and Matthiessen, who strenuously insist on reading *Moby-Dick* as drama, use the term *drama* loosely. And both are forced to confront the limits of its valence. "Melville's 'wicked book,'" writes Olson, "is the drama of Ahab, his hot hate for the White Whale, and his vengeful pursuit of it into the Atlantic. It is that action, not the complete novel *Moby-Dick*" (54). Matthiessen, too, claims that the dramatic nature of Ahab's action justifies classifying aspects of the book as drama. He calls the three days of the final chase "the finest piece of dramatic writing in American literature, though shaped with no reference to a stage" (421). These discussions of Melville and Shakespeare, *Moby-Dick* and drama, ultimately seem incomplete for two reasons. First, they do not define the parameters of the drama. As a result, they do not probe deeply enough the explicit structural and thematic tensions between narrative form and dramatic form in *Moby-Dick*. And, second, they do not adequately historicize Shakespeare, or the drama, in nineteenth-century America. They do not allow enough room for Melville's interest in contemporary theater and the peculiar relationship of that theater to American social experience.

More recently, Walter E. Bezanson, who also claims that *Moby-Dick* should be read, at least in part, as drama, notes, "What should not get lost, whatever narrative concept one adopts, is the live, powerful, dominant presence of Ishmael which surrounds the entire book" (185). Ishmael's impulse to narrate, however, is complicated and sometimes obviated by his impulse to experience events that are not easily represented in narrative form. Bezanson notes this problem when he writes that "a modern reader's fascination with *Moby-Dick* might well begin with attention to Ishmael's search for forms—a sermon, a dream, a comic set-piece, a midnight ballet, a meditation, an emblematic reading. It is as if finding a temporary form would in itself constitute one of those 'meanings' which Ishmael is always so portentously in search of" (185). The peculiar nature of Ishmael's presence in and disappearences from *Moby-Dick,* the various forms assumed by his narrative impulse, and his motivations for narrating at all (let alone for going on a whaling voyage) suggest that the relationship between narrative and drama in *Moby-Dick* may, at certain intersections, be especially productive of "meanings" for the text as a whole.

Moby-Dick is one instance of what Lawrence Buell calls "observer-hero narrative," a story told by a dramatized first-person narrator about his relationship with another person. Observer and hero are both opposites and counterparts; the hero contrasts with the observer in outlook or lifestyle while also embodying in purer or more extreme form qualities that the observer has or with which he (for it is nearly always he) sympathizes. The observer's world seems like our world, while that of the hero seems more romantic.[2] The most fundamental convention of observer-hero narratives, notes Buell, is the inseparability of the two main figures. Ishmael, for example, "needs a definite focus like Ahab's quest as a field of action for his sensibility" (94). Yet what exactly is Ishmael's "sensibility"? What fields of action is Ishmael drawn to besides Ahab's quest, and what is it about Ahab's quest which draws him?

A field of action is a public space, a "space of appearance."[3] It comes into being wherever people gather together for a common purpose whose outcome is to be revealed; the field of action requires the potential of revelation. It is constructed not by physical work but by the shared sense of potentiality. White-Jacket refers to this space when he says, "You cannot save a ship by working out a problem in the cabin; the deck is the field of action" (33). The relationship between narrator and reader, on the other hand, is private and intimate. Private space is a space of subjectivity and is, therefore, set apart from action; for action has the objective character of "reality." The private narrator-reader relationship occurs in a space not of potentiality but of interpretation and illumination. Admittedly, however, to discuss a *space* of narration is somewhat misleading. For, though the narrator-reader relationship is often represented spatially, narrative occupies a fundamentally different experiential dimension than dramatic action. In *Moby-Dick* the reader's relationship to Ishmael is not generally realized in space but in time. For example, our relationship with the narrator begins with the imperative "Call" (the aural), whereas Ishmael's relationship with Ahab begins with a physical appearance: "I levelled my glance," "He looked like . . ." (i.e., the visual).[4] Certain fields of action eventuate in stylistic disruptions or lacunae in the narrative form. Central chapters in the book are not in the form of narrative at all but assume a dramatic form, with dialogue printed as in a play-text, stage directions, and dramatic speech patterns. In *Moby-Dick* drama, or the dramatic, often represents that which narrative cannot express.

Ahab is clearly the most compelling performer Ishmael encounters. His magnetism and the violence he provokes conjure up stories of some of the period's most charismatic actors and especially their ability to sway volatile crowds. As Joel Porte has shown, an appreciation of Ahab's similarity to certain Shakespearean actors of his day significantly complicates more conventional readings of Shakespearean language in his speech.[5] The King Lear of Edwin Forrest, for example, was said to affect audiences "physically as well as mentally," to be "beyond the power of pen to describe." As Lear, Forrest's "defiance of the elements was grand and magnificent . . . gigantic, awful, fearful in its sublimity" (Rees 172). In a similar spirit, when Ishmael first sees Ahab, he remarks: "I levelled my glance towards the taffrail, foreboding shivers ran over me. Reality outran apprehension; Captain Ahab stood upon his quarter-deck." When reality outruns apprehension, Ishmael's narrative impulse must confront its limits.

The attempt to circumscribe the public space of action indicates a crucial social-political problem: how does a literary form experienced privately through the act of reading represent the quality of being immersed in a public experience that is socially crowded and diverse? Narrative, in this view, may be inadequate to represent what Walt Whitman calls the "full play of human nature" (*Democratic Vistas*), the spirit of the "common people" and their public life. Melville's use of both narrative and dramatic modes is based partly on such sociological and political considerations, which were stimulated to some degree by important events in the history of American theater occurring in the years that Melville was writing both *White-Jacket* and *Moby-Dick*. Therefore, Melville's interest in theater, both in New York and in London, in the two years leading up to the publication of *Moby-Dick,* also suggests a place for the book in contemporary discourse about the theater.

Many American authors in the nineteenth century claimed that their work had more in common with drama than with the English novel, and one feature of this difference was a tendency of American authors to privilege "action" over character. Here *action* is defined in terms of nineteenth-century melodrama, and a close study of contemporary theater will shed new light on Ahab, not as a tragic hero but as a melodramatic figure. In numerous works, from *The Confidence-Man* to "Benito Cereno," Melville shows that in comparison to the "truthful" excesses of the melodramatic theater, the realism of the novel appears epistemologically naive. Ahab represents in part a kind of theater that seems to offer, if not solutions, at least alternative approaches to problems that Ishmael cannot represent in narrative alone. A reading of *Moby-Dick* in the context of theater history indicates deep thinking about the theater on Melville's part as well as new possible readings of the symbolic importance of the whale. In such an interpretation the symbolism of the catastrophe at the drama's end may be understood to have implications for the form of the novel itself.

REPRESENTING THE PEOPLE

"When I go to sea, I go as a simple sailor, right before the mast," writes Ishmael (14). This statement is, of course, both true and false. Though shipping before the mast, Ishmael is no simple sailor. Melville's sailor/narrators, like Melville himself, are red-blooded democrats, proud of shipping with the roughs, the common seamen, but they are also representatives of a cultured elite, a fact felt not only by themselves but often, especially in *Omoo* and *White-Jacket,* by the other sailors as well. "Culture" was a hotly contested notion in mid-nineteenth-century America. In "The Young American" (1844), for example, Emerson notes that "it is remarkable, that our people have their intellectual culture from one country, and their duties from another" (213). Of all social-artistic venues the American theater in the 1840s and 1850s was especially resistant to culture. Edwin Forrest, the great American actor, who relished his working-class following and range of acquaintances, was never comfortable with intellectuals. Peculiarly, however, he married an elegant Englishwoman, Catherine Norton Sinclair, said to be of "the highest intellectual culture." When the marriage ended in a highly publicized divorce in 1852, the actor received huge ovations in the theaters and, on one occasion, was greeted by a banner on which was printed, "THIS IS THE PEOPLE'S VERDICT" (McConachie 69–72). Culture, in this sense, is a notion that anticipates by some twenty years Matthew Arnold's "idea of perfection as an *inward* condition of the mind and spirit" (34). In Arnold's view culture is fundamentally at variance with "material civilization" and public action; it comes from the pursuit of perfection through knowledge, through reading "the best which has been thought and said in the world." As Lawrence Levine remarks, in Arnold's view "anything that produced a group atmosphere, a mass ethos, was culturally suspect" (164). It is the sense of private and "internal" cultivation that I intend to evoke with the word *culture,* and it is this cultivation that sets Melville's narrators and "gentlemen" apart from other seamen.

In *Germinie Lacerteux* (1864) Edmond and Jules de Goncourt describe a discrepancy between political revolutions that have resulted in "a time of universal suffrage, of democracy, of liberalism" and literary developments that have produced novels that disdain "the people." Why, they ask, must the lower classes "remain under the literary interdict" of novelists? Anticipating the Goncourts, Melville seeks to incorporate just such lower orders without also rejecting the idea of culture and interior experience. Yet in novels ranging from *Omoo* to *Moby-Dick* the problem of representing adequately an illiterate and unreflective social body in a novelistic form quickly becomes apparent. To represent the people and their field of action Melville turns to the theater. For, as he writes in *White-Jacket,* "if ever there was a continual theatre in the world, playing by night and day, and without intervals between the acts, a man-of-war is that theatre, and her planks are the boards indeed" (93).

In *Omoo* and *White-Jacket* the tensions of class difference are acute, and the differences are cultural rather than economic. The narrator of *Omoo* becomes fast friends with Doctor Long Ghost first by sharing books and then other interests. Their relationship represents a particular form of cultural elitism. Common interests, in reading, in playing chess, not only establish a bond between them but also privilege them in the eyes of the people: "Aside from the pleasure of his society, my intimacy with Long Ghost was of great service to me in other respects. His disgrace in the cabin only confirmed the good-will of the democracy in the forecastle; and they not only treated him in the most friendly manner, but looked up to him with the utmost deference . . . As his chosen associate, this feeling for him extended to me; and gradually we came to be regarded in the light of distinguished guests" (363). White-Jacket has a similar relationship with Jack Chase and the few other cultured sailors aboard the *Neversink*.

White-Jacket wants to be recognized as a rough and hardy sailor but, at the same time, continually asserts his difference from the common seamen, the "people," the vulgar mob. The words *gentleman* and *gentlemanly* pervade his narrative. The "gentlemen" of the after-guard on the *Neversink,* for example, are the least robust, the least hardy, and the least "sailorlike" of the crew and, therefore, relatively contemptible: "They lounge away the most part of their time, in reading novels and romances; talking over their lover affairs ashore; and comparing notes concerning the melancholy and sentimental career which drove them—poor young gentlemen—into the hard-hearted Navy. Indeed, many of them show tokens of having moved in very respectable society" (9). Seamen/gentlemen, like Jack Chase and White-Jacket himself, however, also are distinguished by how much they have read and how many languages they speak. One of the most important distinguishing characteristics of Melville's gentlemen, for good and for bad, is their literacy, often projected as a love of books and generally related to their capacity as narrators.

The sense of the narrator's ambivalence toward the people and the often conflicted representations of class difference frequently manifest themselves in an ambivalence to literature itself and the sense that literature is not exactly "democratic." In short, Melville represents a set of complex social attitudes in his depiction of the contemporary cultural hierarchy that assigned a privileged status to literature while regarding theater as a vehicle for public, or *popular,* expression. It has often been noted that Melville's narrators are both cultured elitists and "ruthless democrats." What I aim to contribute to the discussion is a sense of how theater and the dramatic work in these books to clarify and illustrate the nature of this ambivalence.

The tensions between cultured elitist and political democrat stem in part from a blurring of private and public life for the ordinary sailor aboard ship. It is easy for the commodore to maintain his difference from the crew, for he has a private space, to which he can retreat. This private space, the "curtained cabin," the narrator tells us, is like a "sealed volume." There is no privacy for the common sailor on a man-of-war: "To a common sailor the living on board a man-of-war is like living in a market" (36). White-Jacket, the uncommon sailor, compensates for this lack of privacy by living in his jacket, which is associated, like the captain's cabin, with writing. The jacket, "like a confidential writing-desk, abounded in snug little out-of-the-way lairs and hiding-places" (37). The jacket, which visibly marks the narrator's difference, also provides a metaphorical space for the intimate relationship between narrator and reader: "Come under the lee of my white jacket, reader" (124).

Gentlemen express themselves in writing, and the people express themselves on the "field of action," which is the deck. Melville's texts generate different strategies of representation for different classes of the population. One of the few occasions on which *the people* are given free rein to express themselves on the man-of-war is the principal democratic holiday, the Fourth of July. The only mode of celebration available to the crew on the *Neversink* is to stage a theatrical event. Three days before the anniversary "it was publicly announced that free permission was given to the sailors to get up any sort of theatricals they desired, wherewith to honor the Fourth" (92). The Fourth of July may be the first time the sailors are allowed to stage a play, but it is not the first time they have tried. Weeks before sailing from home, we are told, "some of the seamen had clubbed together, and made up a considerable purse, for the purpose of purchasing a theatrical outfit" (93). In a Peruvian harbor they had asked permission to produce a "much-admired drama," *The Ruffian Boy,* but had been assured by the captain that there were already too many ruffian boys on board and had been forced to stow all the theatrical equipment in the bottom of the sailors' bags. Theater as a mode of both self and group expression is taken seriously by the ship's officers. In this case the captain reads the play as a literal, or potentially literal, representation of actual characters on his ship. The danger in Captain Claret's eyes is that, if the people are allowed to express themselves in this way, they will have appropriated the capacity for self-definition and will therefore undermine the navy's structures of authority. The captain clearly understands the reciprocal relationship between theatrical production and real life on deck.

The Fourth of July, however, is set off from the rest of the year, and both the drama and its aftermath bear certain resemblances to carnival. The production actually begins as a quasi-literary form. Lemsford, the "gun-deck poet," draws up the playbill, and "upon this one occasion his literary abilities were far from being underrated, even by the least intellectual person on board." Captain Claret asserts authority over the text by acting as censor, to make sure nothing in the manuscript could breed dissatisfaction against "lawful authority." The theater itself is set up to reinforce structures of authority. The curtain is composed of a large ensign. The commodore does not appear on deck to witness the event, but the wardroom officers seat themselves centrally upon camp stools, and "*that* was the royal box."

All of this public display establishes the ship's social hierarchy. But the theatrical event itself, once under way, is intensely festive. Expanding beyond the official sphere, the play inverts hierarchical rank, substituting special forms of speech and gesture. The play begins when four sailors, dressed as Maltese mariners, stagger onto the stage in a feigned state of intoxication. "The truthfulness of the representation," remarks the narrator, "was much heightened by the roll of the ship" (96). Even nature, in the incessant role of the waves, is appropriated in the theatrical event. The production of the Cape Horn Theatre aims to represent but also to parody life on board the ship itself. The officers, including "The Commodore," "Old Luff," "The Mayor," and "Gin and Sugar Sall," are played to the admiration of all, receiving great applause. Things begin to get out of hand, however, when Jack Chase appears on the boards:

> Matchless Jack, *in full fig,* bowed again and again, with true quarter-deck grace and self-possession . . . "Hurrah! hurrah! hurrah!—go on! go on! go on!—stop hollering—hurrah!" was now heard on all sides, till at last seeing no end to the enthusiasm of his ardent admirers, matchless Jack stepped forward, and, with his lips moving in pantomime, plunged into the thick of the part. Silence soon followed, but was fifty times broken by uncontrollable bursts of applause. At length,

> when the heart-thrilling scene came on, where Percy Royal-Mast rescues fifteen oppressed sailors . . . the audience leaped to their feet, overturned the capstan bars, and to a man hurled their hats on the stage in a delirium of delight . . . The commotion was now terrific; all discipline seemed gone forever, the lieutenants ran in among the men, the captain darted from his cabin, and the commodore nervously questioned the armed sentry at his door as to what the deuce *the people* were about. (96–97)

The play has licensed a rupture of discipline which includes the mingling of officers and common seamen in the most violent commotion. It is unclear, however, what exactly White-Jacket's position has been throughout these events. White-Jacket is, throughout the book, as infatuated with Jack Chase as anyone, and the vigor of his description of the previous scene might indicate that he has been enjoying it with everyone else. But his reaction when the commotion subsides is quite different from Ishmael's enthusiastic comment, for example, after the fight on the forecastle in *Moby-Dick:* "I, Ishmael, was one of that crew, my shouts had gone up with the rest" (155). Instead, White-Jacket asserts himself nervously, even fussily, as a squall appears to be bearing down on the maddened ship: "There is no knowing what would have ensued, had not the brass drum suddenly been heard, calling all hands to quarters, a summons not to be withstood." Whose side is he on anyway? He refers to "the sailors" both in the third person, as if he were not one of them, and in the first, as if he were:

> And here White-Jacket must moralize a bit. The unwonted spectacle of the row of gun-room officers mingling with *the people* in applauding a mere seaman like Jack Chase, filled me at the time with the most pleasurable emotions. It is a sweet thing, I thought, to see these officers confess a human brotherhood with us . . . Nor was it without similar pleasurable feelings that I witnessed the *temporary* rupture of the ship's stern discipline, consequent upon the tumult of the theatricals. (97; my emph.)

There is a kind of intellectual detachment to White-Jacket's description. He *witnessed* the rupture of discipline, but did he not participate? The narrator's "pleasurable feelings" seem tepid compared to the frenzy of the rest of the crew. And why does he need to call attention to his moralizing? Certainly, Melville's narrators do plenty of moralizing, but the marker, "And here I must moralize," seems overdetermined.

There is ample evidence to show that in 1850 Melville had simmering in his mind a particularly vivid event in the history of American theater, one in which the will of the people was asserted to a violent and catastrophic end. The Astor Place Riot, on 10 May 1849, which involved the loss of over twenty lives and injuries to many more, marked the climax of audience participation in American theaters. At the time the event was both understood and clearly projected by the participants as a class conflict of a distinctly cultural nature. The following notice appeared around New York shortly before the "silk-stockinged" English actor, William Charles Macready, arrived there to conclude his tour:

> Workingmen, shall Americans or English rule in this city? The crew of the British steamer have threatened all Americans who shall dare to express their opinion this night at the ENGLISH AUTOCRATIC *Opera House!* We advocate no violence, but a free expression of opinion to all public men. WASHINGTON FOREVER! Stand by your *Lawful Rights!*
>
> AMERICAN COMMITTEE[6]

The right that the people demands is twofold. It is, on the one hand, the right of the people to express themselves as audience members. But it is also the right of the people to choose their own representative, in this case an artistic representative, the actor Edwin Forrest, to *act for* them.

The professional (and personal) feud of actors William Charles Macready and Edwin Forrest already had a long history in 1849. The two men were the leading tragedians of the day but had radically different acting styles and personalities. The root of the rivalry, wrote Philip Hone, had "no cause that I can discover, except that one is a gentleman, and the other is a vulgar, arrogant loafer, with a pack of kindred rowdies at his heels" (2:359–60). Macready was well-known for his cerebral acting style and the psychological complexity of his character portrayals. He was meticulous in his technique, and on stage he was intellectual and restrained. Forrest, physically powerful and bombastic, aimed to achieve striking effects on stage; he eschewed subtlety and was most famous for excessive interpretations of heroes like Lear and Richard III. He was renowned especially for an overpowering voice, which seemed to explode in certain climactic scenes. "His voice," remarked one of his fellow actors, "surged and roared like the angry sea, lashed into fury by a storm; till, as it reached its boiling, seething climax, in which the serpent hiss of hate was heard, at intervals, amidst its louder, deeper, hoarser tones, it was like the falls of Niagara, in its tremendous down-sweeping cadence" (qtd. in Moses 428).

For all of these reasons the two actors appealed to different audiences. Macready's circle of friends and acquaintances included most of the outstanding literary men of his day: Dickens, Victor Hugo, Washington Irving, even Emerson. The *Literary World,* run by Melville's friends the Duyckincks and to which Melville contributed work, including his 1851 essay on Hawthorne and Shakespeare, were overt Macready partisans. Of Forrest, Evert Duyckinck wrote: "He tramps and staggers and is convulsed like an ox in shambles. If a bull could act, he would act like Forrest" (qtd. in Porte 203). But Forrest also had many outspoken supporters. And, given the ambivalence expressed toward charismatic performers in his books, Melville, it seems safe to say, may have felt some kind of allegiance to both actors. In Melville's magazine sketch "The Two Temples," for example, he parodies uncritical enthusiasm for Macready. The comical young narrator of the story finds himself in the gallery of a stately theater in London. Gazing uncritically upon his surroundings, including the performance on the stage in which Macready plays the Cardinal Richelieu, he exclaims: "Hark! The same measured, courtly, noble tone. See! the same imposing attitude. Excellent actor is this Richelieu!" (GSW 164). The ejaculations alone render the descriptions of the performance suspect.

Forrest was not only a popular favorite in the United States among the working people but also was himself deeply patriotic and frequently made extravagant expressions of love for the American people and country.[7] Unlike foreign stars who seemed indifferent to the development of American drama, Forrest also was famous for encouraging American dramatists by sponsoring playwriting competitions. A number of important plays were written for Forrest and performed by him throughout his career, and they came to be seen as "representative of the Forrest régime" (Moses 427). They included *Metamora, The Gladiator, The Broker of Bogota,* and a play by Robert T. Conrad which not only highlights the relationship between theater and class conflict but also reminds us of the matchless Jack Chase. This was a play first performed by Forrest in 1841 called *Jack Cade.* Jack Cade, of course, is the rebel leader of the people, of the commons, in *2 Henry VI.*

Space will not permit a thorough comparison of Shakespeare's Jack with Conrad's and with Melville's Jack Chase, but a few points can be stated simply. First, the rebel antihero of Shakespeare's play becomes in Conrad's melodrama the democratic hero, a wholly virtuous knight-in-shining-armor who has, indeed, every conceivable motive for rebellion: the evil aristocrats have flogged his father to death, beaten then burned his old mother, starved his infant son, and, finally, raped his wife, driving her first to madness then to death. Although, as the Duke of York grudgingly admits, Shakespeare's Jack resembles a nobleman "in face, in gait, in speech," he remains intensely opposed to all forms of cultural elitism; in particular, he is deeply suspicious of literacy and knowledge of foreign languages. Conrad's Jack Cade has spent ten years in Italy and has earned his Ph.D. degree (being "graced / With the mind's title of nobility / And known as Doctor Aylmere"). Like Melville's Jack, he is a man of the people but a cultured elitist ("in his breeding loftier than a peasant" and even called, at one point, "King o' the Commons"). But Conrad shows little self-awareness of this paradox. There is no irony in this portrayal of Jack as the complete melodramatic hero. Most important, Shakespeare's Jack dies an ignominious death, grubbing for food in a garden, while Conrad's Jack dies like Prince Hamlet by a poisoned blade, completely vindicated, exclaiming with his last breath: "Free! Free! The bondman is avenged, my country free!" Conrad's aim in *Jack Cade* was to invest the part completely with the self-evident truths of popular liberty and equality, qualities he understood as inherently, and categorically, good. Conrad's Jack bridles self-righteously when Buckingham tells him, "The greatness which is born in anarchy, / And thrown aloft in tumult, cannot last." The role of Jack Cade, moreover, became publicly recognized as Edwin Forrest's "incarnate tribuneship of the people" (Moses 429).[8]

If Melville admired Forrest and extravagant expressions of democratic feeling, however, he was no less critical of Forrest and what Forrest represented than he was of Macready. The complex position of Jack Chase in *White-Jacket* may be one indicator of Melville's attitude regarding the theatrical commoner and the popular audience. For example, Melville's Jack is also a people's general. In fact, he has fought throughout the world in wars of independence: "Though bowing to naval discipline afloat, yet ashore, he was a stickler for the Rights of Man, and the liberties of the world. He went to draw a partisan blade in the civil commotions of Peru, and befriend, heart and soul, what he deemed the cause of the Right" (17). Yet to accept hierarchies in one sphere while advocating the Rights of Man (i.e., democracy) in another is a serious inconsistency. While serving as an officer on a Peruvian warship, Jack is spotted as a deserter from the *Neversink* and is retaken. Upon retrieving him, Captain Claret initially regards Jack with a mixture of irony and displeasure, to which the fine-looking, bearded Jack replies, "Your most devoted and penitent captain of the maintop, sir; and one who, in his very humility of contrition, is yet proud to call Captain Claret his commander." After this conciliatory speech Jack makes a glorious bow and "tragically" throws his Peruvian sword overboard. Theatricality here seems a substitute for real authority. As Tony Tanner comments, "Jack Chase can only be a 'hero' in the amateur theatricals, in which he plays the 'chivalric' character of Percy Royal Mast and rescues fifteen oppressed sailors to great applause . . . Looked at closely, he is, in Melville's larger vocabulary, as much a 'slave' as anyone on the ship" (xxii). The theatrical gesture, like the play, which parodies life on a ship, functions in a discreet system of social relations in which, simultaneously, theatricality is an expression of subversion toward the dominant power structure but is also contained by that power structure, in fact, reinforcing it.[9]

Most theatergoers seemed to feel a strong loyalty to either Forrest or Macready by the time Macready arrived in New York in 1849. Shortly before the riot, during Macready's 7 May performance of *Macbeth* in New York, a house, overcrowded with "b'hoys" from the Bowery, expressed themselves against English attempts to govern the "mimic world," generating so much noise with cheering, hissing, whistling, and groaning that *Macbeth* became virtually a dumb show. There were cries of "Three groans for the codfish aristocracy," "down with the English hog," and "remember how Edwin Forrest was used in London!" Rotten eggs were thrown, and then chairs crashed onto the stage. Macready's friends shouted, "Shame! Shame!" Ladies and gentlemen hurried from the boxes. "Thus ended the first attempt of Mr. Macready to play in opposition to the popular voice," wrote James Rees. "Had he adopted a different course—one more suited to our national feelings, and the well-known good nature of the American people, —we question if the scenes which followed would have occurred" (330–33). The Astor Place Riot is remarkable for the clarity with which the issues at

FIG. 10. Forrest as Macbeth.

stake were understood and represented by people with dramatically different points of view. An interpretation from the perspective opposite to that of Rees shows that, whether for Forrest or Macready, Americans understood the fundamental nature of the conflict in the same way. Philip Hone, for example, wrote in his own diary after the 7 May fiasco, "The respectable part of our citizens will never consent to be put down by a mob raised to serve the purpose of such a fellow as Forrest" (2:360). The coherence of ideological interpretations in the most divergent sources has endowed the history of the Forrest-Macready rivalry with the status of teleological inevitability (see figs. 10 to 13).

Macready's 1848–49 tour of America started and ended in New York. But troubles really began in November, when Macready was performing *Macbeth* at the Arch Street Theatre in Philadelphia and Forrest chose to appear at another theater across town in the same role. A Forrest partisan newspaper, the *Philadelphia Public Ledger,* excitedly announced "a week of theatrical rivalry." Macready fumed privately but acted with great discretion in public. His was a highly sensitive, often obsessive, personality, turning for relief most often to his private journal. On 8 November 1848, after a performance of *King Lear,* Macready wrote: "The audience, who would have cheered on a thick-headed, thick-legged *brute* like Mr Forrest, took no notice of this, my best performance. This is civilization—the growing *taste* of the United States!" (254). Forrest outraged Macready's sense of refinement both on the stage and off. In his journals Macready insisted repeatedly that Forrest was no artist and certainly *not* a gentleman. Two weeks later Forrest attacked Macready openly in a "Card" published in the *Public Ledger:* "Mr. Macready, in his speech, last night, to the audience assembled at the Arch Street Theatre, made allusion, I understand, to 'an American actor' who had the temerity, on one occasion, 'openly to hiss him.' This is true . . . But why say 'an American actor'? Why not openly charge me with the act? for I did it, and publicly avowed it in the *Times* newspaper of London, and at the same time asserted my right to do so" (qtd. in Rees 323). In general Macready managed to avoid Forrest's attempts to drag him into a public confrontation. Though occasionally forced to stare down, or even to lecture, a particularly rambunctious audience, Macready did not challenge Forrest or his supporters directly from the stage. As David Grimsted has remarked, "The different vehicles generally chosen for expressing their feel-

FIG. 11. Macready as Macbeth.

FIG. 12. Forrest, that "mountain of a man," as the shirtless and pugilistic gladiator. The original caption proclaims: "Mr. Edwin Forrest: The American Tragedian as The Gladiator."

FIG. 13. Monument to William Charles Macready depicting Macready as a paragon of culture, surrounded by muses with books. The testimonial printed beneath the monument celebrates not only Macready's "personation of Characters" but also his "Restoration of the Text, and his illustration by the best intellectual Aids of the Historical Tracts and Poetical Creations of the Plays of Shakspeare [*sic*]."

ings—the public press and the private diary—gave clues to the personalities of the combatants."[10]

After the 7 May performance Macready was ready to leave the country, but an open letter published in the *New York Herald* on 9 May strongly urged him to go on. Forty-seven of New York's most "highly respectable citizens," including Washington Irving, Evert Duyckinck, and Herman Melville, signed the petition, which encouraged Macready to finish his engagement at the Astor Place, with the implied pledge that they would stand by him. On 10 May Macready was to play Macbeth, while Forrest played Spartacus in *The Gladiator* across town at the Old Broadway Theatre. The theaters themselves were weighted with ideological significance. The architecture and interior design of the two theaters reflected important class, as well as artistic, differences. The Astor Place, which had opened only two years earlier, was one of the most fashionable theaters in the city, with a fine open front and "excellent ventilation." It was capable of seating eighteen hundred people in parquet, dress circle, family circle, and gallery. The Old Broadway Theatre, on the other hand, could accommodate forty-five hundred people. The Broadway had an immense pit (parquet) to which only men and boys were admitted. The pit was the most democratic space in nineteenth-century theaters. It seated mostly the working classes, but it was also the best place from which to see and to hear the play, being closest to the stage. The price of admission was twenty-five cents, and the seats were plain benches without backs. On crowded nights, notes T. Allston Brown, "the jam used to be terrific" (1:368). The first and second galleries (dress and family circles) contained three rows of benches set apart for "colored persons." It was, according to Brown, "one of the best arranged places of amusement in the city."

On the evening of 10 May, as early as half-past six o'clock, people began to assemble outside the Astor Place. At seven the rush to gain admittance became particularly intense. The crowd that packed the theater, however, did not seem nearly as dangerous as that which filled the streets outside. Forrest partisans were out in numbers, organized by the head of the American Committee, E.Z.C. Judson, a notorious rabble-rouser, also known as Ned Buntline.[11] When the curtain rose there was an outburst of hisses, groans, cheers, and "miscellaneous sounds." A few arrests were made in the theater, and the play was able to proceed, miraculously. Though virtually inaudible through the first act, there was otherwise no serious incident inside the theater. The real trouble came afterward in the street, when news of a police action reached the mob. When the police were unable to disperse the people, they called in the militia. What followed, including the rioters' misreadings of the situation and its potential dangers, lends a deeply ironic cast to this theatrical tragedy (a term used advisedly). When the Seventh Regiment arrived, a rumor spread that they were using only blanks and not real bullets. The rumor, of course, was false. The second round of fire proved the reality of the ammunition.

Another explanation for the people's refusal to subside is that the mob took the military show for just an act. One rioter is reported to have shouted: "Take the life out of a free born American for a bloody British actor! Do it, aye, you daresn't" (qtd. in Rees 343). The democracy of early nineteenth-century theater frequently degenerated into mob rule, but there seemed to be a tacit understanding between audience members and performers that the arrangement was extralegal. The most violent manifestations of disapproval or approval of one's representatives, restricted in ordinary social intercourse, were understood by the people and the authorities alike to be licensed in and around the theater. Spectators notoriously resented any reference to riot acts or police enforcement.[12] The Astor Place Riot marked an irrevocable change in direction in the course of American theater history, for it fundamentally altered notions of theater as a popular forum.

The one piece of direct, written evidence concerning Melville's involvement in events surrounding the riot—the petition he signed encouraging Macready to perform and lamenting mob rule—can hardly be read as a genuine and deep endorsement of Macready over Forrest. Six months later, after seeing Macready play Othello at the Haymarket Theatre in London, Melville disparaged the English actor in his journal: "McCready [panted/painted?] hideously. Didn't like him very much upon the whole—bad voice, it seemed" (ML 1:334). Moreover, in his work Melville often seems to celebrate excessive performances and violent acts of audience participation. Ahab is hardly a model of restraint. It is also clear, however, that Melville was far from being an average Forrest supporter. In "Hawthorne and His Mosses" (1850) Melville remarks: "'Off with his head! so much for Buckingham!' this sort of rant, interlined by another hand brings down the house,—those mistaken souls, who dream of Shakespeare as a mere man of Richard-the-Third humps, and Macbeth daggers. But it is those deep far-away things in him; those occasional flashings forth of the intuitive Truth in him; those short quick probings at the very axis of reality:—these are the things that make Shakespeare, Shakespeare" (541). Only the mistaken souls in the house are excited by ranting presentations of Shakespeare. The best form of admiration is that which is excited by the subtle, hidden aspects of genius. This view is essentially, and explicitly, literary.

Melville clearly establishes a dichotomy between readers and the mob: "If very few who extol [Shakespeare] have ever read him deeply, or, perhaps, only have seen him on the tricky stage (which alone made, and is still making him his mere mob renown)," then who can wonder that Hawthorne still goes unappreciated? Those accustomed by tradition to expect the next great literary genius to be a writer of dramas, Melville suggests, will wait in vain. Literarity and theatricality seem, in his mind, almost antithetical. The proper kind of appreciation for Shakespeare ought to be deep, difficult, and literary, a far cry from the blind, unbridled admiration expressed by the vulgar mob for Edwin Forrest. And, finally, not only will the best literature require patience and restraint, but it will also be best enjoyed in private, "in some quiet arm-chair in the noisy town, or some deep nook among the noiseless mountains" (542). The problem, then, is how to comprehend Melville's seemingly divergent attitudes and, if they are comprehensible, to consider how they may bear upon the ultimate subject of this study, the narrative/dramatic tensions in *Moby-Dick*.

Joel Porte has recently brought into question the Shakespearean qualities of *Moby-Dick* praised by Charles Olson and F. O. Matthiessen. In particular, he finds Ahab's rhetorical overopulance troublesome. Is Melville really trying to reproduce a Shakespearean hero in this whaling captain? The crucial question, writes Porte, "is that of the singlemindedness of Melville's intent" (197). In chapter 33, "The Specksynder" (literally "Fat-Cutter"), Porte suggests that Ishmael "shrewdly and gently deconstructs Ahab the histrio." "The Specksynder" provides a crucial discussion of two different strategies or modes of representation, and even Porte's rich emphasis on this chapter misses some of its significance as a commentary on theatricality. This chapter reveals the complexity of Melville's ambivalence to class, culture, and representation at its most sophisticated. It brilliantly sets the stage for the first group of drama chapters, anticipating, in particular, chapter 36, "The Quarter-deck."

"The Specksynder" centers on the trappings of authority, how social authority is established and maintained. Without directly challenging the conventional forms of power, the chapter is endlessly self-deconstructing. In particular, it achieves this effect grammatically, through a layering of conditionals, qualifying conjunctions and adverbs: *nevertheless, although, and yet, for all that.* The narrator, for example, stresses the importance of the social hierarchy of the ship, despite factors that may contribute to more democracy on a whaling vessel than on other ships; here Ishmael is extraordinarily convoluted:

> *Though* the long period of a Southern whaling voyage . . . the peculiar perils of it, and the community of interest prevailing among the company, all of whom, high or low, depend for their profits, *not* upon fixed wages, *but* upon their common luck, together with their common vigilance, intrepidity and hard work; *though* all these things do *in some cases* tend to beget a less rigorous discipline than in merchantmen *generally; yet, never mind* how much like an old Mesopotamian family these whalemen *may,* in some primitive instances, live together; *for all that,* the punctilious externals, *at least,* of the quarter-deck are *seldom* relaxed, and in no instance done away with. (128–29; my emph.)

Never mind the actual fact of equality among men aboard a whaling vessel? A brief synopsis of the passage (one sentence with elisions) might read: "On a whaling ship, officers and men must pull together, but sometimes, for the better working of the ship, authority must be asserted according to old codes." Ishmael's peculiar way of expressing himself tends to emphasize the artificiality of the trappings of authority. The history he gives of the office of Specksynder also manifests a significant degeneration from real to nominal authority. The title designates a particular office on board the whaling ship, one that for many years shared equal authority with the Captain. If the authority of Specksynder has come to be abridged over time, the appearance of authority and social difference still, for some reason, ought to be asserted. This character, therefore, "*should nominally* live apart from the men before the mast . . . *though always,* by them, familiarly regarded as their social equal" (my emph.). The subjunctive mood and the stress on purely nominal privilege, however, render even the usages of authority suspect.

The primary subject of chapter 33 is, of course, ultimately not the Specksynder at all, but Ahab, the Captain. Ahab, too, is introduced in the chapter in a one-sentence paragraph modified by four dependent clauses. In this paragraph Ishmael insists that Ahab, unlike captains who parade their quarter-decks with elated grandeur, is least given to such shallow assumptions of power and that he commands only implicit obedience (both points later turn out to be patently untrue). Whatever effect these statements have on our understanding of Ahab, we have been invited implicitly to be skeptical about the trappings of authority. Presumably, our skepticism about the theatricality of power increases with each "and though" until the paragraph's end, when Ishmael finally assures us, in typically roundabout fashion and double negation: "*yet even Captain Ahab was by no means unobservant of the paramount usages of the sea.*" Captain Ahab does employ the usages of the sea, these having been designed for a public end—the well functioning of the vessel and the people on it. Yet the character of Ahab's monomania, here only hinted, brings that simple aim into question as well.

One problem with life on the *Pequod,* Ishmael begrudgingly admits, is that Ahab sometimes makes use of forms "for other and more private ends than they were legitimately intended to subserve." This point is at the core of the chapter's deepest confusion. What usages, if any, or what forms of expression, are "legitimate"? Ultimately, Ishmael argues, public recognition cannot be achieved without a performance from the hustings; "true" authority, however, employs no trappings:

> Be a man's intellectual superiority what it will, it can never assume the practical, available supremacy over other men, without the aid of some sort of external arts and entrenchments, always, in themselves, more or less paltry and base. This it is, that for ever keeps God's true princes of the Empire from the world's hustings; and leaves the highest honors that this air can give to those men who become famous more through their infinite inferiority to the choice hidden of the Divine Inert, than through their undoubted superiority over the dead level of the mass . . . Nor, will the tragic dramatist who would depict moral indomitableness in its fullest sweep and direst swing, ever forget a hint, incidentally so important in his art, as the one now alluded to. (129–30)

External arts and entrenchments, unlike the deep faraway things and intuitive truths stressed in the Hawthorne essay, are inherently paltry and base, and yet they are necessary to achieve any kind of public action. This passage may provide insight into Melville's deep ambivalence about his own career—his desire for public recognition of his genius but also his disgust with paltry usages required to effect it. There can be no doubt of Melville's sense of affinity for his mad, theatrical captain, who, despite Ishmael's assertions that he does not overuse the trappings of the "tricky stage," can hardly be said to keep from the hustings and who, only three chapters later, self-consciously rants and raves in the most theatrical manner possible.

Does Ahab's theatricality, therefore, mean that he is not a true prince, that he is somehow inferior? The term *inferiority* itself, of course, has a couple of possible, important meanings in this passage. It seems literally to mean inferior in genius to God's true princes. But, unavoidably, it also has the connotation of social inferiority. Moreover, inferiority, in this passage, is fundamentally related to the mode of theatrical expression. When Ahab usurps the text, as he does in "The Quarter-deck," he may *act* like a king. But, the hustings available to Ahab are denied Ishmael, the writer.[13] Ishmael suggests that, when it comes to sitting down and *writing* this "episode," Ahab cannot but be deflated, for he is, after all, only a common man:

> But Ahab, my Captain, still moves before me in all his Nantucket grimness and shagginess; and in this episode touching Emperors and Kings, I must not conceal that I have only to do with a poor old whale-hunter like him; and, therefore, all outward majestical trappings and housings are denied me. Oh, Ahab! what shall be grand in thee, it must needs be plucked at from the skies, and dived for in the deep, and featured in the unbodied air! (130)

Ishmael, as narrator, circumscribes the theatrical Ahab. This assertion of the narrating self in order to conclude the chapter is also an assertion of the narrative form. Here it is the narrator who seems to have ultimate authority. The narrative contains, like a Chinese box, the hustings, which are Ahab's vehicle. But Ishmael's authority is also suspect. In this last paragraph Melville deconstructs the authority of the narrative mode as well, positing an endless interplay between narrative and dramatic form. The drama cannot be contained in language, he implies; the poet's pen can only give it local habitation and a name, a "melodramatic" view, emphasizing the ineffable. Moreover, the tacit allusion to *A Midsummer Night's Dream* ("As imagination bodies forth / The forms of things unknown, the poet's pen / Turns them to shapes, and gives to aery nothing / A local habitation and a name") implicitly raises the question of the narrator's capability: is Ishmael like the lunatic or lover? *A Midsummer Night's Dream* is a play, moreover, in which the mode of expression allowed to working men is theater. And, as the play also concerns, implicitly, the trappings and authenticity of power, the play within the play, though comical, has a deeply subversive element. The poet's pen may give shape to airy nothings, but, as Peter Quince says in the prologue to the working people's play: "By their [the people's] show, you shall know all, that you are like to know." The poet's pen and the people's theater, the cultured elite and the socially inferior, contend in an endless cycle of negotiation.

Ahab is and is not a king. He both requires and does not require outward trappings. Ahab is a common man, who in reality is not much higher than the dead level of the mass. But, in Melville's view, lowness of birth and education can also indicate a nobility beyond the grasp of the more cultured. A thief in jail is as honorable as George Washington, Melville wrote to Hawthorne. "The Specksynder" presents what can only be understood as an unresolvable paradox: Ahab becomes kingly when he is histrionic, but he is at his most kingly when he is least theatrical. In other words, Ahab the old whaleman can be a king when he is stomping on his quarter-deck/stage. Ironically, however, his true kingliness is what he shares with every man, something internal and beyond the expressive powers of his own theatrical self-display or of the narrator. This emphasis upon the ineffability of the soul is at the core of Melville's ruthless democracy. As readers, we are asked to pause in "The Specksynder" before we have even seen Ahab challenge his crew to the central drama of the book and to consider how he may best express himself. It is, therefore, a problem that is comprehensible only in rereading. We are invited by the narrator to consider the problem of representation itself. In the end, after going down with the whale, Ahab disappears to where even language cannot reach. What seemed corporal melts as breath into the wind.

Finally, *Moby-Dick,* in a far more sophisticated way than Melville's other books, manipulates the tone of the narrator's condescension and plays with his elitist tendencies. As narrator, Ishmael is proud, if not condescending, not only in "The Specksynder" but throughout the book. "What the white whale was to Ahab, has been hinted; what, at times, he was to me, as yet remains unsaid," Ishmael proclaims self-importantly in "The Whiteness of the Whale." The tone of superiority, and its association with Ishmael's sense of his role as narrator, is explicitly thematized in "The Town-Ho's Story." There the sense of the social difference that comes with control over narrative is manifested in the telling. Significantly, "The Town-Ho's Story" is about a kind of class conflict—seamen (particularly "a Lakeman and desperado from Buffalo") against officers—and it is a conflict that climaxes in one of Melville's favorite subjects, a mutiny. Notably, however, this mutiny, unlike many moments of high drama or conflict on the decks of the *Pequod,* is contained entirely within Ishmael's narrative: it is not represented in dramatic form. Michael Paul Rogin attempts to explain why Ishmael includes the story of a mutiny that has occurred not on the *Pequod* but on another ship: "Mutiny takes place offstage in *Moby-Dick,* on the *Town-Ho,* as if to contrast the subversive threat from democratic man on that ship with Ahab's power on the *Pequod*" (129). But the contrast established in the telling of this story seems to be more between Ishmael and Steelkilt than between Ahab and Steelkilt.

In fact, Ahab and Steelkilt have much in common when it comes to the performance of power (though, unlike Ahab, Steelkilt is notably not in the official power structure) and the ability to hold men in thrall. Ishmael and Steelkilt, on the other hand, seem at a glance to be virtual opposites. The contrast between narrator and hero of the drama again exemplifies the tension between narrative and dramatic form. Whereas the story is told in private, Steelkilt's rebellion happens in the open; the only way to disempower him is to force him into the forecastle, to keep him off the deck/stage, the field of action. Like Ahab, Steelkilt is "a fine dramatic hero." Ishmael, on the other hand, is presented nowhere else in *Moby-Dick* with his nose higher in the air: "For my humor's sake, I shall preserve the style in which I once narrated [the story] at Lima, to a lounging circle of my Spanish friends, one saint's eve, smoking upon the thick-gilt tiled piazza of the Golden Inn. Of those fine cavaliers, the young dons, Pedro and Sebastian, were on the closer terms with me; and hence the interluding questions they occasionally put, and which are duly answered at the time" (208).

The story Ishmael narrates is, he insists, a kind of private property. The circumstance of the white whale's vengeance on the first mate, Radney, is transmitted selectively by word of mouth. Originally, it was the "private property of three confederate white seamen" of the Town-Ho, one of whom told the story to Tashtego with intense injunctions to secrecy which are only violated when Tashtego is overheard talking in his sleep. In Lima Ishmael's auditors depend on him for definitions and explanations as well as for the basic story. The process of putting the narrative together and transmitting it, therefore, is inherently undemocratic; the narrator has received, not earned, the power that comes with knowledge, and the story is not accessible to all. Moreover, the sense of privilege that comes from knowing is heightened by the sense of social privilege which surrounds the telling: the thick-gilt tiled piazza, the sybaritic young dons swinging on mats of grass, the "dull, warm, mostly lazy, and hereditary land." And Lima, as one of the cavaliers points out, is well-known to be as corrupt as Venice. Both Peru and Venice, moreover, are corrupt republics, that is, oligarchies.[14] Ishmael's way of speaking to the dons, perhaps self-parodying, shows him to be, at the very least, at home with the cultured elite: "I crave your courtesy," "Thus, gentlemen," "Will you be so good . . . ," etc. But among the aristocracy it is clear that Ishmael is also different. He is called "sir sailor," a designation that captures, more concisely than any other, a sense of the dualism of Ishmael's character in *Moby-Dick*. As narrator he is an aristocrat, but as sailor he is one of the roughs, a ruthless democrat. He gently mocks these Peruvian gentlemen, for, in the final analysis, he has had experience of the world, including the heroism of common men, and they have not.

"I can well perceive," Melville wrote to Hawthorne in 1851, "how a man of superior mind can, by its intense cultivation, bring himself, as it were, into a certain spontaneous aristocracy of feeling." He insists, in what seems an intense struggle to convince himself, on the basic equality of all men, that all are equally "honorable." "It seems an inconsistency to assert an unconditional democracy in all things, and yet confess a dislike to all mankind—in the mass. But not so." In the end the conflict between narrative form and dramatic form in *Moby-Dick* leaves us with a sense of Melville's deeply conflicted thinking about democracy itself as well as his deep honesty. Edwin Forrest represented the fulfillment of the dramatic, the democratic, but his was a position that Melville could not comfortably obtain. Forrest represented an enthusiasm for the people which was repaid in extraordinary popular acclaim, to which Melville could not have been insensible. On the night of the Astor Place Riot, Edwin Forrest, as Spartacus in Robert Montgomery Bird's play *The Gladiator,* proclaimed:

I thank the gods that I am a barbarian;
For I can better teach the grace-begot

> And heaven supported masters of the earth,
> How a mere dweller of a desert rock
> Can bow their crown'd heads to his chariot wheels.
> Man is heaven's work, and beggar's brats may 'herit
> A soul to mount them up the steeps of fortune,
> With regal necks to be their stepping blocks.
> (IV.iii)

It is a speech characteristic of *The Gladiator,* one of Forrest's favorite roles, and of Forrest's career in general. In Forrest's idiom it is natural for a thief in jail to be as honorable as General George Washington—a notion that Melville believed true but ludicrous (letter to Hawthorne, 1 June 1851). Myths sprang up around Forrest's life. Forrest became the hero of the drama that was his life, and America itself was transformed into his stage.

One such story brings Shakespeare to the common man and exalts the lowest condition of the human experience:

> It was at Columbus, Ohio, in the railroad station at midnight. It was cold, bleak, biting weather, and the old fellow [Forrest] hobbled up and down the platform, but there was majesty even in his very hobble. An undertaker's wagon pulled up at the station, and a corpse was removed from it. The baggageman carelessly hustled the body into his dray and wheeled it down the platform. As he halted, old Forrest broke out into the most horrible cursing, and with his tongue lashed the baggageman for his careless handling of the human clay. Then he turned, approached the corpse, and broke into the oration of Marc Antony over the body of Caesar. No one was there but the frightened baggageman and a handful of actors. The great actor's voice rose and fell, and the subtle tears and resolute thunder of the oration awoke the echoes of the station as a grand organ in a majestic cathedral. He read every line of the oration, and said in an aside speech, as a climax: "There, take that, you poor clay in the coffin, I'll be dead myself inside a year." And he was.[15]

Here Forrest invests the remains of an anonymous American with the majesty of Caesar and transforms an obscure railway depot into a great cathedral, while he, himself, is simultaneously a hobbling old fellow and Marc Antony. For Forrest every public space is a stage, and he becomes, therefore, a representative figure of American public life. Among supporters and detractors he excited the most extreme emotions, but few, if any, felt neutral toward him. Whatever Melville's emotional engagement with Forrest or Ahab, his use of the dramatic hero in his prose indicates an intense and complex struggle between the ruthless democrat and the cultured elitist.

CHARACTER DRAMATICALLY REGARDED

One reason that literary critics have had difficulty in classing Melville's works as novels is that many of his major characters are highly gestural and "charismatic," with vestiges of the original religious meaning of the word. They act publicly in ways that only professional performers acted in the mid-nineteenth century. Captains Bildad and Peleg, for example, the prototypes for Ahab, are fighting Quakers—Quakers with a vengeance. These seamen are not fully realized individuals but eccentrics, remarkable for "a thousand bold dashes of character" (71). Peleg flies into a short-lived comic rage that anticipates Ahab's longer "tragic" one, when he screams at Bildad, "Fiery pit! fiery pit! ye insult me, man; past all natural bearing ye insult me" (75). Despite the differences between Peleg and Ahab, for Ishmael each man's temper is upsetting, exciting, but ultimately inexplicable. Intimacy with such characters is impossible; their personal lives have been left on shore. With their "bold and nervous lofty language" they talk as no one exactly talks and act as no one exactly acts.

Chapter 16, "The Ship," sets the stage for Ahab, "a mighty pageant creature, formed for noble tragedies," whom Ishmael, in his capacity as narrator, anticipates in a gnomic aside: "Nor will it at all detract from him, *dramatically regarded,* if either by birth or other circumstances, he have what seems a half wilful [*sic*] over-ruling morbidness at the bottom of his nature. For all men tragically great are made so through a certain morbidness" (71; my emph.). But what exactly does it mean to "regard dramatically"? Earlier we saw how Melville thematized writing and theatricality to represent different aspects of a particular social reality. Here we probe a "little, lower layer" and question the very mode of perception, ostensibly a dramatic mode, which, through Ishmael, Melville asks us to adopt in the presence of the whaling captain. As Melville implies, the mode of perception is conditioned by the nature of the object perceived; we regard Ahab dramatically because he is tragic. But, beyond the vagaries of "a certain morbidness," how are we to understand the tragic in *Moby-Dick?*

In his influential discussion of the novel and the romance Richard Chase suggests that in a novel "the comic or tragic actions of the narrative will have the primary purpose of enhancing our knowledge of and feeling for an important character, a group of characters, or a way of life." Character, in other words, is more important than action. The romance, on the other hand, tends to prefer "action" or plot, terms that Chase employs more or less interchangeably.[16] Action in the romance, he argues, tends to be violent or sensational, to depict astonishing and often highly symbolistic events, and to explore dramatic (or melodramatic) possibilities of form. The form of melodrama and the romance, unlike that of the English novel, is characterized by radical and irreconcilable contradictions and highly wrought fragments of experience. As a result, characters in romances frequently appear to be little more than a function of plot. Such characters may be shallow or abstract and unrealistic, but, due to the suggestion of deeper truths at which they can only gesture, they may also be more dramatic. Chase's argument has obvious insufficiencies for describing an American tradition, but it is still a compelling position when applied to the tensions in *Moby-Dick* between narrative form and dramatic form as well as to what may be called a dialectic between the very notions of narrative and drama in the book.[17]

Many American authors in the nineteenth century used the term *romance* to understand how their work differed from that of novelists across the sea. In 1835, for example, William Gilmore Simms of South Carolina writes that the romance "differs much more seriously from the English novel than it does from the epic and the drama, because the difference is one of material, even more than of fabrication." "Our Romance," Simms concludes, "is the substitute of modern times for the epic or the drama" (qtd. in Chase 16). Simms was not the only one who understood the new brand of American fiction to bear a fundamental relation to the drama, one more important than that which it bore to the English novel and the novel's representations of normative social life. In *The Confidence-Man* Melville admonishes readers who demand an unwavering "fidelity to real life" that the task of the fictionist is to present a scene, an atmosphere, a world that is, if anything, more real than their experience:

> There is another class [of readers], and with this class we side, who sit down to a work of amusement tolerantly as they sit at a play, and with much the same expectations and feelings. They look that fancy shall evoke scenes different from those of the same old crowd round the custom-house counter, and same old dishes on the boarding-house table, with characters unlike those of the same old acquaintances they meet in the same old way every day in the same old street. And as, in real life, the proprieties will not allow people to act themselves with that unreserve permitted on stage; so, in books of fiction, they look not only for more entertainment, but, at bottom, even for more reality than real life itself can show . . . In this way of thinking, the people in a fiction, like the people in a play, must dress as nobody exactly dresses, talk as nobody exactly talks, act as nobody exactly acts. It is with fiction as with religion; it should present another world, and yet one to which we feel the tie. (243–44)

Characters on stage are more real than those in real life because it is clear that they are acting.[18] In the nineteenth century character on stage and character on the street were moving in opposite directions. In the melodramas or historical romances on stage, actors were self-consciously histrionic; they performed with extravagant and significant gestures, elaborately costumed and accompanied by theme music intended to convey some sense of moral purpose. In the theater the audience members knew exactly with whom they were dealing from the first entrance. Villains slunk, and heroes strode boldly. Actors like Edwin Forrest thundered across the stage. Forrest as Macbeth, writes James Rees, "threw around his impersonation of this character, an air of wild, startling romance, which we consider as perfectly just, for the whole play of Macbeth, with its witches, its ghosts, and its music, is a melo-dramatic play, and as such was rendered by Mr. Forrest" (262). Similarly, Junius Booth "possessed the power of combining a meaning in every gesture, and a silent glance was equivalent to a delivered sentence" (Clarke 65). The one place where expressiveness and spontaneity, authenticity and interpretability, were celebrated was the stage.[19] On the street, however, people attempted to be more and more nondescript; one did not draw attention to oneself before strangers. The cities were filled with multitudes, like Melville's seagazers, who not only did not express themselves but did not even speak to one another.

The dramatic world of the ship, Ishmael asserts time and again in *Moby-Dick,* bears a heightened relation to the commercial-bound, insular city of Manhattoes which he leaves behind. To that which is old and familiar are added "new and marvellous features." Nantucket also, like New York and life ashore in general, is a normative place. It is the place of private life and the family. There, left behind, are Ahab's young bride and child, whose existence proves, in Peleg's mind at least, that Ahab is a real, ordinary person like other men: "Think of that; by that sweet girl that old man has a child: hold ye then there can be any utter, hopeless harm in Ahab? No, no, my lad: stricken, blasted, if he be, Ahab has his humanities!" (77). The claim that Ahab's private life is significant because it helps us to understand his public character indicates an early, but important, stage in the blurring of the public and the private. In light of the drama that follows, the attempt to locate the real Ahab in his Nantucket life seems fatuous indeed. He is "more real" on the *Pequod.*

On the deck of the *Pequod* Ahab is less a person than a personality. "In the midst of the personified impersonal, a personality stands here," he exclaims in "The Candles" (417). In the increasingly secular world of nineteenth-century America the mysterious notion of personality, or character, was replacing other mysteries of the universe. When Ishmael hears Ahab described in "The Ship," he notes, "I also felt a strange awe of him; but that sort of awe, which I cannot at all describe, was not exactly awe; I do not know what it was. But I felt it; and it did not disincline me towards him; though I felt impatience at what seemed like mystery in him" (77). Like the passive seagazers of chapter 1, Ishmael embodies the prevailing mode of behavior in public: he observes other people while trying not to draw attention to himself. Ahab, on the other hand, expresses himself "dramatically" in the public view.

The nature of Ahab's drama is further clarified when read in the context of contemporary writing for the stage. For example, in George Henry Boker's play *Francesca da Rimini,* a romantic drama first performed about a year after the publication of *Moby-Dick,* two of the principal characters are dramatic in ways that are directly relevant to Ahab. The central theme of *Francesca da Rimini* is the inability to make moral judgments based upon the reading of visible signs. The problematic hero, Lanciotto, is a hunchback and a warrior who, like Ahab, is set apart from other men by physical marks and scars. While he is not also inwardly deformed (like his prototype

Richard III), Lanciotto is violent, and he is deeply tortured by the lack of correspondences between appearance and reality. He is himself referred to as a "chaos of a man," a "bulk of wretched contraries," and he struggles both against the injustice of his deformity and then against his misfortunes that arise because of it.[20] Lanciotto is compelled (it is his raison d'être) to embody and dramatize the wrongs done to him.

The second character who resembles Ahab is the villain, Pepe, who ultimately destroys the court world of Rimini. Pepe is both the fool and the self-proclaimed "anointed man of truth." His ambition, motivated by what seems to be sheer vindictiveness, is little short of total destruction of his world:

> I am a very firebrand of truth—
> A self-consuming, doomed, devoted brand—
> That burns to ashes while I light the world!
> I feel it in me. I am moved, inspired,
> Stirred into utterance, by some mystic power
> Of which I am the humble instrument.

Significantly, Pepe is a model of the professional performer. As fool, he is kept to entertain the court. Pepe, unlike fools in Shakespeare, is a full-fledged antagonist; he is the drama's villain. He shows the cracks in the surfaces of the court, and his actions play a large role in the eventual destruction of his world. The integrity of the world created in the drama depends far more upon Pepe than it does on soldiers, clergy, or statesmen. The notion of revealing the constructions upon which public behavior is based has become the quintessentially dramatic act. For this reason the metaphor of shining a spotlight, the Drummond light, the burning brand,[21] becomes central to dramatic action in melodrama. As Melville comments in *The Confidence-Man:* "The original character, essentially such, is like a revolving Drummond light, raying away from itself all round it—everything is lit by it, everything starts up to it (mark how it is with Hamlet), so that, in certain minds, there follows upon the adequate conception of such a character, an effect, in its way, akin to that which in Genesis attends upon the beginning of things" (318). Images of light and darkness, moreover, indicate the essentially spatial (visual/gestural) continuum in which melodrama occurs. *Moby-Dick* appropriates and inverts this imagery, when Ahab claims to be "darkness leaping out of light" (417), a self-conscious complication of the melodramatic symbology. Truth is not necessarily revealed in light.

The chapter in *Moby-Dick* which represents most clearly melodramatic assumptions about light and darkness, the visual image, the fragility of the temporal world, and the overburdened significance of gesture is chapter 119 ("The Candles"). Here the typhoon unleashed upon the *Pequod* creates a series of scenarios or scenes of intense purity; each is a sharp-edged, incorruptible projection. "The Candles" makes extended use of the tableau, the freezing of attitudes and gestures to capture a state of being or a powerful emotion. When the three tall masts first catch fire, "silently burning in that sulphurous air, like three gigantic wax tapers before an altar," the crew congregates in a moment of superstitious dread, enchanted, eyes gleaming. Daggoo, the African harpooner, "the gigantic jet negro," looms at three times his real stature, like a black cloud. Specific physical markers of the harpooners which have been noted in the narrative are invested with a new kind of signifying power. Tashteego's sharklike teeth "strangely" gleam, and Queequeg's tattooing burns like "Satanic blue flames on his body."

The tableaux themselves are highly ritualistic. The masts burn as if "before an altar." Each tableau, illuminated by a flash from the sky, conjoins the visible and the cosmic. Starbuck and Stubb bump into each other and briefly attempt to interpret the first tableau, but the appearance of a new image overwhelms them and undermines the process of interpretation or syntactical integration.[22] A second flash occurs:

> At the base of the mainmast, full beneath the doubloon and the flame, the Parsee was kneeling at Ahab's front, but with his head bowed away from him; while near by, from the arched and overhanging rigging, where they had just been engaged securing a spar, a number of the seamen, arrested by the glare, now cohered together, and hung pendulous, like a knot of numbed wasps from a drooping orchard twig. In various enchanted attitudes, like the standing or stepping, or running skeletons in Herculaneum, others remained rooted to the deck; but all their eyes upcast. (416)

This passage stresses a visual image, a spatial arrangement, an impression. Ahab cries out: "Oh! thou spirit of clear fire . . . I now know thee . . . I own thy *speechless, placeless power;* but to the last gasp of my earthquake life will dispute its unconditional, unintegral mastery in me" (417; my emph.). Ahab's own speech may be understood as a counterpart to the crew's dumb awe. Hyperbolic speech and muteness are similar reactions because both imply that certain meanings are ineffable.

Ahab's speech is often melodramatic, and, as Joel Porte suggests, Melville's sophisticated, and often ironic, regard for the theater of his own day ought to lead us to revise long-held conceptions about the Shakespearean and tragic qualities of both Ahab and *Moby-Dick*. A crucial example of Melville's dramaturgical imagination at work in the representation of character is evidenced in the way he reimagines the form of the tragic soliloquy. In chapter 107, for example, we find the Carpenter, who spends "a great part of the time soliloquizing; but only like an unreasoning wheel, which also hummingly soliloquizes" (389). This notion of the soliloquy as pure self-expression characterizes the major actors in this drama as well. In Ahab's soliloquies in chapters 30 and 99 the speeches represent not a mind divided against itself, the dilemma of a situation in which choice is both impossible and necessary,[23] but, rather, moments of pure self-expression, of nomination: "I'm demoniac, I am madness maddened! That wild madness that's only calm to comprehend itself! The prophesy was that I should be dismembered; and Aye! I lost this leg. I now prophesy that I will dismember my dismemberer." The repeated exclamations represent the inadequacy of language to express psychological content or anything, for that matter, beyond wild emotionalism and a condition of being ("I am madness maddened!"). The rhetoric is highly gestural, burdened with the weight of hatred for which there is no adequate means of expression. The meaning of the passage is located in the signifier for which Ahab can find no adequate signified: his dismembered body. Each choked phrase is a gesture at transcendence confined by the frustrations of materiality and presence. The gestural nature of the rhetoric, moreover, is heightened by two important stage directions: "The cabin; by the stern windows; Ahab sitting alone, and gazing out" and then "waving his hand, he moves from the window." Both suggest a tension between immanence and transcendence.

The space in which Ahab appears, speaks, gestures, is marked by a sense that the actor moves dialectically between extremes. With a dismissive gesture, but also a gesture toward the unreachable, Ahab turns back into the concrete, knowable world of the ship. His dramatic action is predicated on a paradox: "Gifted with the high perception, I lack the low, enjoying power; damned most subtly and most malignantly in the midst of Paradise!" Like Lanciotto, Ahab is deeply incoherent: "Ahab had cherished a wild vindictiveness against the whale, all the more fell that in his frantic morbidness he at last came to identify with him" (160). This notion of incoherence of character is at the core of Melville's attempt to represent character truthfully. In *The Confidence-Man* he disparages "psychological novelists" for being reductive, for attempting the revelation of human nature based on fixed principles. Rather, he argues that "the author who draws a character, even though to common view incongruous in its parts, as the flying-squirrel, and, at different periods, as much at variance with itself as the caterpillar is with the butterfly into which it changes, may yet, in so doing, be not false but faithful to facts" (90).

Moby-Dick represents, then, a basic conflict not only between the dramatic and the novelistic character but also, implicitly, between the dramatic and novelistic storyteller, for Ishmael functions both as interdiegetic author and audience. Beginning in the first chapter, the reader is alerted to the fact that, as a narrator, Ishmael's ability to represent his experiences will be severely limited. Significantly, the experiences for which he goes in quest are imagined dramatically. His initial statement of motives for going to sea explicitly involves two of the most basic, traditional definitions of *catharsis,* the medical view (purgation) and the moral view (purification), and subsequent action bears out a third, the mystical view (possession with a view to deliverance).[24] A trip to sea is Ishmael's way of "driving off the spleen, and regulating the circulation." His amusing tone belies not only what we are in for but his own reasons for setting out a whaleman:

> Whenever my hypos get such an upper hand of me, that it requires a strong moral principle to prevent me from deliberately stepping into the street, and methodically knocking people's hats off—then, I account it high time to get to sea as soon as I can. This is my substitute for pistol and ball. With a philosophical flourish Cato throws himself upon his sword; I quietly take to the ship. There is nothing surprising in this. If they but knew it, almost all men in their degree, some time or other, cherish very nearly the same feelings towards the ocean with me. (12)

Ishmael goes to sea not only because he feels depressed on land but also because his violent impulses are frustrated in ordinary social space. In the insular city of Manhattoes every citizen has become a kind of Narcissus, longing for the sea but isolated both from it and from other people. Everyone seems entirely self-absorbed. A whaling ship, on the other hand, is a place where men live so close together that the potentialities of action are always present.

The incongruity between tone and subject on the first page indicates an important division, for the Ishmael who greets us no longer is overcome, presumably, by his hypos. He is back on land, a narrator, recounting past events. The Ishmael who put to sea was a different kind of person, a participant not a narrator: "The transition is a keen one, I assure you, from a schoolmaster to a sailor" (14). The transition in reverse, the reader can assume, is equally keen. In this way Melville establishes from the start a dichotomy between narrating self and experiencing self. There is, as Ishmael's submergence and resurfacing in both chapter 41 and in the epilogue most powerfully attest, a discontinuity between action and cognition. Roland Barthes calls this sense of discontinuity the "obtuse meaning." "Obtuse," Barthes points out, has connotations of being "greater than," being excessive and expansive. Because the obtuse meaning is "outside (articulated) language" and is, in a sense, "*indifferent* to the story," Barthes suggests, it is "the epitome of counter-narrative" (55–57).

The problem of representing the discontinuity between action and cognition is one reason for Ishmael's (and Melville's) attempt to present large portions of the experience as a drama. In fact, Ishmael introduces the notion that experience is best represented as drama in a kind of playbill:

> My going on this whaling voyage, formed part of the grand programme of Providence that was drawn up a long time ago. It came in as a sort of brief interlude and solo between more extensive performances. I take it that this part of the bill must have run something like this:
>
> *Grand Contested Election for the Presidency*
> *of the United States.*
> "WHALING VOYAGE BY ONE ISHMAEL."
> "BLOODY BATTLE IN AFFGHANISTAN [*sic*]."

> Though I cannot tell why it was exactly that those stage managers, the Fates, put me down for this shabby part of a whaling voyage, when others were set down for magnificent parts in high tragedies, and short and easy parts in genteel comedies, and jolly parts in farces . . . I think I can see a little into the springs and motives, which being cunningly presented to me under various disguises, induced me to set about performing the part I did. (16)

Sandwiched between election and war, Ishmael's "cathartic" voyage is to be understood as both productive, generating a new state, and destructive of the old order. The field of action is characterized by conflict and violence. Equally important, this cross between metaphysical speculation and Barnumlike advertisement is presented with the strange disclaimer that the whole thing has been orchestrated by invisible stage managers; the narrator is not responsible for imposing form upon the events, which are better rendered in scenes than in narrative. As readers, we have to wait until chapter 29 ("Enter Ahab; To Him Stubb") for the first explicit privileging of dramatic over narrative presentation, but in the opening chapter Melville establishes two representational strategies (narrative and dramatic) which will generate contrapuntal tensions and resolutions throughout the book. With Ishmael, even in this first quarter of the text, in which the narrative form is privileged, we are continually drawn to scenes.[25]

From early in *Moby-Dick* there is a tension between the narrating "I" and the kinds of performances which furnish him with experience. Ishmael is drawn, almost in spite of himself, to performance spaces that represent intense fields of action. Such spaces provide the pleasures of spectatorship but also represent dangerous seductions. Starting out in New Bedford, Ishmael stumbles into a "negro church" filled with a hundred black faces and led by a black Angel of Doom beating a book in a pulpit: "Ha, *Ishmael,* muttered *I,* backing out, Wretched entertainment at the sign of 'The Trap!'" (18; my emph.). The trap here, posed by the power of blackness, is in part the danger of self-obliteration; the performance threatens to absorb the narrator. This kind of seduction is repeated on several occasions before reaching Nantucket. In "The Spouter Inn," in which Ishmael meets Queequeg, he finds himself enraptured, from the vantage point of his bed, in the cannibal's devotions: "I thought it was high time . . . to break the strange spell in which I had so long been bound" (30).

By far the most exciting performance space and most charismatic actor to whom Ishmael is drawn, before the appearance of Ahab, is Father Mapple in the theatrical Whaleman's Chapel. At first, the scene (chaps. 7–9) beginning with "The Chapel" is presented, significantly, as a space of reading, in which each person sits silently in grief that is "insular and incommunicable . . . eyeing several marble tablets." This space of reading is emphasized graphically by rendering the various scripts of the engraved tablets in the book itself. We read the texts that the interdiegetic congregation reads. In the chapel, however, there is one person "who could not read, and, therefore, was not reading those frigid inscriptions" (40). Queequeg alone is aware of other people; he is aware of the "solemnity of the *scene*" (my emph.). And Queequeg alone notices Ishmael's entrance. Here writing is clearly associated with death: "What despair in those immovable inscriptions! What deadly voids." The atmosphere of frigidity is dispelled when Father Mapple enters and climbs up to the prowlike pulpit, drawing his rope ladder after him. Although Ishmael protests, "I could not suspect him of courting notoriety by any mere tricks of the stage," he is clearly pleased when the chapel is transformed from a space of private and incommunicable grief into one of excitement and theatricality (43). In chapter 8, "The Pulpit," for the first time Melville actually privileges the theatrical scene. In the next chapter ("The Sermon") the narrator disappears during Father Mapple's monologue.

Despite Father Mapple's dramatic sermon, however, and two earlier references to a doomed Shakespearean vessel called the "The Whale-ship Globe" ("Extracts" 9),[26] nothing can really prepare Ishmael, or us, for the dramatic appearance of Ahab: "reality outruns apprehension." When Ahab appears in chapter 28 the book is invested with a new kind of energy: "He looked like a man cut away from the stake, when the fire has overrunningly wasted all the limbs without consuming them . . . So powerfully did the whole grim aspect of Ahab affect me, and the livid brand which streaked it, that for the first few moments I hardly noted that not a little of this overbearing grimness was owing to the barbaric white leg upon which he partly stood . . . I was struck with the singular posture he maintained" (109–10). Ishmael is so powerfully affected by the sight of Ahab that he misses crucial details at first, the most important being the white, whalebone leg. More important, he recognizes in Ahab some cosmic quality that he is unable to represent in words. Ishmael sees in Ahab an "*infinity* of firmest fortitude" (my emph.). Here the obtuse meaning is suggested by a subtle stylistic joke.

The "infinity of firmest fortitude" is manifested in the "fixed and fearless, forward dedication of [Ahab's] glance." The awkwardness of the alliteration, which highlights the writerliness of this paragraph, indicates the inability of language to represent the full force of Ahab's presence.

Ishmael's "innocence" as a spectator is a precondition for the representation of Ahab's power as a performer. Thus, the pivotal quarter-deck scene, in which Ahab exerts himself dramatically to win the crew to his mission, is anticipated in a culminating example of Ishmael's susceptibility to absorption in experience. Chapter 35 ("The Mast-head") explores the unique role of the spectator in *Moby-Dick.* Ishmael is the paradigmatic spectator because he tends to lose himself in whatever he is contemplating, but, in the worst case, he is extremely susceptible to both demagoguery and mob action. In "The Mast-head" Ishmael stands his watch for the first time on the cruise. One clue to reading this chapter dramatically is its emphasis upon the spatial dimension. Ishmael is alone high above the deck and informs us ingenuously: "I kept but a sorry guard. With the problems of the universe revolving in me, how could I—being left completely to myself in such a thought-engendering attitude,—how could I but lightly hold my obligations to observe all whale-ships' standing orders, 'Keep your weather eye open, and sing out every time' " (139). The weather is pleasant, and the masthead "to a dreamy, meditative man" is delightful. But, though it is neither violent nor overtly dangerous, the masthead presents the seduction of spectatorship, the danger that, lulled into an opiumlike listlessness, an absent-minded youth may at last lose his identity.[27]

In the magazine sketch "The Two Temples" (1853) Melville expands on the theme of theatrical spectatorship raised in "The Mast-head." In "Temple Second" a wandering young man, much like Ishmael, finds himself penniless in London. As he makes his way through the immensity of great London, which he calls "the Leviathan," like the narrator at the end of *Moby-Dick,* he feels himself floating on the edges of a maelstrom. At last emerging from the crowd, he finds himself standing in a quiet street in front of a beautifully appointed theater. Procuring a ticket to the cheapest seats, he climbs up to the gallery and at last attains the dizzy altitude of the lofty platform:

> The more I looked about me in this lofty gallery, the more was I delighted with its occupants. It was not spacious. It was, if anything, rather contracted . . . embracing merely the very crown of the top-most

> semi-circle; and so commanding . . . the whole theatre, with the expanded stage directly opposite, though some hundred feet below . . . I stood here, at the very main mast-head of all the interior edifice.
>
> Such was the decorum of this special theatre, that nothing objectionable was admitted within its walls. With an unhurt eye of perfect love, I sat serenely in the gallery, gazing upon the pleasing scene, around me and below. (GSW 163)

Like the impressionable, and somewhat naive, Ishmael, this comical young narrator gazes from his masthead uncritically upon his surroundings, including the performance on the stage, in which the famous William Charles Macready plays the Cardinal Richelieu. The narrator's eulogy of Macready's performance, however, is mere parody (e.g., "Excellent actor is this Richelieu!"). Like the narrator of "The Two Temples," Ishmael can be a dreamy and unthoughtful spectator. In "The Mast-head" he serenely gazes upon the pleasing scene, losing himself in the infinite series of the sea. Very often, he tells us, captains take such "absent-minded young philosophers to task" for not keeping their wits about them. In this enchanted mood the watch hovers over "Descartian vortices," and we will do well to recall that a vortex consumes the *Pequod* in the end. Following "The Mast-head" Ishmael *is* consumed only to resurface six chapters later to comment on his experience of the dramatic central chapters. In "The Quarter-deck" drama usurps the text.

The text becomes a drama because Ahab finally asserts himself. He appears in the subhead title, in the stage direction: "*Enter Ahab: Then, all.*" His order to have the crew assemble is extraordinary, disrupting the normal workings of the ship, arousing curiosity and surprise among mates and men alike. Maintaining his silence for the moment, Ahab paces up and down the quarter-deck. Though he may appear wrapt in thought, he knows how to play his audience: "When the entire ship's company were assembled, and with curious and not wholly unapprehensive faces, were eyeing him . . . Ahab, after rapidly glancing over the bulwarks, and then darting his eyes among the crew, started from his standpoint; and as though not a soul were nigh him resumed his heavy turns upon the deck. With bent head and half-slouched hat he continued to pace, unmindful of the wondering whisperings among the men" (141).[28] Unlike the narrator, Ahab generates an atmosphere, an *aura,* and is inseparable from it. The description of his posture, his silent pacing, and the great spell that he casts upon his audience nearly duplicates the language with which Whitman described the aura of the great Junius Brutus Booth, who as Richard III similarly enthralled his audience. Aura, however, is not simply projected outward by the performer toward the spectator; it is reciprocally generated and, therefore, also involves a way of perceiving or experiencing. Of course, *Moby-Dick* cannot literally produce the action of Ahab's pacing, but it can represent, symbolically, the quality of being present, the weave of time and space, by presenting the action as drama rather than narrative.

Like other great performers of his day, Ahab has what audiences of the nineteenth century called "influence," a mysterious force that "binds human beings together, so that the heart of one answers to the heart of another . . . The link is often silent and unperceived, like the rolling in of a wave in a quiet sea; but like that same wave it is mighty and resistless" (Halttunen 1982, 4). Ahab works his crew into a strange, fierce gladness; "the mariners began to gaze curiously at each other, as if marvelling how it was that they themselves became so excited" (141–42). Much of the scene is characterized by features that could be found in productions of the "all-popular Shakespeare" which Melville seems to disparage in "Hawthorne and his Mosses": "the popularizing noise and show of broad farce, and blood-besmeared tragedy" that obscure the "flashings forth of the intuitive Truth." At one point Ahab shouts "with a terrific, loud, animal sob, like that of a heart-stricken moose; 'Aye, aye! it was that accursed white whale that razeed [*sic*] me!'" And when he first confronts Starbuck's opposition, he hoots and hollers and smites his chest, a gesture that strikes even poor Stubb as a little extreme; Stubb responds appropriately in quasi-Elizabethan language, "He smites his chest . . . what's that for? methinks it rings most vast, but hollow."

While narrative arises from a single perspective, drama is fundamentally dialectical. Narrative can unfold the inner life of a single individual, but drama requires conflict. The drama of "The Quarter-deck" is enhanced by the conflict of Ahab and Starbuck. Starbuck, who recalls that the white whale took Ahab's leg, voices a rational objection, a claim that everyone, including Ahab, must recognize as valid. "I am game for [the white whale's] crooked jaw," he says, "and for the jaws of Death too, Captain Ahab, if it fairly comes in the way of the business we follow; but I came to hunt whales, not my commander's vengeance" (143). Ahab's response is quintessentially dramatic; he appropriates Starbuck's objection, subsuming the interpersonal conflict in his larger conflict with Moby-Dick:

> Hark ye yet again,—the little lower layer. All visible objects, man, are but as pasteboard masks. But in each event—in the living act, the undoubted deed—there some unknown but still reasoning thing puts forth the mouldings of its features from behind the unreasoning mask. If man will strike, strike through the mask! . . . Ah! constrainings seize thee; I see! the billow lifts thee! Speak, but speak!—Aye, aye! thy silence, then, *that* voices thee. (*Aside*) Something shot from my dilated nostrils, he has inhaled it in his lungs. Starbuck now is mine; cannot oppose me now, without rebellion. (144)

This scene presents an example of *acting for* which is structurally similar to Ahab's relationship with Ishmael. Donald Pease writes that, "in taking Starbuck down onto *his* lower layer, he *acts out* Starbuck's motive for mutiny" (386). Ahab dominates the scene physically, but he also contains it verbally. According to Pease, "Ahab's scene of persuasion collapses the space of argument, where dissent would otherwise be acknowledged, into an opposition—that between him and cosmic forces—whose terms carry the conclusion within their organization" (388). Starbuck can recognize in Ahab's outrage at the whale an impulse that he too possesses. Significantly, this dramatic moment of acting out disrupts normative social and economic life on the ship, and it is located in the sacralized, symbolistic space of the quarter-deck. So, while symbolic action may be reconsidered in retrospect, it is overwhelming to participants who are swept up in the flow. And Ishmael is a far more susceptible spectator than Starbuck. Not only is his autonomy entirely subsumed in Ahab's performance, but Ishmael continues to be utterly absorbed in the action as the crew dramatizes Ahab's "strike through the mask" speech in the wild revelry of chapter 40 ("Midnight, Forecastle"). "A wild, mystical, sympathetical feeling was in me," he comments, upon his reemergence as narrator in chapter 41; "Ahab's quenchless feud seemed mine" (155).

In declaring *Hamlet* an artistic failure, T. S. Eliot famously observed that Hamlet's disgust with his mother is excessive: "It is thus a feeling which he cannot understand; he cannot objectify it . . . None of the possible actions can satisfy it; and nothing that Shakespeare can do with the plot can express Hamlet for him" (48). Hamlet seems, to Eliot, more a personality than a person; Eliot understands Shakespeare's play, in other words, as melodrama. Most important, he concludes that, because the character Hamlet is so drawn (so melodramatic), Hamlet attracts the attention of writers who are somehow frustrated or weak in their own experience and who, therefore, exploit his character to achieve "artistic realization": "Hamlet the character has had an especial temptation for that most dangerous type of critic: the critic with a mind which is naturally of the creative order, but which through some weakness in creative power exercises itself in criticism instead. These minds often find in Hamlet a vicarious existence for their own artistic realization. Such a mind had Goethe . . . and such had Coleridge" (45). Such a mind has Ishmael, when faced with the whiteness of Moby-Dick or the standing spectacle of Ahab.

In representing the tension between narrative and drama, Melville shows this mind at work and shows its limitations. When Ishmael asserts, comically, that he has been "blessed with an opportunity to dissect him [the whale] in miniature," the reader will hear echoes of "we murder to dissect," and Ishmael's aim to narrate the whale's deepest, darkest parts contrasts with his own caveat that it is vain to popularize profundities (373). As Carolyn Porter remarks, the purpose of Ishmael's ventures into cetology is not only to parody such discourse "but to circumscribe and reify it, so that its boundaries come into view, set in relief as an artificial limit against the expanse of alien knowledge Ishmael has no direct means of communicating" (1986a, 96). The irony of Ishmael's attempt to comprehend and communicate the heart of the whale is the comic counterpart to the impossibility of narrating Ahab's deeper, darker parts. Character that is both dramatic and "original" will compel a reading of surfaces, of signs, which are in and of themselves manifestly inadequate to convey the significance that is assigned. *Dramatic character,* by definition, eludes the scope of narrative, for some part of him eludes the scope of language. The narrator, on the other hand, must ultimately detach himself from the drama. Otherwise, the unmediated experience could not be comprehended. Thus, *Moby-Dick* concludes: "*The drama's done. Why then here does any one step forth?—Because one did survive the wreck*" (470).

Between Herman Melville and the French actor and theoretician Antonin Artaud (1896–1949) there are remarkable coincidences of rhetoric. Artaud's actor gesturing through the flames seems like Ahab "cut away from the stake, when the fire has overrunningly wasted all the limbs without consuming them." Artaud's dolphins diving into the obscurity of the deep seem to be analogues of the white whale sounding. Both authors speak of vortices that destroy language and, with it, the subject. And then there is a similar notion of the body as hieroglyph (in Melville, Queequeg's, Ahab's, and, of course, the whale's). In "Writing and Sounding the Whale" Anthony Kubiak argues that, while American theater seems to lack a theoretical or intellectual tradition, such theorizing may be found in certain theatrical novels, of which *Moby-Dick* is a paradigm, and that these novels reveal a "profound sensitivity to the problematic phenomenology of the stage" (108). There is in Melville's work, Kubiak suggests, a kind of silent or submerged theory of the theater in American culture. He also believes that there exists a relationship between Melville and Artaud; both seek to realize a theater that is not bound by re-presentation.

Although it is difficult to define exactly what Artaud means by "theater of cruelty,"[29] it seems clear that similarities between Melville and Artaud are not merely coincidences in rhetoric. In their own ways both writers make an explicit and profound connection between theater and violence. And they share a similar frame of reference, for the vision of both writers is fundamentally conditioned by nineteenth-century melodrama. Nineteenth-century melodrama provides the context for their thinking about theater. They are speaking, on the one hand, of a particular relationship of art in performance to a public audience. They are also criticizing, on the other hand, art that is essentially literary and private and which fosters passivity in its spectators. The drama they imagine exists in the liminal landscape between the immanent and the transcendent, a concrete reality that bodies forth cosmic truths. In this sense drama shares much with ritual. Although we might not say that Melville advocates melodrama or is a proponent of melodrama, as Artaud is and does, melodrama informs Melville's work on a deep level. For both men melodrama represents a strategy to express the inexpressible, a highly gestural form of representation, and a mode of excess. Both men, moreover, are writing against a notion of psychological realism. They are interested in bold, theatrical dashes of character which sweep up all in their path. In fact, Ahab may represent exactly the kind of Artaudian hero which many critics find so deeply disturbing, a kind of fascistic figure whose actions seem to preclude rational analysis on the part of his audience.

There can be no calm evaluation in the theater of cruelty. The spectator is absorbed in the spectacle, losing his individuality and, with it, it seems, his capacity to judge critically. But the violence of this kind of theater may also provoke a deeper kind of thinking—about the very *origins* of meaning, about the relationship of form to content. In this sense such a theater may be intended to foster an even more intense kind of critical judgment. "The theater," writes Artaud, "restores us all our dormant conflicts and all their powers, and gives these powers names we hail as symbols: and behold! before our eyes is fought a battle of symbols, one charging against another in an impossible melée" (T&D 27). In the true theater a play disturbs the senses' repose, Artaud tells us. Symbols burst forth in the guise of incredible images. Consciousness that was repressed is liberated. There is no cruelty without consciousness nor, for that matter, without the application of consciousness.

"Benito Cereno" is perhaps the work, with *Moby-Dick,* which lends itself most provocatively to an Artaudian reading. In this great novella the underside of theatricality is terror, and every gesture is charged intensely with a latent violence. Again, it would be a mistake to read the story too simply as a sort of prototype of Artaud's theater, but the climax is represented as a particularly specular and theatrical epiphany for the gullible spectator, Captain Delano, a moment when he recognizes that what he has been witnessing is theater, and for that very reason the scene erupts into violence: "Glancing down at his feet, Captain Delano saw the freed hand of the servant aiming with a second dagger . . . with this he was snakishly writhing up from the boat's bottom, at the heart of his master, his countenance lividly vindictive, expressing the central purpose of his soul; while the Spaniard, half-choked, was vainly shrinking away." Aboard the *San Dominick* each awkward gesture points to the constructedness, the artificiality, of the signs. But it is the black servant Babo's "lividly, vindictive" countenance that serves, finally, as the Drummond light or, perhaps more accurately, as Ahab's "darkness leaping out of light," to the long-benighted mind of Captain Delano. Babo's expression produces a "flash of revelation . . . illuminating, in unexpected clearness" his previous behavior. But, as Melville deftly shows throughout his work, the brilliance of an expressive image or a moment of an especially intense action is comprehensible only within its theatrical context. "Too much clarity," as Philip Fisher remarks, "is the mark not of fact but of performance" (1988, 94).

In the opening pages of "Benito Cereno," Melville contrasts the experience of entering a house (the realm of the domestic, the normative, and the private) with that of entering a ship. "Both house and ship," he notes, "hoard from view their interiors till the last moment; but in the case of the ship there is this addition: that the living spectacle it contains, upon its sudden and complete disclosure, has, in contrast with the blank ocean which zones it, something of the effect of enchantment. The ship seems unreal; these strange costumes, gestures, and faces, but a shadowy tableau just emerged from the deep, which directly must receive back what it gave" (GSW 242). The "seeming unreality" of the ship is another one of Melville's characteristic and wonderful double negatives. The seeming unreality, as the benighted Amasa Delano is unable quite to fathom, is a version of experience more real than reality. And it is precisely for this more intense version of experience that, like Ishmael, we readers go to sea. We go to Melville's ships as we go to a play, not to see the same old crowd round the customhouse counter, the same old dishes on the boardinghouse table, with characters like those of the same old acquaintances we meet in the same old way every day in the same old street. We want at bottom even more reality than real life itself can show, another world, and yet one to which we feel the tie.

FOUR

The Right to Privacy

William Dean Howells and the Rise of Dramatic Realism

> The American plays have to do with man as a family man; and I hope that a little thought about them will confirm the reader in any impression he may have that with us the main human interest is the home . . . Its interest does not live from man to man, but from men to women, and from women to men.
>
> WILLIAM DEAN HOWELLS, "Some New American Plays"

> The curtain falls. The audience rises and departs. We move out with the chatting crowd. The street sparkles and roars. The old life receives us at the portal. But on the old life a new thread is woven; the golden thread of a fresh vision of beauty.
>
> GEORGE WILLIAM CURTIS, after seeing Edwin Booth's *Hamlet*

In 1858 George Pullman began experiments with railroad cars which would revolutionize travel in America. More than any other single technology at that time, the railroad symbolized American "progress." Trains hurtled through the landscape carrying a community of strangers organized by economic forces that were represented by the tickets they held in their pockets. In many imaginations the railroad represented the powerful energies, if not the violence, of the young nation. In "To a Locomotive in Winter" Walt Whitman apostrophizes the mythological train: "Type of the modern—emblem of motion and power—pulse of the continent." For Nathaniel Hawthorne the image of the railroad represented a feeling of "a whole world, both morally and physically . . . detached from its old standfasts and set in rapid motion."[1] Pullman profoundly altered notions of the railroad by transforming the railroad car, literally and symbolically, into a domestic interior, a space of privacy, often intimacy, and familiarity. For the price of a ticket one could mitigate all the discomforts of travel; one could have, in fact, the comforts of home. Certain Pullman cars, such as the sleeping cars, were transformed during the journey itself, as seats were replaced by beds.

"We are reminded of a prophesy which we heard some three years since," announced the *Illinois Journal* in 1865,

> that the time was not far distant when a radical change would be introduced in the manner of constructing railroad cars; the public would travel upon them with as much ease as though sitting in their parlors, and sleep and eat on board of them with more ease and comfort than it would be possible to do on a first-class steamer. We believed the words of the seer at the time, but did not think they were so near fulfillment until Friday last, when we were invited to the Chicago & Alton depot in this city to examine an improved sleeping car, manufactured by Messrs. Field and Pullman, patentees after a design by George M. Pullman, Esq., Chicago. (Qtd. in Boorstin 332).

By 1876 "Pullman car style" had become a common generic name.

In a letter to William Dean Howells in 1882 Edmund Gosse confesses, "We are all talking about you. I see ladies giggling over little books in the trains, and then I know they must be reading 'The Parlour Car'" (qtd. in CP 23). A generation earlier the notion of a literary theater, at which Howells's one-act drama *The Parlor Car* is an early thrust, would have seemed as contradictory as trains and domesticity. The injection of private experience into public space, however, became a crucial aspect of American life as the century wore on, and Howells was one of the primary theorists of this shift. It is, therefore, no mere coincidence that four of Howells's situational comedies, a genre to which he devoted considerable energies for more than thirty-five years, are set in railroad cars or depots. *The Parlor Car* (1876) was not only the first of the railroad plays but was, in fact, the first of Howells's twenty-five one-act dramas. Moreover, the parlor car in question is not only the scene of an intimate drama between two lovers, but it actually becomes disengaged from the rest of the train midway through the play and is left standing on the tracks, "nowhere in particular."

In general Howells's plays mock overt theatricality and focus on the ordinary and intimate experiences of the upper-middle class, experiences that are represented primarily in talk. The refinement, or "culture," of the characters and the literary quality of the plays themselves are thrown into relief particularly when they are set in erstwhile public or quasi-public spaces such as railroads or hotels.[2] Howells's dramas are interestingly situated, therefore, in what may be understood as a trajectory from a publicly oriented theater to a realist theater in America. In these situational comedies of the 1870s and 1880s theater re-presents private life.

"In the creation of the farce comedy," claims Arthur Hobson Quinn, Howells is surpassed by no other writer in English. It is a genre, Quinn remarks, that "depends for its effect upon the delicate contrast of domestic and social values" (1:67). Howells's interest in this delicate contrast is, indeed, the defining feature of many of his best dramatic compositions; it is also evident in his critical writings on the theater and in his advocacy of a new kind of drama. In his novel *The Story of a Play* (1898), which is at the same time the story of a marriage, Howells reflects on a disagreement between his two principal characters, Brice and Louise Maxwell, the playwright and his wife: "Their tiffs came out of their love for each other, and no other quarrels could have the bitterness that these got from the very innermost sweetness of life. It would be hard to show this dramatically, but if it could be done the success would be worth all the toil it would cost" (165). Maxwell struggles against the prevailing orthodoxy in the popular theater, the notion that to represent domestic experience "dramatically" is a contradiction in terms. The quasi-Ibsenist play that Maxwell is both writing and trying to sell "daringly portrayed a woman in circumstances where it was the convention to ignore that she ever was placed" (128). Howells himself chose public or semipublic settings, such as railroad cars or hotel parlors, for his domestic dramas, in order to represent the contrast between private and public more effectively. The dramatic energy of his comedies and farces is largely generated by his characters' awareness of, or resistance to, the fact that their private lives are contingent to a world of markets, immigration, class tensions, politics, and technology.

THE RAILROAD

In Howells's four plays set either in railroad cars or a railroad depot several features assume particular importance in representing the contrast between inner (domestic) life and outer (societal) experience. To begin with, the distinction between private and public is spatialized. Windows, for example, are an important metaphor for defining types of space. They establish an inside and an outside, and, in Howells's plays, windows serve as a vital threshold between the familiar and the unfamiliar. Of course, the railroad car itself is the most important structure for defining space in these plays. The Pullman car represents a self-enclosed compartment that moves within a larger setting (geographic, societal, economic, and technological). Second, the private-public contrast is gendered.[3] By and large, in Howells's plays it is the role of women, as representatives of private life, to determine the character of the action even in public spaces. While female characters retain their domestic function, they are no longer relegated to the home; thus, the plays emphasize the problem of private-public negotiations. If, in the railroad one encounters a world of strangers, a major objective of Howells's women is to identify familiar people (family or friends) among the sea of unknown faces. And, third, the railroad brings Howells's middle-class families into contact with the "great unwashed," including both railroad employees and fellow travelers as well as folk waiting in a depot. This aspect of the contrast is represented primarily, though not exclusively, in language, through differences in dialect, idiom, or pronunciation between the speech of upper-middle-class ladies and gentlemen and that of black porters or Irish chorewomen.

When the curtain rises on *The Parlor Car* the set is empty but for a "gentleman," Mr. Allen Richards, who sits facing one of the windows. Allen is not gazing out of the window, however. Apparently, he is asleep; his hat is drawn over his eyes. He seems to remain asleep when the rear door opens and Miss Lucy Galbraith, escorted by the porter, bustles in. Lucy / Miss Galbraith seems preoccupied. She goes to the large mirror to pin her veil, sits down, fidgets in her chair, leans forward, and, finally, attempts to raise the window, which falls with a crash, catching her dress, which she finds herself unable to release. To be caught in a window is the epitome of a condition betwixt and between public and private worlds. When Allen / Mr. Richards comes to her assistance, they both receive a shock of recognition. It appears, remarkably, that these two people are not only acquainted but that they are lovers who have recently parted in a huff and are thrown together by what seems to be a coincidence.

Mr. Allen Richards: Will you allow me to open the window for you? (*Starting back*) Miss Galbraith!

Miss Galbraith: Al—Mr. Richards!

There is a silence for some moments, in which they remain looking at each other; then—

Mr. Richards: Lucy—

Miss Galbraith: I forbid you to address me in that way, Mr. Richards.
Mr. Richards: Why, you were just going to call me Allen!

The terms of address, whether familiar or formal (Lucy or Miss Galbraith, Allen or Mr. Richards), are contested throughout the play and, for that matter, in many of Howells's plays. In an important sense the terms of address foreground the play's central theme: is this a public meeting or the continuation of an intimate relationship? This question is the source of the play's dramatic energy. In the semiprivacy of this parlor car the characters can enact their intimate drama of quarrel and reconciliation. The drama in the railroad car epitomizes the expansion of the world of intimate feeling. Private lives are not confined to the home, in part because the Pullman car is a space that has all the appurtenances of home but also because of an increasing sense, in nineteenth-century social experience, of isolation in public.[4] Of course, it is also the couple's great good fortune to have the car entirely to themselves.

Yet there is another, and a far more dramatic, action that renders this public space separate and private. By some fluke, in the middle of the drama the car literally becomes disconnected (or disengaged) from the rest of the train. The train somehow has sped on ahead and left them standing on the track, "nowhere in particular." Moreover, to emphasize the couple's isolation, it is raining outside, and, in an additional though gratuitous detail, the exit door is locked. "Oh, the outside door is locked," cries Miss Galbraith, "and we are trapped, trapped, trapped!" Of course, Miss Galbraith is less dismayed than she seems. Being trapped in a car is the best thing that could happen to the couple. Howells was peculiarly drawn to this type of situation. In *The Elevator* (1884) the drama revolves around the occupants of a passenger elevator (originally, in the 1850s, called the "vertical railway") which becomes stuck between floors. By establishing a confined dramatic space, the railroad plays express succinctly what historian John Higham has described as a transformation of American culture "from boundlessness to consolidation" in the third quarter of the nineteenth century.[5] The railroad, which contributed to an enormous widening of horizons in the landscape of the American imagination, is reimagined by an author whose work epitomizes a new quest for order in the theater and quiet on the stage. We see a similar shift from boundlessness to consolidation in popular acting styles and productions, in the transition, for example, from Edwin Forrest's tempestuous Macbeth to Edwin Booth's intellectual Hamlet.[6]

In the isolated setting of *The Parlor Car,* of course, the lovers hash out their quarrel. When an elevator becomes stuck or a car unhitched, characters are licensed to express their private thoughts, feelings, and fears. Innermost feelings are safely dramatized. Eventually, the train will return, and Lucy and Allen will be recoupled in every sense. The urgency of their drama is to accomplish a reconciliation and return to intimate relations before the train returns: "A sound as of the approaching train is heard in the distance. She gives a start, and then leaves her chair for one a little nearer his." When the porter finally returns, he finds them caught in an embrace, Lucy fainting on Allen's breast.

> *Miss Galbraith, in a fearful whisper:* Allen! What will he ever think of us? I'm sure he saw us!
> *Mr. Richards:* I don't know what he'll think *now.* He *did* think you were frightened; but you told him you were not. However, it isn't important what he thinks. Probably he thinks I'm your long lost brother. It had a kind of family look.
> *Miss Galbraith:* Ridiculous!
> *Mr. Richards:* Why he'd never suppose that I was a jilted lover of yours!

It isn't important what the porter thinks, for he is accustomed to such scenes and, paradoxically, makes them feel more private. This minor but important character also resembles the railroad employee in Howells's novel *A Modern Instance* who, on entering a similar situation, "was far too familiar with the love that vaunts itself on all railroad trains to feel that he was an intruder." Enhancing rather than diminishing the cozy intimacy of a traveling couple, "he scarcely looked at them, and went out, when he had mended the fire" (131). Thus, for Allen and Lucy it may not be important what the porter thinks, but the mere possibility that he is a voyeur adds to their sense of intimacy and even supplies them with a mildly erotic pleasure. Finally, as the car is about to pull into Schenectady, harmony is restored; they are engaged again.

As they prepare to depart their bower of bliss, Lucy is struck by an idea. Perhaps Mr. Pullman could be induced to sell the car. They could live in it always. It could be fitted up for a sort of summerhouse and kept in the garden. Allen considers this suggestion "admirable," but he has a better idea. He mentally removes the car from the marketplace entirely. It will be better, he suggests, to "simply keep it as a precious souvenir, a sacred memory—and let it go on fulfilling its destiny all the same." In this spirit they conjugally bless the little car as a kind of domestic heaven:

> *She kisses her hand to the car, upon which they both look back as they slowly leave it.*
> *Mr. Richards, kissing his hand in the like manner:* Good-by sweet chariot! May you never carry any but bridal couples!
> *Miss Galbraith:* Or engaged ones!
> *Mr. Richards:* Or husbands going home to their wives!
> *Miss Galbraith:* Or wives hastening to their husbands.
> *Mr. Richards:* Or young ladies who have waited one train over, so as to be with the young men they hate.
> *Miss Galbraith:* Or young men who are so indifferent that they pretend to be asleep when the young ladies come in! (*They pause in the door and look back again.*) And I must leave thee, Paradise? (*They both kiss their hands to the car again, and, their faces being very close together, they impulsively kiss each other. Then Miss Galbraith throws back her head, and solemnly confronts him.*) Only think, Allen! If this car hadn't broken its engagement, we might never have mended ours.

The Parlor Car is a neo-morality play for modern, urban America. Heaven has become the happy home; Everyman is the married man. And intimacy can be achieved only with an uncoupling from the economic forces of which the railroad was such a powerful emblem. It is a drama about the upper-middle class for the upper-middle class. This little play transforms a public space into a private situation, and in doing so it is emblematic also of transformations of American theater in the second half of the nineteenth century. The trajectory of American theater from rowdy spaces of audience visibility and audibility to darkened auditoriums habituated by only a small cross-section of the population (the kind of theater which we have today) may be imagined, for better or worse, as this parlor car, disengaged from the speeding train, left quietly on the tracks.

The concerns, instructions, and language of women tend to govern the action that occurs in these public spaces turned private, even when such spaces are principally occupied by men. One of the most common actions in these plays is the attempt to identify familiars among strangers, or to strike up intimate relations with people whom one is meeting for the first time. And women generally initiate this action. *The Sleeping Car* (1882) is a farce in which Mrs. Agnes Roberts keeps all of the male passengers awake with her conversation and her haphazard attempts to identify her brother Willis, whom she has not seen for ten years, among a world of strangers. And it is Mrs. Roberts again in *The Albany Depot* (1889) who hires the cook and then leaves her husband in charge of identifying the woman without providing him with a description.[7]

In *The Smoking Car* (1898) it is a strange woman who sets the action going. When the curtain rises, we discover Mr. Roberts, "seated, deeply absorbed in a book which he is reading." As Roberts sits and reads, a young mother with a child in her arms enters and addresses him. This flighty, young woman simply leaves her baby with Roberts, a stranger, while she runs off to do an errand. The comedy centers on the problem of maternity. When Roberts's brother-in-law Willis Campbell comes in and discovers the situation, he suggests that the woman has simply abandoned her baby. The main action of the drama is the attempt of those inside the smoking car, eventually the two related couples (Roberts and Campbells), to locate the mother in the crowd outside. To the Roberts and Campbells the mother is literally one of the crowd, an outsider who has intruded to complicate their lives. In an important sense the problem of class also defines the inside-outside contrast. The mother is one of the lower orders; she is the wife of a "prosperous mechanic" and a "village person." Without this intrusion by the outside world, Howells implies, the cozy car would be "quite like your own fireside."

The humor of a situation-comedy depends upon two kinds of familiarity: the principal characters' familiarity with one another and the middle-class audience's familiarity with the principal characters. The characters, moreover, are not only familiar because they are like the audience members but also because the same characters have been seen in previous sketches. Familiarity of character, in Howells's farces, as in modern television sitcoms, is the starting point for every episode. Each episode requires a slight variation in the situation to set the characters in motion or to reveal some aspect of their personalities, to impel them to an action that is both ordinary and *extra*ordinary. Howells is totally uninterested in "dramatic" plots. Instead, in both his critical essays and his plays he continually advocates character sketches. The success of a play, he claims, depends "upon incident and character, without those crucial events which in life are so rarely dramatic, but which when they come, arrive with as little ceremony as the event of dinner or of death" ("The Play and the Problem," AR 60).

As usual, in *The Smoking Car* the Roberts and Campbells are in a domestic interior that is complicated by the fact that it is on a train, and a strange woman's baby is in their midst. The issue of privacy-in-public conditions their conversation. Overwrought, Amy Campbell informs her husband that she is going to "make a scene and disgrace you before the whole car." To which he replies, "As long as there's nobody in the car I shan't mind your making a scene, and as we're likely to have the smoker to ourselves on a 9:30 train, why not sit down and wait here till Roberts gets back?" Paradoxically, however, the station is extremely crowded. It is rush hour, after all. The contrast between the crowded station and the empty smoking car is emphasized, again, by the important position of the window. The couples in the car are continually pressing to the window, straining to catch a glimpse of the young mother. "Mrs. Roberts, pressing to the window and looking out," complains that Campbell, who has gone in search of the mother, has "disappeared already! I shouldn't like to look for anyone in that crowded station." Howells's plays are conditioned by a tension around their spatial borders. There is a world outside, flying by; the family unit, however, like the work of art, requires borders to define it.

The young mother, who enters, leaves, and reenters the smoking car where Mr. Roberts sits waiting for his family, comes from the working-class world of Bangor, Maine. She is an outsider to the Roberts-Campbell milieu, yet she is more like than unlike these affluent Bostonians in both language and manner. Indeed, as a scatter-brained young mother, she closely resembles Agnes Roberts and Amy Campbell. Occasionally, she lapses into colloquialisms. She exclaims, for example, "I sh'd be in a perfect fidge to know whether I'd got on the right train." But there is little other evidence of her connection to the "folk." Walter J. Meserve has suggested that her weakness "as a far Downeaster . . . is a dominant weakness of the play itself" (CP 518). Moreover, her function in the play, leaving her baby in a car with utter strangers, has a quality of sheer silliness. The "delicate contrast" between the intimate Roberts-Campbell circle and unfamiliar society is not as well developed here as in Howells's earlier railroad dramas, in which the tension seems less contrived.

The railroad is one of the few places where Howells's principal characters come into brief contact with characters not of their own white, upper-middle-class, Protestant, Boston milieu. The combination of contact and distance between social classes is established at the beginning of Howells's first railroad drama, *The Parlor Car,* when the porter tells Lucy Galbraith, "I'll be right here, at de end of de cah, if you should happen to want anything miss." The porter, like most railroad employees in these plays, represents not only social and economic difference but also racial difference. And the profundity of that difference is indicated not only by the color of his skin or by his uniform but also by the job he does and the language he speaks. As Elsa Nettels has noted, most of the non-Anglo-Saxon figures in Howells's work "occupy a position low on the social scale and speak a nonstandard English that not only signals their social inferiority but in itself calls to mind the familiar stereotypes of racial jokes and cartoons" (90). Peripheral characters introduce aspects of the unfamiliar into the sanctum sanctorum of intimate relations. They also represent intrusions of the marketplace. After escorting Miss Galbraith in and assuring her that he will be nearby, the porter hesitates before leaving the car, "takes off his cap, and scratches his head with a murmur of embarrassment. Miss Galbraith looks up at him inquiringly and then suddenly takes out her portemonnaie, and fees him." The railroad is an area where non-Brahmin characters are required by economic necessity to enter the protagonists' lives.

Like *The Parlor Car, The Albany Depot* begins with an exchange between social unequals. Mrs. Roberts, who is looking for her husband (a typical Howells opening), encounters a chorewoman who is mopping up. The woman, who barely stops her work, speaks in a thick brogue: "There's a gentleman over there beyant, readin', that's just come in. He seemed to be lukin' for somebody." Periodically throughout the play, characters representing hierarchies of the marketplace brush up against or intrude into the domestic comedy: the chorewoman mops the floor near Mrs. Roberts's skirts, forcing her to tiptoe away. The "Colored Man, who cries the trains" repeatedly walks halfway into the room, makes his announcements, and leaves. The initial exchange, moreover, between Mrs. Roberts and the chorewoman, is an inverted prefiguration of the main action of the play, which is the attempt of Mr. Roberts and Mr. Campbell to identify an Irish cook, just hired by Mrs. Roberts, while they wait for their train.

The central dramatic interest of the play, in other words, is the negotiation between these sheltered families and the great underclass of servants and immigrants (often one and the same, as in the case of the cook). In this play the contrast is dramatized especially in Roberts's conflict with a stereotypical drunken Irishman whose wife Roberts mistakes for the cook. The "small and wiry" Irishman corners the bewildered Roberts and Campbell: "Fwhat made ye take my wife for a cuke? Did she luke anny more like a cuke than yer own wife? Her family is the best in County Mayo. Her father kept six cows, and she never put her hands in wather. And ye come up to her in a public place like this, where ye're afraid to spake aboove yer own breath, and ask her if she's after beun' the cuke yer wife's engaged. Fwhat do ye mane by ut?" The crucial problem for Roberts in *The Albany Depot* is how to establish employer-employee relations with someone he has never seen before and the dangers of attempting to establish those relations with the wrong people. All the little Irishman wants to know, he insists, is "what this mahn [Roberts] meant by preshumin' to speak to a lady he didn't know."

Howells's intimate dramas depend on an understanding that the railroad is not generally considered to be a space of privacy. The intimate dramas are enabled by two conditions, isolation and visibility, which two generations earlier had inspired Poe's proto-existentialist and deeply anxious story, "The Man of the Crowd." Howells's dramatic vision reverses Poe's unhappy notion that intimate knowledge of other people is impossible in public space. The counterpart of Poe's narrator/observer is the extradramatic audience that Howells's drama necessarily implies. Paradoxically, Howells's private couples are knowable *because* they are in a public place. The conclusion of his novel *The Story of a Play* emphasizes the fundamental relatedness of personal intimacy and public staging. Not only does the play, which depicts the most intimate details of the playwright's married life, achieve an unqualified success, but the principal actor and actress in it become engaged to be married. In fact, the acting couple chooses to inform the playwriting couple of their engagement in the theater after the play. Backstage, both couples discuss the play as a metaphor for their respective relationships. Public staging nourishes private relationships, and vice versa. The evidence that the dramatic roles of husband and wife continue to be played to perfection even a year later, we are informed, is that the actors "have not yet been divorced." A happy marriage on stage indicates happiness in private life, while a happy private life enables the domestic drama.

THE HOTEL

The hotel, like the railroad car, in nineteenth-century America, was remarkable for being a public space into which private affairs could intrude. Hotels in America were, as the *National Intelligencer* proclaimed in 1827, "Palaces of the Public." European visitors to antebellum America found the hotel to be a "'peculiar institution' of this country." One English observer in the 1840s described the difference succinctly in terms of public and private life: "With us [in England] hotels are regarded as purely private property, and it is seldom that, in their appearance, they stand out from the mass of private houses around them. In America they are looked upon much more in the light of public concerns, and generally assume in their exterior the character of public buildings" (qtd. in Boorstin 1965, 135). Like the Pullman car, the hotel was a space to which Howells seemed irresistibly drawn. And a number of his dramas, including two early full-length plays, are set in hotels. In fact, in his one-act farce, *Room Forty-Five* (1899), the hotel is repeatedly associated with various aspects of the railroad: the couple who are put into room forty-five have just arrived by the last train; the man downstairs snores like a locomotive; and, twice, Mr. Trenmore compares their situation to being in a sleeping car. Much of the tension of the play derives from the question of how much privacy this couple has a right to demand as transients in a public place. Trying to dissuade his hypersensitive and thoroughly unreasonable wife from making a ruckus when she is disturbed by the snoring in the room below, Mr. Trenmore expostulates: "We're in a public house, and we have no right to make a noise and wake everybody up. They can arrest us, I believe." But Mrs. Trenmore will not be pacified and proceeds to smash umbrellas, pitchers, parasols, and trunks.

Both of Howells's first attempts at full-length dramas, *Out of the Question* and *A Counterfeit Presentment,* were written in 1877, immediately following *The Parlor Car.* Both are set in the parlor of the Ponkwasset Hotel. And both plays involve a quest for privacy which is complicated by an infortuitous meeting in the hotel, a crisis that is reconciled by the establishment of intimate relations between the antagonists. The title of the first play, *Out of the Question,* refers to the possibility of marriage between a debutante and a member of a lower social class. The curtain rises on the parlor of the Ponkwasset Hotel, where "two young ladies [sit] with what they call work."

Although we later discover that the hotel is full (there isn't an empty room in the house), there are no unfamiliar faces to intrude on this domestic scene. In fact, the two friends are anticipating the arrival of a third, the "refined and cultivated" (and rich) Leslie Bellingham. Leslie arrives with an entourage that includes her mother, her intensely elitist Aunt Kate, and a young man who is "free and equal as the Declaration of Independence." Stephen Blake has come up with the ladies on the stage and altruistically has seen to their every need during the journey, but now Blake complicates the family retreat because he will not go away; he plans to stop at the same hotel. The position of the parlor into which we are introduced itself portends trouble, specifically through the location of the window, which "commands a magnificent prospect of Ponkwasset Mountain" yet also "condescends to overlook so common a thing as the road up to the house." The prospect of the road cannot be ignored in the parlor, and the hotel, as a kind of intersection, functions as a space of tension between different social orders.

The central issue in *Out of the Question* is the problem of introducing an outsider into a private social circle. Can a representative of a different social order and an apparent stranger—we later find that Mr. Blake is actually known by the family, and this fact dramatically facilitates his inclusion—be admitted to intimate relations, and, if so, can the social circle be reconstituted as private, or does his inclusion vitiate the possibility of privacy? In other words, though *Out of the Question* seems to be focused on the problem of eroding social hierarchy ("We're all on the same level at the Ponkwasset Hotel," says Lilly Roberts), the ultimate concern is constitution of the private. Private life is *made up* in the public space of the hotel:

> *Leslie, very graciously:* Don't let our private afflictions drive you from a public room, Mr.—
> *Blake:* Blake.
> *Leslie:* Mr. Blake. This is my mother, Mr. Blake, who wishes to thank you for all your kindness to us.
> *Mrs. Bellingham:* Yes, indeed, Mr. Blake, we are truly grateful to you.
> *Leslie, with increasing significance:* And my aunt, Mrs. Murray; and my friend, Miss Wallace; and Miss Roberts. (*Blake bows to each of the ladies as they are named, but persists in his movement to quit the room; Leslie impressively offers him her hand.*) *Must* you go? Thank you, ever, ever so much!

Although in this last line Leslie is ostensibly thanking Blake for his many kindnesses and attempting to vindicate him to her excessively rude Aunt Kate, it sounds suspiciously as if she is thanking him for quitting the parlor that she and her friends and family have totally possessed. Indeed, Leslie goes so far as to make her toilet at a mirror in the parlor. Although this room is known as "the parlor of the 'transients,'" Blake is called an "intruder" when he accidentally comes upon Leslie in the midst of applying her makeup.

> *Blake:* Excuse me. I expected to find your mother here. I didn't mean to disturb—
> *Leslie, haughtily:* There's no disturbance. It's a public room. I had forgotten that. Mama has gone to tea. I thought it was my friend Miss Wallace. I—(*With a flash of indignation*) When you knew it wasn't, why did you let me speak to you in that way?

The intrusion is clearly gendered. Significantly, in the text itself the young ladies are designated by their first names (Leslie, Maggie, Lilly), while Stephen Blake is "Blake" and Charles Bellingham is "Bellingham."[8] Women, in other words, are constituted by the script itself as private creatures, while men are designated primarily as public beings. Women, as Leslie's mother is aware, are not permitted the freedoms in public that men are: "You are a young lady, and you can't be as gentlemanly as you like without being liable to misinterpretation. I shall expect you to behave very discreetly indeed from this time forth. We must consider now how our new friend can be kindly, yet firmly and promptly dropped."

There are several important peripeteias in *Out of the Question,* and each leads to a heightened sense of intimacy between characters. The first occurs in the "fayre forest," a Chaucerian space inhabited by the ultimate transients, a pair of tramps. With remarkable eloquence and detachment (though with a slight brogue) one of the tramps, a "hideous little Irish wretch," explains, "I'm not the lazy, dirty vagabond I look, at all; I'm the inevitable result of the conflict between labor and capital; I'm the logical consequence of the prevailing corruption." Howells may be having his fun here, but there is an element of truth to this absurdly allegorical claim, for the tramps do represent a certain quality of the "real world," the inequities of the marketplace, which haunts the fringes of most of Howells's domestic situations. Leslie and her friends, in what seems an unconscious effort to colonize the entire world as their own private property, come out for a stroll in what obviously will be the most troubled space for their own interests. The smell of tobacco alerts them to the ominous fact that men are somewhere present: "This scent of tobacco is an unheard of intrusion." In fact, it was Blake who gave the tramps his tobacco, earning from them, if not from Leslie, the title of "gentleman." Despite the warning of the smoke, however, Leslie stops to sketch the beauties of nature while her friends go on. In one of the most dramatically effective scenes of the play the tramps attack her and attempt to steal her watch. Naturally, Blake returns in the nick of time to save the day (and the watch), but in the process his wrist is broken. Leslie is left unhurt, though polluted: "Oh, it was—Oh, oh, I feel as if I should never be clean again! How *can* I endure it? That filthy hand on my mouth! Their loathsome rags, their sickening faces! Ugh! Oh, I shall dream of it as long as I live! Why, why did I ever come to this horrid place?" The immediate result of this crisis is that Leslie becomes Blake's devoted nurse; a pretext for intimate relations has been established by a crisis in public space.

Leslie quickly comes to know and, of course, to love the up-and-coming young Mr. Blake, who, among many accomplishments, has invented an improved locomotive driving wheel. Together Leslie and Blake philosophically discuss the definition of the term *gentleman*. It is abundantly clear that Blake has all the makings of one when he explains that driving wheels, like railroads, are not inherently interesting but "good to get you there." When Leslie asks him what exactly he means by "there," he explains:

> *Blake:* Well, in my case, away from a good deal of drudgery I don't like, and a life I don't altogether fancy, and a kind of world I know too well. I should like to go to Europe I suppose, if the wheel succeeded. I've a curiosity to see what the apple is like on the other side; whether it's riper or only rottener. And I always believed I should quiet down somewhere, and read all the books I wanted to, and make up for lost time in several ways. I don't think I should look at any sort of machine for a year.
>
> *Leslie, earnestly:* And all that would happen if you had the money to get the driving-wheel going?

Yet, when Leslie, the embodiment of the private sphere, proposes to lend Blake some money from her own abundant store for building railroad parts, he is shocked and recoils in horror. When her mother hears of the little scene, she too is deeply troubled: "But what a thing for a young lady to propose! I can't imagine how you could approach the matter." In what seems the most bizarre reaction to Leslie's offer and Blake's refusal, Leslie compares her interaction with Blake to the attack by the tramps. Amazingly, the difference, for her, seems only to be one of degree: "Oh dear, dear—he thought—that I w-w-anted to—to marry him! Oh, how shall I endure it? It was a thousand times worse than the tramps,—a thousand times."

Of course, Leslie does want to marry Blake, though Mrs. Bellingham suggests that she might as well marry a locomotive driver as this "clever artisan." The question is not only whether or not Blake is a gentleman but also whether a person of his background will be accepted by others in their "society," as Leslie's Aunt Kate is pleased to call it. This question is yet another formulation of the private-public issue, for, while one is always already a member of society, one must be elected to the restrictive sphere of society as Aunt Kate means it. Society in the latter sense is not a fit place for former steamboat engineers prone to working with rolled-up sleeves. But, when Leslie's brother Charles arrives to reveal a previous acquaintance with Blake (an acquaintance of no ordinary kind) and to vouch for Blake's native refinement, the road to marriage begins to be smoothed over. Blake and Bellingham had served together in the war, and Blake had saved Charles's life, fishing him out of the Mississippi (like the railroad, the river is a crucial space of public traffic), where Charles had nearly drowned. There is, it may be argued, no more intimate or personal debt than that owed to the saver of one's life, though notably Blake never demanded and never demands recognition of this debt. Blake, Charles asserts, is a "natural gentleman."[9] Miraculously, it seems that this man of humble origins has never uttered a word or displayed a trait that wasn't "refined."

Moreover, in a seemingly irrelevant detail—but, for Howells, a significant one—Charles asserts that the Blake he knew was "a reader in his way, and most of the time he had some particularly hard-headed book in his hand when he was off duty." This is the second reference to reading as a symptom, or token, of Blake's refinement, and it is a statement with broader implications in terms of Howells's aesthetic criteria. *Out of the Question* is, after all, a play, but the only mention of theater in it is a disparaging one. Mrs. Murray (Aunt Kate) compares Leslie's relation to the lowly Mr. Blake with a sensation play: "From beginning to end it has been quite a sensation play. Leslie must feel herself a heroine of melodrama. She is sojourning at a county inn, and she goes sketching in the woods, when two ruffians set upon her and try to rob her. Her screams reach the ear of the young man of humble life but noble heart, who professed to have gone away but who was still opportunely hanging about; he rushes on the scene and disperses the brigands, from whom he rends their prey." Despite her sarcasm, Aunt Kate gives a perfectly accurate description of the events. And yet are we not to take this action as a sensation play or a melodrama? Within the play Howells clearly privileges reading over theater.[10] In doing so, he privileges a private aesthetic experience over a public one. In a letter to John Hay in 1877, regarding *Out of the Question,* Howells remarks that "the play is too short to have any strong effect, I suppose, but it seems to me to prove that there is a middle form between narrative and drama, which may be developed into something very pleasant to the reader, and convenient to the fictionist. At any rate my story wouldn't take another shape."[11] Significantly, Howells refers to this work not as a drama but as a "story."

In Howells's novel *Private Theatricals* (1875), written only two years earlier, *theatricality* is a term laden with both moral and aesthetic value.[12] Two Civil War buddies, Easton and Gilbert, both fall for the erotically charged and apparently irresistible young widow, Mrs. Farrell, who is staying at a summer boardinghouse with other women whose husbands are working in Boston. Mrs. Farrell epitomizes theatricality: she "does everything for an effect," and her "flirtatiousness is vast enough for the whole world." On the one hand, Mrs. Farrell's talents as a flirt, her theatrical qualities, are only effective in the sphere of intimate relations. And yet, on the other, the sphere of intimate relations has expanded to fill the world. When Easton "sat down beside her, in whatever presence, he always seemed to be alone with her" (118).

Howells's interest in private relationships leads him, in this early novel, to reimagine both theatricality and, at the conclusion of the novel, the nature of the professional theater itself. Theater has become what women do in "society." Predictably, Mrs. Farrell becomes a professional actress in the end: "She's a novice to the stage, but she's been an actress all her life." Her reception on the professional stage by "the public," however, is interesting and complex. In 1875 the professional stage is not used to representing the lives of women and sexual relations (no matter how theatrical they are):

> Those who remember the impression made among people who knew of her, by the announcement that Mrs. Farrell was going upon the stage, will recall the curiosity which attended her appearance in Boston, after her debut in a Western city, where she had played a season. There is always something vastly pitiable in the first attempts of a woman to please the public from the stage; this is especially the case if she is not to the theatre born, and confronts in her audience the faces she has known in the world: at any rate it showed itself the kindest of houses, and seized with eager applause every good point of her performance.

Yet, despite the kindness of the audience and her genius for looking and dressing the character, Mrs. Farrell's debut on the Boston stage is finally a failure. The audience members cannot exactly put their finger on her inadequacy as Juliet, but her performance, says one critic, "wasn't so much art as it was nature and artifice . . . Perhaps she wasn't artistically large enough for the theatre. I shouldn't have said, at first, that she was particularly suggestive of the home circle; very likely, if I'd met her off the stage, I should have pronounced her too theatrical; and yet there was a sort of appealing domesticity about her, after all." Off the stage Mrs. Farrell is clearly not the ideal homemaker, but on the stage her capacity as an actress ought to be limited to domestic types. Mrs. Farrell, this intelligent observer concludes, is perfectly suited for character sketches, "little morsels of drama that she could have all to herself, with the audience in her confidence—a sort of partner in the enterprise, like the audience at private theatricals" (264).

Howells's profound contribution to American theater was to recognize and advocate the importance of "little morsels of drama," character sketches, and ordinary exchanges between people with intimate knowledge of one another. Significantly, Howells's plays were largely restricted to amateur performances. His one-act farces and comedies privilege private life not only in their content but also in their formal demands. Indeed, the best experience in theater, in Howells's view, is akin to reading a novel. As a reader, one can be audience to a private domestic scene even in a crowded public place: "The novelist sets up his stage here and there, and then plays the whole piece through to the reader . . . and the audience of the portable theatre enjoys privileges impossible in the stationary theatre. The witness of the dramatic action of the novel may go away and return when he likes; he can always take up the piece at the point where he left it; he can retrace his steps in it for a verification of his impressions, or advance with it to the end at such a pace as he pleases" (RT 10).

Howells's advocacy of a domestic drama and his ability to dramatize intimate exchanges in swift and intelligent dialogue has led to his recognition as the foremost theorist of dramatic realism in America between 1865 and 1916.[13] The early hotel comedies are some of the best examples of his attempts to imagine intimate relations in spaces occupied by a variety of people. These plays exemplify the intrusion of private affairs into public space, and, in doing so, they anticipate a new brand of theater, a domestic theater that represents action that had been previously considered "untheatrical." *A Counterfeit Presentment,* Howells's first play to have a successful stage life, was performed by one of America's foremost actors, Lawrence Barrett.[14] While relatively successful for Howells, however, the play was hardly a popular favorite. Generally regarded as charmingly written, *A Counterfeit Presentment* was also felt to be lacking in action. In this play, too, characters disparage the theater. When he is told the "tragic" story of a young lady who has come infelicitously to the hotel, a lady whom he is destined to wed, the hero Bartlett exclaims, tellingly: "Oh, come now! You don't expect me to believe that! It isn't a stage-play."

FIVE

The Theater of Private Life

Acting Out in the Families of Louisa May Alcott

There is no form of amusement more generally popular at the present day than that of private theatricals, and although at first sight it may appear strange that people should take great delight in seeing their friends play at acting, when with less trouble they could see the real thing done by trained actors, it is actually not difficult to find an explanation for the enjoyment which attaches to these performances.

—*A Practical Guide to Amateur Theatricals* (1881)

In the second half of the nineteenth century, both in Europe and America, middle-class families came increasingly to recognize their own theatricality. The "genteel performance" of middle-class social relationships, as Karen Halttunen has persuasively shown, became increasingly self-conscious in the 1850s and 1860s. Nowhere, Halttunen argues, "was the new direction of middle-class culture more evident than in the vogue of private theatricals that swept the parlors of America" (1982, 153). Private theatricals dramatized what was otherwise a widely accepted metaphor. "The primary theatre of private life in the nineteenth century," writes Michelle Perrot, "was the family." The family, she claims, "established the characters and roles, the practices and rites, the intrigues and conflicts, typical of the private sphere" (97).

If the language of theatricality, however, was increasingly employed to describe and understand the private sphere, it was also a language with serious limitations, confined by the epistemological boundaries of melodrama and farce. Both in the parlor and in the commercial theater ethical ambiguities were simplified and characterological nuances erased. For example, in his 1866 *Amateur's Handbook and Guide to Home or Drawing-Room Theatricals* Tony Denier strongly advocates a "natural" style of acting, but, paradoxically, he also limits the range of such acting to the "types of humanity." And, in a similarly restricted view of dramatic character, the playwright Bronson Howard in 1886 insists, as one of his "axioms" of the theater, that "the death, in an ordinary play [not a tragedy], of a woman who is not pure . . . is inevitable" (30). While parlor theatricals and popular melodramas commonly depicted domestic scenes (e.g., George Aiken's 1852 dramatization of *Uncle Tom's Cabin*), it would be years before Americans would accept the domestic realism of Ibsen or dramatic portrayals of women's social and sexual desires in contemporary private life without being scandalized. William Dean Howells, one of Ibsen's great defenders in America, remarked in 1899 that "the latest performance of Ibsen's *Ghosts* . . . has been followed by quite as loud and long an outburst of wounded delicacy in public and private criticism as the earliest [performance] provoked. Now, as then, the play has been found immoral, pathological, and revolting" (100).[1] James A. Herne's "epoch-making" *Margaret Fleming* (1890), an unsentimental exploration of a woman's character, was a critical success but a popular failure when first produced, unable even to find a theater in New York.[2] Despite such setbacks for playwrights in the commercial theater and limitations on actors in the private sphere, there were unrecognized venues in which dramatic realism began to penetrate the domestic ethos.

In various stories and novels written between 1854 and 1886, Louisa May Alcott reimagines inherited notions of theater and theatricality to represent a newly complex vision of the relationship between theatricality and domestic life. In these texts an incipient form of dramatic realism appears when plays are staged in domestic space. Alcott has two basic, and often interlocking, strategies for showing a relationship between theater and the private sphere. The first is to convert the home, or some part of the home, into a theatrical space—often, literally, into a theater. And the second is to represent the private life of a professional actress. Independently, these strategies may not appear particularly original, but, where they operate together, Alcott's work illustrates how fictional re-presentations of theater, or meta-private-theatricals, can produce unsentimental glimpses of domestic life.

In a number of ways Alcott's representations of theater indicate a continuation and a reassessment of Jane Austen's representation of theater in *Mansfield Park* (1814). Although the antitheatricalism of *Mansfield Park* no longer seemed relevant in the elaborately theatrical culture of late-nineteenth-century America, Austen's representation of theater was well-known, if widely misinterpreted. Ironically, guidebooks for amateur actors, such as O. A. Roorbach's *Practical Guide to Amateur Theatricals* (1881), cite Austen approvingly in order to lend their works authority. It is useful, therefore, to consider briefly how Austen did, in fact, construct the domestic theater of her novel.

Theater is posed as a direct threat to a particularized notion of domestic space. "What signifies a theatre?" asks Austen's young, brilliant, and superficial Henry Crawford. "Any room in this house might suffice" (149). As a visitor to Mansfield Park from London, Crawford is addicted to excitement. Although he has no formal experience of acting, he longs to give it a try, and, it turns out, he has a natural gift. When he reads Shakespeare in the parlor he is able, with the "happiest knack," to render every character with equal skill: "Whether it were dignity or pride, or tenderness or remorse, or whatever were to be expressed, he could do it with equal beauty.—It was truly dramatic" (335). Crawford's opposite, of course, is the quiet and passive Fanny Price, and his attempt to woo and marry her some time after the private theatricals have been attempted becomes the central crisis of the novel; their relationship is virtually an allegory of the tension between forces of change and those of conservation. During the rehearsals Fanny finds herself drawn, in spite of her better promptings, to Crawford's excellent acting: "She did not like him as a man, but she must admit him to be the best actor." Fanny, naturally, is the one young person in the home who refuses to act in the play.

Opposition to theater in *Mansfield Park* is strongly and repeatedly asserted, principally by Sir Thomas Bertram's younger son, Edmund. Ironically, Edmund's eventual participation in the theatricals results from his anxiety to protect the privacy of the house. He is finally prevailed upon to take a role when the rest of the players threaten to invite an outsider to take the one male part yet to be filled—or, in other words, to violate the family circle. Edmund complains: "This is the end of all the privacy and propriety which was talked about at first. I know no harm of Charles Maddox; but the excessive intimacy—the familiarity. I cannot think of it with any patience." He tries to explain his inconsistency to the unimpeachable Fanny: "Perhaps you are not so much aware as I am, of the mischief that may, of the unpleasantness that must, arise from a young man's being received in this manner—domesticated among us—authorized to come at all hours—and placed suddenly on a footing which must do away with all restraints. To think only of the license which every rehearsal must tend to create" (175). If the theater must be private, Edmund determines, it must be completely private. The danger is in the blurring of the public and the private. He therefore sets out, by participating, to exclude all strangers and thus attempts to be the means of "restraining the publicity of the business." Edmund's capitulation is against his better judgment, and he knows that Fanny disapproves, but the others are overjoyed, for "to have it quite within their own family circle was what they particularly wished."

The integrity of the family is the central theme of the novel. Every locus of action outside of Mansfield Park is characterized by dysfunctional families. The Crawfords come from a home in London characterized by incompatible stepparents, and the home of Fanny's parents in Portsmouth is an "abode of noise, disorder, and impropriety." The intensity of Fanny's longing for the domestic felicity of Mansfield Park after three months of exile at Portsmouth leads her to realize the essential distinctness of Mansfield from every other place. Mansfield Park is an oasis of old-fashioned order. The most exceptionable character in the theatricals episode is the one person who has no family bonds whatsoever. It is the outsider, the Honorable John Yates, who introduces the notion of theater, or "the infection," into Mansfield Park to begin with and who eventually elopes with the younger daughter, Julia. The self-serving Yates has little concern for this, or any, family, "having never been with those who thought much of parental claims, or family confidence." From beginning to end *Mansfield Park* is a profound commentary both on the family and various intrusive, destabilizing forces of the nineteenth century which threaten it, and it is in this context that the antitheatrical prejudice in the novel makes sense. The density and sophistication of Austen's ironies may lead the reader to question the essential distinctness of the two social spheres—the theatrical world of John Yates, on the one hand, and, on the other, the quiet home epitomized by the passive Fanny. But the superficial resolution of the theatricals episode, the suppression of theater by Sir Thomas and Fanny's apparent vindication, must also lead the reader to view the theater as subversive of family interests at this historical moment.

As in *Mansfield Park,* in Alcott's *Little Women* (1868) the absent father is a precondition for theatricals in the home. The discussion of the absent father which frames private theatricals in both novels emphasizes paradoxically both the self-sufficiency and the vulnerability of the domestic sphere. The

March family's *Operatic Tragedy* is, however, more purely private than the Bertrams' *Lovers' Vows*.[3] The four March sisters are the only actors; they both invent the drama and play every role. Moreover, even when playing theatrical roles, in an important sense their extradramatic personalities and their specific roles in the family are affirmed. Jo is always Jo, rebellious daughter and headstrong sister. The theatricals allow her to "act out" but ultimately emphasize her basic conformity to familial expectations. Her sister Meg (Anna) makes this clear when she writes:

> Jo, of course, played the villains, ghosts, bandits, and disdainful queens; for her tragedy-loving soul delighted in lurid parts, and no drama was perfect in her eyes without a touch of the demonic or supernatural. Meg loved the sentimental rôles, the tender maiden with the airy robes and flowing locks, who made impossible sacrifices for ideal lovers, or the cavalier, singing soft serenades and performing lofty acts of gallantry and prowess. Amy was the fairy sprite, while Beth enacted the page or messenger when the scene required their aid. (*Comic Tragedies* 8)

The roles assumed by the sisters reinforce notions of family, for they confirm the sisters' identities in the family independent of the play. Thus, in *Little Women* theatricals seem to have a moral orientation directly opposed to that of theatricals in *Mansfield Park*. Unlike the situation at Mansfield Park, the interest in private theatricals in the March home contributes to "the idealization of the family as an institution that could restrain the forces of conflict and diversity in American society and curb the radical individualism of Jacksonian democratic culture" (Halttunen 1984, 234).

In Alcott's fiction, however, in which the line between public and private is less clearly defined, moral complacency about the theater and theatricality becomes more problematic. Like Jane Austen, Louisa May Alcott represents theater with a strongly moralistic tone, but Alcott's representations are also often caught in a web of contradictions; the good actress, for example, cannot easily be a "good woman" too. For Alcott theater is a standing challenge to the separateness of private and public, female and male, social spheres and the ideological systems that the separate spheres entail. There are many interesting examples of theater in Alcott's fiction in which the borders of home are more permeable than they are in *Little Women*. And the paradox of the good actress and good woman is a pervasive problem both in Alcott's domestic-tutelary novels and in her sensation fiction.[4]

As a metatheatrical device, the play-within-a-play (or within-a-novel) brings into focus particular dramaturgical assumptions. If a theatrical production implicitly privileges character over plot, for example, this bias will be reflected with a special clarity in a play-within-a-play. And, while the play-within-a-play may also reflect on a kind of plot (e.g., it may parody melodramatic action or the form of a well-made play), representations of theater in the novel, like realist productions in the theater, tend to focus on the problem of character. In Louisa May Alcott's fiction metatheatricality indicates, most significantly, something about character. In this sense especially, Alcott's fictional representations of theater clearly reflect dramaturgical assumptions of her day. In the years between 1860 and 1880 an increasing concern about the nature of dramatic character is represented both in new kinds of drama and in new productions of old works.

An important feature of dramas written in the third quarter of the nineteenth century for private or drawing-room entertainment is the defamiliarization of the domestic ethos. By transforming their parlors into theaters, middle-class performers self-consciously played with the conventions of everyday life. Of the countless parlor theatricals published and produced in Alcott's day, *Mr. John Smith* (1868), by Sarah Annie Frost, collected in *Amateur Theatricals and Fairy-Tale Dramas: A Collection of Original Plays, Expressly Designed for Drawing-Room Performance* (1868), is a particularly good example of a play that defamiliarizes the domestic ethos. The drama opens with Mr. John Smith still shaking the snow from his clothes after a train ride from New York City and a long hike through a disorienting blizzard. The transition from the cold "outside" world to that of the warm and supposedly safe drawing room will ultimately prove to be highly ironic.

Mr. Smith mistakenly believes that he has arrived at the home of his eccentric old friend, Dr. Harris. In fact, Smith has stumbled into a party of amateur actors and actresses preparing for their first performance. It is, moreover, no ordinary performance, for it is not to be of a single drama but, since all the guests wish to be stars, a patchwork of tragedies and comedies, ranging from *Macbeth* to *School for Scandal.* As characters enter and exit, in costume, posing, reciting, acting, they incorporate Smith into the scenes, assuming that he is aware that it is all theater. In comparison with actors in a play-within-a-play, characters such as John Smith who are outside the represented drama are theatrically unhistrionic. Smith, of course, is totally confused; he assumes that he has come to a lunatic asylum or that he is witnessing some bizarre new experiment of his unusual friend, the doctor. In this setting theater and "reality" merge seamlessly. One character calls to another, "Macbeth, Ophelia wants you!" Smith is unaware that characters are either rehearsing or indulging in mock-theatrical dialogue offstage. Ophelia seems to him a poor young lady who has gone quite insane, Macduff a dangerous psychopath. An extensive familiarity with dramaturgical methods (e.g., the stride of Forrest or the "style" of Macready) is assumed by all of the characters except John Smith, who insists in the end, "I was never in a theatre, sir, in my life, and know nothing about it!" Also, a comprehensive knowledge of dramatic literature is assumed, both of the actors in the play and of the audience members for whom *Mr. John Smith* is intended. The audience members are, presumably, sitting in a parlor in which, and of which, this stage-parlor is a re-presentation.

The comic idea at the center of *Mr. John Smith* is that in unfamiliar society one may not know when people are playing roles and when they are being "themselves." For it is not only John Smith who is confused by these actors; they are also mistaken about who he is. They are expecting another Mr. John Smith from New York and welcome this John Smith as a familiar member of their group, complicit in all the same assumptions. But their John Smith is a professional actor affiliated with a theater in the city who has promised to write their prologue, interludes, and epilogue, and to act as prompter. "Such a remarkable name!" exclaims Lily Jones when she learns of the mistake in the end. The central problem from which all other comic possibilities follow, therefore, as the title character's generic name suggests, is to mistake a private citizen for a professional actor. Here the professional theater has come, or is wrongly supposed to have come, into the private home. On the one hand, there is an implication that the private sphere is irremediably theatricalized. But, at the same time, the recalcitrance of John Smith indicates a theatrical space outside of "theatricality." Whether or not Alcott knew *Mr. John Smith,* she undoubtedly knew plays like it. And she was able to employ such epistemological comedy in complex and socially incisive ways. In particular, Alcott uses the *mise-en-abyme* to show how skepticism about character in a theatrical society could redound most seriously to the disadvantage of women who did not have a clear allegiance to the public or the private sphere, and for these women the actress was an important paradigm.

In *Behind a Mask; or, A Woman's Power* (1866), Alcott's last and, arguably, her best sensation story, she inverts the premise of *Mr. John Smith*. In Alcott's story the theatrical Jean Muir enters the home of the affluent and untheatrical Coventry family. Despite soliciting a governess for younger sister Bella, the family is extremely reluctant to receive a stranger in their home. Jean Muir, a close cousin of Becky Sharp, is literally a *little* woman with extraordinary talents: she is charming, sings like an angel, plays the piano, speaks perfect French, and appears willing to cater to the family's every need. (Younger brother Ned actually calls her "a capital little woman" after she miraculously tames his horse Hector.) Jean Muir is also recovering from a dangerous fever, contracted, naturally, in France, though she assures Mrs. Coventry that there is no danger of infection. Furthermore, like the Honorable John Yates, the intruder who brought the theatrical infection to Mansfield Park, Jean Muir has no serious family attachments.

Miss Muir's first scene with the Coventry family involves many theatrical moments, such as an unexpected fainting spell while playing the piano, and the family members themselves understand the scene as theater: " 'Scene first, very well done,' whispered Gerald to his cousin." Overhearing this remark, Jean looks over her shoulder with a "gesture like Rachel" and replies in a penetrating voice, "Thanks, the last scene shall be still better" (101).[5] But it is only in her room, when "the curtain is down" and Jean literally disrobes, that Alcott allows us a peek at the "real" Jean Muir: "The metamorphosis was wonderful, but the disguise was more in the expression she assumed than in any art of costume or false adornment. Now she was alone, and her mobile features settled into their natural expression, weary, hard, and bitter" (106). Jean is an excellent actress but, the story seems to suggest, a bad, and very dangerous, woman. " 'Theatricality,' " as Nina Auerbach notes, "is such a rich and fearful word in Victorian culture that it is most accurately defined . . . in relation to what it is not. Sincerity is sanctified and it is not sincere" (1990, 4).

Moreover, this form of private theatricality has distinctly gendered overtones. Whereas theatricality in public spaces is often a metaphor for a kind of masculine self-promotion, private theatricality tends to have connotations of feminine promiscuity, the phenomenon of Becky Sharp, a view clearly articulated around this time by Schopenhauer in his notoriously misogynist notions of feminine wiles: "In the girl nature has had in view what could in theatrical terms be called a stage-effect: it has provided her with super-abundant beauty and charm for a few years at the expense of the whole remainder of her life, so that during these years she may so capture the imagination of a man that he is carried away into undertaking to support her honorably in some form or other for the rest of her life, a step he would hardly seem to take for purely rational considerations" ("On Women" 81). Such is the most serious danger of theatricality in private life, the ability of insincere women to subvert masculine self-interest. Thus, the Coventry family is defenseless against Jean. By virtue of her theatrical powers she soon becomes the life of the house, a favorite of the servants, and the object of every man's desire. In fact, jealous of her relationship with his older brother Gerald, Ned Coventry attacks his brother with a pruning knife.

In *Behind a Mask* Alcott seeks to create in the actress a heroine who is both financially and personally secure but one who can also share a domestic space with other intimates. In chapter 5, "How the Girl Did It," a blithe company of young people assembles to stage a series of *tableaux vivants* in Sir John Coventry's saloon. Jean Muir, of course, is the focus of each tableau, the most successful of which is a picture of two lovers which she performs with Gerald. This tableau is successful not principally because of its effect upon the audience but because of its effect on Gerald:

> It lasted but a moment; yet in that moment Coventry experienced another new sensation. Many women had smiled on him, but he had remained heart-whole, cool, and careless, quite unconscious of the power which a woman possesses and knows how to use, for the weal or woe of man. Now, as he knelt there with a soft arm about him, a slender waist yielding to his touch, and a maiden heart throbbing against his cheek, for the first time in his life he felt the indescribable spell of womanhood, and looked the ardent lover to perfection. (149)

The irony, of course, is that Gerald's first experience of "real" womanhood takes place in an explicitly theatrical scene. Encouraged by the audience's enthusiastic response, the lovers perform another tableau even more moving, both to the others and to themselves, than the first. It takes a jealous woman, cousin Lucia, who is in love with Gerald, to disrupt Jean and Gerald's performance. The cousin, who is part of the family but not one of the narrow group under Jean Muir's spell, attempts to break up the party: "Others thought it fine acting; Coventry tried to believe so; but Lucia set her teeth, and, as the curtain fell on that second picture, she left her place to hurry behind the scenes, bent on putting an end to such dangerous play" (149). Lucia, however, is too late. Gerald is under the little woman's power, and they glide away together to a "secluded little nook, half boudoir, half conservatory" in order to enact what Jean later refers to as "strictly private theatricals, in which Monsieur and myself were the only actors" (198). There they achieve a deeper level of intimacy, or so it seems to Gerald. "We are acting our parts in reality now," Jean sighs beneath his velvet cloak. But the tension between the inner "Coventry" world and the extrafamilial world symbolized by the professional actress intensifies as Jean comes closer to winning the heart of each member of the nuclear family.

Ultimately, Jean aims to marry into the family. While Gerald falls deeper into love, however, the threat of information about Jean's past looms on the horizon; she is forced to work for the match nearest at hand, marriage with the elderly Sir John. As Judith Fetterly comments: "The job requires extraordinary self-discipline and self-control. Jean must continually act as if she is not acting and pretend that she is not pretending; she must never let the ultimate mask of 'real self' slip" (7). Jean seeks to provoke Sir John into a proposal without overstepping "the bounds of maiden modesty" (*Behind a Mask* 177). When she does, in fact, achieve her match, provoking the gentle Sir John to propose (this event being the "last scene [which is] better than the first"), "the blessed sense of safety which came to her filled Jean Muir with such intense satisfaction that tears of real feeling stood in her eyes, and the glad assent she gave was the truest word that had passed her lips for months" (181). At this point one may feel licensed to view Jean Muir with more sympathy than earlier sections of the novella invited. Her end (a happy marriage), to some degree, belies the means (theatricality). The fact that Jean Muir's first, basic ambition was to have a home of her own is, finally, the greatest argument on her behalf. And her wedding to Sir John is the climax to which the novella builds insistently: "When the ring was fairly on, a smile broke over her face. When Sir John kissed and called her his 'little wife,' she shed a tear or two of sincere happiness" (192). We are never permitted to forget, moreover, that financial necessity is one of the most pressing factors compelling Jean to her theatrical devices.

As in *Mr. John Smith,* the meeting of the self-consciously theatrical and the unconsciously theatrical defamiliarizes conventions of social behavior which, because they occur in private, are supposedly more "natural" than those of public life. Through Jean's letters to a friend, for example, Alcott invites us to take an unsentimental view both of Jean's character and of the family unit in explicitly theatrical terms. "Bah!" Jean writes, "How I hate sentiment! I drank your health from your own little flask, and went to bed to dream that I was playing Lady Tartuffe—as I am." Jean's construction of all that has happened since her coming to the home indicates the detachment of a character who knows the value of being a member of a family but one who has not idealized the institution. In one letter she comments on each member of the family in turn: "The cadet of the family [brother Ned] adores horses. I risked my neck to pet his beast, and he was charmed. The little girl is romantic about flowers; I made a posy and was sentimental, and she was charmed . . . I get on well and meanwhile privately fascinate Sir J. by being daughterly and devoted" (196). Because her appreciation of the family is not sentimental, Jean renders family life in vivid colors, exposing its corruptions.

Implicit in all her mockery, however, is a basic acceptance of the importance of the family and the rules of family life. Jean actually seeks to punish those members of the family who do not appreciate what they have, who do not, in other words, respect one another or the family as a unit: "I laugh at the farce and enjoy it, for I only wait till the prize I desire is fairly mine, to turn and reject this lover who has proved himself false to brother, mistress, and his own conscience. For my sake he cast off the beautiful woman who truly loved him; he forgot his promise to his brother; and put by his pride to beg of me the worn-out heart that is not worth a good man's love" (199).

The story projects a sense of Jean Muir's alienatedness from sentimental hypocrisy while also emphasizing her need of a family unit in order to survive. Once they have read what Jean has written, each member of the family is shocked, but they do not seem to learn anything about themselves. The truth of the sentiments expressed in the letters only leads the family group to start up, cry out, and weep with outrage. Mrs. Coventry clasps her daughter "as if Jean Muir would burst in to annihilate the whole family." The story's great point, however, is that annihilation of the family is the last thing that Jean wants. She wants the family to survive, and she wants to be part of it. In the end Jean (now Lady Coventry) and Sir John enter the family circle, literally (for they come into the parlor) and figuratively. Sarcasm passes away from Jean's voice and defiance from her eye, as she turns to Ned and Bella.

"For [Sir John's] sake forgive me," she says. "And let there be peace between us" (201). The family accedes, and the "game is won." Jean may remain a problematic heroine, for she is never fully exonerated for her earlier insincerity, but, as will become increasingly clear, her victory is substantial.

Jean Muir's position in the Coventry household is characterized by two basic conditions: first, her cynical detachment and, second, her profound dependence. These two conditions come to characterize representations of the family on the American stage for a century and, arguably, reach their apotheosis in Eugene O'Neill's *Long Day's Journey into Night* (1941), also a metatheatrical play. But even in the 1860s and 1870s a profound change was taking place on the American stage, and it is in the context of that change that Alcott's fiction should be read. In Edwin Booth's *Hamlet,* for example, Alcott felt that she had seen "my ideal done at last" (LLJ 102). *Hamlet* was her favorite play and Edwin Booth her favorite actor.[6] Booth's *Hamlet* strongly emphasized character over plot, reversing the priorities of melodramatic productions a generation earlier. Booth's famous 1870 production especially dramatized relations among the family members, and to this end a new and highly sensitive staging of the play-within-the-play was achieved.[7]

Booth's interpretation of *Hamlet* marked a radical departure from that of the waning school of American acting epitomized by Edwin Forrest, whose robust and athletic Dane was a far cry from Booth's gentlemanly, and even effeminate, hero. In the play-within-the-play scene, wrote one reviewer, Forrest had "more the air of some huge gipsy, watching with roguish glance an opportunity to rob the hen-roost, than a highly intellectual analyzer of nature trying to decry on the human countenance the evidence of guilt" (14). In short, the interest that Forrest's Hamlet takes in the play-within-the-play privileges plot over character. Forrest's Hamlet, apparently, has already made up his mind about his uncle and is simply watching the play for the action he expects it to provoke. This interpretation of the scene clearly indicates dramaturgical assumptions about the play as a whole; Forrest's production is not realistic but melodramatic. For Booth, on the other hand, this scene is a crucial indicator of Hamlet's basic weakness and intellectuality. First of all, in Booth's staging the emphasis has shifted from the play staged for the royal family to the royal family members themselves. In the "traditional" staging *The Mousetrap* had been presented up-stage center, with the family split (Hamlet and Ophelia on one side and Claudius and

Gertrude on the other), looking back toward the play. In Booth's "modern" staging Hamlet and Ophelia are up-stage center, Claudius and Gertrude stage right, and the play itself occupies the weakest space of action, stage left. The family has become the focus of interest, with Hamlet at the center, while Claudius and Gertrude assume a chiasmic relation to the Player King and Queen (see figs. 14 and 15). This arrangement, remarked the reporter for the *Sunday Times,* "cannot but be deemed an improvement, for the counter-workings of the features of both Hamlet and Claudius are not only brought more into direct antithesis, but also more plainly put in sight of the audience" (9 January 1870). The subversive content of the *Mousetrap* is thus dramatized in the relations between the family members, as the emphasis on the players is downplayed and the contrast between Hamlet and Claudius heightened.

Toward the Queen, his mother, in the play-within-the-play scene, Booth's Hamlet displays a "fine mixture of deference and irony." His filial affection for both father and mother excited the praise of many critics. "He is inexpressibly gentle," wrote William Winter. "He has honored father and mother with that beautiful filial affection which is rooted in the soul, and which shows the angel in the man" (95). Booth was at the heart of a new cultural sensibility, one in which intellectual refinement was combined crucially with the sanctity of private life. One friendly critic wrote in the New York *Tribune* that Booth was "the first Hamlet for many a day who, in the closet scene, does not consider it necessary to rave and rant at the Queen like a drunken pot-boy—he is the first Hamlet for many a day whose conduct in the same scene would not justify the interference of third parties, on the supposition that he intended to commit assault and battery upon his mother—he is the first Prince of Denmark for many a year who has dared, in this same scene, to conduct himself like a gentleman, and not a blackguard" (27 November 1861, 42).

Here was an actor who knew how to treat his mother. And the reviewer singles out the closet scene as the one, par excellence, in which to differentiate Booth from the Forrest school. Thus, Clarke was not alone in finding this scene, the only one in which Hamlet is alone with his mother and the ghost of his father, the original nuclear family, the most powerful in the play. As Hamlet, Booth was "both gentleman and scholar," refined, quiet, and picturesque. But, above all, he was a tender son. In Booth's *Hamlet* a

FIG. 14. Forrest as Hamlet in the play-within-the-play in 1854 at the Boston Theatre. Forrest staggers from his seat with Ophelia, stage right. The play-within-the-play itself is upstage center.

complex and subtle characterization is theatrically realized in a domestic space—a son alone with his mother in her room. For Alcott the representation of close, yet troubled, family relationships in the theater must have been especially provocative, for in her own life theater had recently seemed a release from emotionally trying family responsibilities.

Three years before Alcott first saw Booth's *Hamlet,* in 1855, the Alcott family had moved to Walpole, New Hampshire. There Louisa and her sister Anna quickly became involved in the Walpole Amateur Dramatic Company. The company, which performed in the Walpole Town Hall with music by the Walpole Serenade Band, confined itself primarily to comedies of the 1840s and 1850s. Louisa tended to play middle-aged, unmarried women, such as the loud-mouthed Widow Pottle in J. R. Planché's *The Jacobite.* In the public house she owns, Widow Pottle, as her daughter's lover laments, "abuses

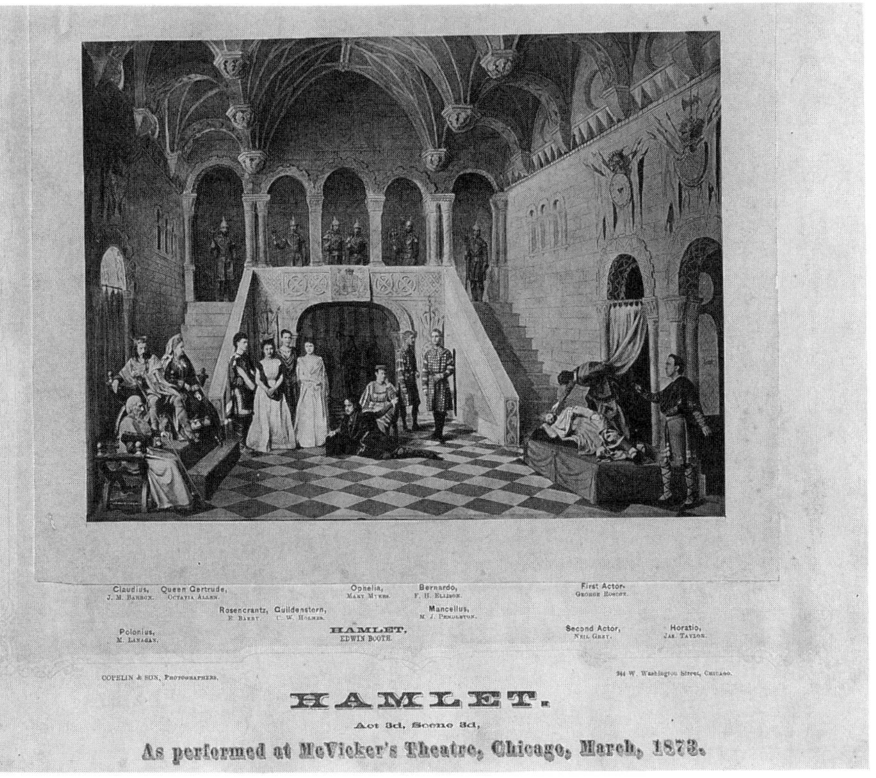

FIG. 15. Booth in the same scene at McVicker's Theatre, Chicago, 1873. Booth rests on the floor upstage center, gazing to his right at the king. The play unfolds ceremoniously downstage left.

the privilege of her sex."[8] As the comic relief, Louisa's characters satirize the ideal of the quiet domestic abode but never fundamentally challenge it. Anna, who was also a gifted actress, tended to play the young beauties destined for domestic happiness. Louisa noted: "Anna was the star, her acting being really very fine. I did 'Mrs. Malaprop [in Sheridan's *The Rivals*],' 'Widow Pottle,' and the old ladies" (LLJ 82).[9]

At this time Alcott also began to have more exposure to the professional theater. Fanny Kemble came to Walpole, where Alcott met her in 1855, and over the course of the year Alcott began, with the help of her uncle,

Dr. Charles Windship, to attempt to place her own plays with Thomas Barry, manager of the Boston Theatre. In 1857 the family moved back to Concord where the Concord Stock Company became a vital escape for Alcott from a home in which in her younger sister, Elizabeth, was dying of the effects of scarlet fever. In Concord, as in Walpole, Alcott played widows and character roles, including many dramatizations of Dickens, while her sister played ingenues, lovers, and young brides. While Louisa attempted to advance her theater career, however, the Alcott family was experiencing its most significant strain. In her journal Alcott explicitly articulates an important dichotomy between home and theater while also indicating their deep relationship in her experience: "I lead two lives. One seems gay with plays, etc. the other very sad,—in Betty's room; for though she wishes us to act, and loves to see us get ready, the shadow is there, and Mother and I see it." The next two entries focus almost entirely on two subjects, theater and her sister's decline:

> December.—Some fine plays for charity.
> January, 1858.—Lizzie much worse; Dr. G. says there is no hope . . . and we tried to bear it bravely for her sake. We gave up plays; Father came home; and Anna took up the housekeeping, so that Mother and I could devote ourselves to her. Sad, quiet days in her room. (LLJ 96–97)

On 14 March Lizzie died quietly in the middle of the night. In June Alcott, who had been given a free pass to the Boston Theatre by Barry, went to see Charlotte Cushman and "had a stage-struck fit." Her dreams seemed nearly realized when Barry agreed to give her a professional break in the role of Widow Pottle. "It was all a secret, and I had hopes of trying a new life; the old one being so changed now, I felt as if I must find interest in something absorbing" (LLJ 98). Unfortunately, however, Barry, who was to play the male lead, broke his leg, and the plan fell through. Louisa's disappointment in the journal is revealing: "I had to give it up; and when it was known, the dear, respectable relations were horrified at the idea. I'll try again by-and-by, and see if I have the gift. Perhaps it is acting, and not writing, I'm meant for. Nature must have a vent somehow . . . Worked off my stage fit in writing a story, and felt better; also a moral tale" (99). The horror of her parents at the idea of Louisa as an actress, her resolution to be an actress nonetheless, her sense of acting and writing as related modes of giving vent to nature, and her catharsis in the end through writing a good moral tale all indicate a dynamic, tense, and also a murky relation between theater and the home in Alcott's imagination as well as the deep tension between acting and writing, public and private modes of creativity.

The moral tale, "Marion Earle; or, Only an Actress," which emerged from these events in 1858, is a story that earnestly seeks to establish a productive, and even a sacred, relationship between the actress and the domestic woman.[10] In the first scene of the story, which itself is constructed in a series of melodramatic set pieces, Marion appears on the stage in a comedy. In her dramatic role she "put by her cares, and was the gay and brilliant creature that she seemed." Soon after leaving the stage, however, with a jest on her lips, a cry is heard backstage. The play continues, "but it now received the divided attention of those who had been absorbed before." When she returns to the stage, Marion struggles unsuccessfully to play her comic role, for she has learned backstage, in the middle of the performance, that her little sister May is dead.

> When, after a long pause, Marion appeared, a quick murmur arose, for in her face there might be read a tale of suffering that brought tears of pity into womanly eyes, and changed the comedy to a tragedy . . . Apparently unconscious of the sympathizing faces looking into hers, or the consoling whispers of her fellow players, Marion went on, mechanically performing every action of her part like one in a dream, except that now and then there flitted across her face a look of intense and eager longing, and her eyes seemed to look in vain for some means of escape; but the stern patience of a martyr seemed to bear her up, and she played on, a shadow in the scene whose brightness she had lately been . . . With the same painful faithfulness, she tried to sing [her concluding song], her voice faltered and failed—her heart was too full.

No longer in her theatrical role, Marion turns to the audience members: "Kind friends, pardon me—I cannot sing—for my little May is dead!" This ingenuous appeal is, paradoxically, the most dramatic utterance of the evening. It is, indeed, a coup de théâtre. Women weep, and men silently throw flowers at the actress's feet. In one respect this story clearly projects Louisa

May Alcott's personal fantasy, an attempt both to reimagine and to affirm her own dual life of the previous year, when she had been, on the one hand, the actress away from home and, on the other, the nurse to her dying sister Lizzie. In this story the sincerity of the private woman validates the performance of the public figure. Marion Earle is an actress as "virtuous and cultivated" as "faithful wives, good mothers, and true-hearted women."

And yet, like other virtuous actresses in Alcott's fiction, Marion is not destined to survive the story. In the end her goodness does her in. Her former lover, Robert Leicester, sick with a "contagious fever," comes to her home, where she happens to be sheltering his abandoned wife and child. After nursing Robert back to health and assuring herself that the nuclear family has been reunited, the saintly actress departs, but, of course, she has been infected with the illness that soon kills her. Marion's death represents a moral crisis, for it is apparent that private life is not conducive to the art of the actress. In fact, despite Marion's talents as both actress and nurturing woman, theater, in this story, represents a standing challenge to the domestic and the feminine. In Alcott's early work it implicitly challenges the "natural characteristics" of the sexes, for theater, in these novels, subverts dichotomies of passive-active, interior-exterior, female-male.[11] The domestic actress, therefore, represents a moral crisis of the utmost importance.

The paradox embodied by the virtuous (and, by definition, domestic) actress was much on Alcott's mind in the 1850s. The play she aimed to produce in 1858, during her sister's decline, was "The Rival Prima Donnas," a dramatization of only her second published story (1854) of the same title. "The Rival Prima Donnas" tells the story of two women, the "fair" and "blameless" Beatrice, who has resigned her position as first lady of the opera in order to make a quiet home, and the up-and-coming "young debutante" Theresa. The opening scene establishes the split architecturally, with Beatrice in the curtained box and Theresa on the stage. Beatrice, moreover, in the middle of the performance, vanishes even from the private box and reappears at home with painter and fiancé, Claude. It is an emblematic transition. "Have I not tried the world and found its flattering homage false?" asks Beatrice of her intended. "Have I not sought for happiness in wealth and fame and sought in vain until I found it in your love? what then do I leave but all I am most weary of, and what do I gain but all I prize and cherish most on the earth? the painter's home I will make beautiful with the useless wealth I have won, and the painter's heart I will make happy by all the blessings a woman's love can give! Then do not fear for me, what *can* I lose in leaving a careless world for a husband and a home?" (12).

This vision of domestic happiness, however, will soon be frustrated and Beatrice's goodness trampled: "As she spoke she laid her proud head trustingly upon his breast, little dreaming of the bitter disappointment her fond words brought to the false heart where all her hope and faith were placed." At midnight Claude departs for a rendezvous with Theresa. The moral polarity of good Beatrice and evil Theresa seems clearly represented when, to the slightly remorseful Claude, Theresa explicitly articulates his choice:

> If Beatrice be still so dear to you, I fear there is no place in your heart for me, therefore choose now between us, for I will have no rival in your love. If Beatrice be dearest, then go and share with her the *quiet home* she longs for and in her calm affection may you find the happiness you seek, but if your many vows be true and Theresa most beloved, then come and tread with me the path that lies before us, share with me the wealth and fame I go to win, and in the *gay brilliant world* find all that makes love pleasant, and happiness in my fond faithful love, both are before you, therefore choose and let all doubts be ended here forever. (15; my emph.)

Naturally, Claude, who is confessedly playing a part himself and, thus, is deeply bound to the world of acting, chooses Theresa. Beatrice, the "deceived, deserted woman," comes to the theater one last time. And, although she hides behind the drooping curtains of her box, she is, Alcott insists, equally as capable of acting the role represented by Theresa on the stage, "with a truth and power that would have thrilled the hearts which beat so quickly now." Instead, when Theresa takes her bows, Beatrice throws down an iron crown concealed in roses which kills her rival and leads, ultimately, to her own insanity.

Although the title of "The Rival Prima Donnas" seems to privilege the professional and public rivalry of the two women, it is clearly the private and domestic aspect that is most important in the story. The story's opening explicitly establishes Beatrice's "generosity" and total lack of jealousy regarding Theresa's ascendance on the stage. In fact, after the first act Beatrice's appreciation of her rival's professional success is most conspicuous, "as forgetful of all but the trembling singer before her she clapped her white hands and cast the flowers from her own bosom at her wondering rival's feet" (11). Moreover, Beatrice loses none of her ability as a performer, as the narrator emphasizes at the climax. Beatrice simply chooses a different sphere of action, the private as opposed to the public. Yet, although the story invites us to favor Beatrice over Theresa, to privilege private over public, it may be wiser to recognize a play between these bipolarities which is not clearly resolved. After all, the most wicked act of the story, murder, is committed in the end by Beatrice, not Theresa. Theresa, moreover, is never despicable; on the contrary, the story manifests a profound appreciation for artistic talent, of which Theresa clearly has plenty. Beatrice may once have been virtuous, but she is disappointed in the end; this is not the tale of goodness rewarded which we expect from melodrama. And Alcott's own enjoyment of playing villains and witches may also provide some context in which to reconsider the "moral" of this tale.

Read in the light of stories such as "Marion Earle" and "The Rival Prima Donnas," *Behind a Mask,* written ten years later, clearly represents an advance for the actress turned domestic, for Jean, though tainted, not only lives, but she also wins a husband. Ultimately, of course, she must reject the handsome Gerald to marry old Sir John, a choice that has much in common with Jo March's rejection of the dashing Laurie and marriage to the avuncular Professor Bhaer. The elder men validate the quiet harmony of the domestic sphere, bringing only minor sexual and "romantic" tension. But, unlike Marion and Beatrice, Jean does manage to negotiate the treacherous terrain between the world of professional theater and the domestic sphere without losing either her life or her mind. She may never be completely absolved of the sin of theatricality, and she clearly remains a problematic heroine, but in her ability to move from the world of theater to the world of the home, Jean, more successfully than either Marion or Beatrice, brings "theatrical" and "authentic" modes of acting into contact with each other. In doing so, Jean manages to represent brief glimpses of realism through the self-consciously theatrical.[12]

After representing actresses in fiction throughout her career, Alcott seems to resolve the good actress / good woman paradox in her last and most sentimental novel, *Jo's Boys.* Miss Cameron, a character apparently modeled on

Fanny Kemble, fulfills not a sensational but a tutelary function.[13] In *Jo's Boys* Miss Cameron faces the same struggle to maintain her privacy which the now famous writer, Mrs. Jo, does. Miss Cameron is a public figure who has retreated to a private space both to refresh herself and to work on her art. This fact alone indicates a new notion of the theater: the space of the actress's real creativity is no longer the stage but the privacy of her own home. At Rocky Nook, where the Laurences (Amy and Laurie) have a house, "Miss Cameron, the great actress, had hired one of the villas and retired thither to rest and 'create' a new part for next season. She saw no one but a friend or two, had a private beach, and was invisible except during her daily drive, or when the opera-glasses of curious gazers were fixed on a blue figure disporting itself in the sea. The Laurences knew her, but respected her privacy" (130). Little Josie Brooke, however, who is staying with her aunt and uncle, pines to meet the great woman who both "thrills thousands by her art" and wins friends by her virtue. Miss Cameron is a model of refinement and cultivation. The notion that one must *cultivate* a "good heart" is a basic lesson of the maternal-tutelary mode, and, ultimately, cultivation becomes the bridge between actress and woman. The virtuous actress, previously understood as a contradiction, is reimagined through the concept of "culture."

As a virtuous actress, moreover, Miss Cameron is doubly validated, and she, in turn, seems to validate both of the spheres (public and private) in which she moves: "The stage needs just such women to purify and elevate the profession which should teach as well as amuse" (130). Consequently, Alcott privileges Miss Cameron to become Josie's mentor. The actress is given access to the private world of Plumfield, which is literally turned into a theater before her eyes in the private theatricals produced by Mrs. Jo and company. Unlike the *tableaux vivants* in *Behind a Mask,* private theatricals at Plumfield require that all participants understand their reality in the same way. Theatricality in *Jo's Boys* implies not insincerity, as it did in *Behind a Mask,* but the "truth" that happiness is in the cultivated private sphere.

Generally, Miss Cameron advises young girls like Josie to be "good wives and happy mothers in quiet homes." Theater and the "quiet home" remain essentially two separate worlds, and those who inhabit them are of two "classes." Culture, however, is now a form of mediation, a quality necessary to fit a girl for either world and to allow a woman to move between them both.

> I can give you no better advice than to go on loving and studying our great master [Shakespeare] . . . It is an education in itself, and a lifetime is not long enough to teach you all his secrets. But there is much to do before you can hope to echo his words . . . Now you will be disappointed, for instead of telling you to come and study with me, or go and act in some second-rate theatre at once, I advise you to go back to school and finish your education. That is the first step, for all accomplishments are needed, and a single talent makes a very imperfect character. Cultivate mind and body, heart and soul, and make yourself an intelligent, graceful, beautiful, and healthy girl. (140–41)

In Miss Cameron's advice Josie recognizes the counsel of her own family. Josie's Aunt Amy feels "that whether her niece was an actress or not she *must* be a gentlewoman" (129). Her family emphasizes education (they run a school) as well as a new form of theater—a fundamentally domestic theater. Uncle Laurie and Aunt Jo, in fact, "plan plays about true and lovely things,—simple domestic scenes that touch people's hearts, and make them laugh and cry and feel better" (142). Her uncle tells her that she must not think of doing tragedy, and Miss Cameron agrees that the girl is not ready for "high art," which includes freezing the blood and firing the imagination.

If in *Jo's Boys,* however, the professional theater seems to capitulate to a sentimental domestic vision—and chapter 14, "Plays at Plumfield," is literally a dramatization of that capitulation—there are also signs of faint and indirect resistance, a sense that the domestic ethos may touch the heart but it also entails a loss of fun. In fact, the "blood-and-thunder" melodramas favored by Jo, as a girl in *Little Women,* exert their presence to the very end, when the narrator remarks that "it is a strong temptation to the weary historian to close the present tale with an earthquake which should engulf Plumfield and its environs so deeply in the bowels of the earth that no youthful Schliemann could ever find a vestige of it. But as that somewhat melodramatic conclusion might shock my gentle readers, I will refrain" (315). Although the narrator does not employ the explosive conventions of the melodramatic theater and, instead, quietly lets "the curtain fall forever on the March family," one is left with the sense that haunting the edges of the happy home is a kind of theater which is incongruous with domestic bliss.

Moreover, though Miss Cameron seems to resolve the good actress / good woman dichotomy, Alcott offers details throughout the novel which undermine this apparent resolution.

Alcott's use of theater to reinforce the sanctity of the home in the domestic novels of the March family appears especially ironic in light of repeated references to *Macbeth.* The play establishes an important link between Jo March, Miss Cameron, and Josie Brooke. In the beginning of *Little Women* Jo exclaims: "I do think *The Witch's Curse, an Operatic Tragedy* is rather a nice thing, but I'd like to try *Macbeth,* if we only had a trapdoor for Banquo. I always wanted to do the killing part. 'Is that a dagger I see before me?' muttered Jo, rolling her eyes and clutching at the air, as she had seen a famous tragedian do" (8). The events of *Little Women* occur when Jo is about fifteen. The famous tragedian to whom she refers is Edwin Forrest, the greatest American Macbeth of his generation, and the dramaturgy she evokes, therefore, is not the rising domestic realism but the melodrama of an earlier period, when the teenaged Louisa, calling herself "Jo," had written *An Operatic Tragedy.* Moreover, the reference to Forrest is significant, because Forrest's *Macbeth* was at the heart of a major public controversy that culminated in 1849 in the Astor Place Riot. That riot, which cost over twenty lives, epitomized the destructive power of the "public" at the theater.[14]

At one time or another all three actresses display an enthusiasm for *Macbeth,* a play with an extraordinarily dark vision of the family, of women generally, and of mothers particularly. Peculiarly, when Nat and Daisy are reunited at the end of *Jo's Boys,* Josie "danced round them like Macbeth's three witches in one" (314). The repeated references to *Macbeth* in Alcott's domestic writing may seem singularly incongruous. In *Macbeth* no home is safe from the ravages of the public sphere. Of the two female characters one imagines herself dashing out her newborn's brains, and the other is unable to protect her children or herself from assassins hired by Macbeth himself. In *Macbeth* there is a deep animus against the very concept of motherhood. Impelled by the witches' prophecy, "none of woman born / Shall harm Macbeth" (4.1.80–81), *Macbeth* imagines what amounts to a motherless world. As Janet Adelman has argued, "the whole of the play represents in very powerful form both the fantasy of a virtually absolute and destructive maternal power and the fantasy of escape from this power" (90).

In *Jo's Boys,* at the crucial moment when Josie begins acting in Miss Cameron's parlor without knowing that Miss Cameron is in the room, she is mouthing Lady Macbeth's last speech. It is a moment, a speech, which connects Josie to a long history of great actresses, to theater history generally, and it is a moment that foreordains her ultimate career choice. Standing alone in Miss Cameron's parlor, waiting for the great actress to appear, Josie forgets herself and, gazing at the portraits of other great actresses, begins "to imitate Mrs. Siddons as Lady Macbeth": "Looking up at the engraving . . . she held her nosegay like the candle in the sleep-walking scene, and knit her youthful brows distressfully while murmuring the speech of the haunted queen. So busy was she that Miss Cameron watched her for several minutes unseen, then startled her by sweeping in with the words upon her lips, the look upon her face, which made that one of her greatest scenes" (136). Lady Macbeth's last speech ("The Thane of Fife had a wife; where is she now?") is the initial point of artistic contact for protégée and mentor, as if this play, which represents the death of families, is the starting point for a career in theater. Miss Cameron, as Josie recalls, had lost a lover years ago and "since had lived only for art" (137). There remains, in other words, an important sense in which family and theater are mutually exclusive.

In *Jo's Boys,* however, Josie's theatrical triumph comes not as Lady Macbeth but as a character much like herself, in a play written not by Shakespeare but by Aunt Jo. Karen Halttunen argues convincingly that, in *Jo's Boys,* "Josie Brooke helps fulfill Miss Cameron's dream to purify American theatre by carrying family theatre onto the public stage" (1984, 249). The play at Plumfield itself is about a simple country family nearly destroyed, as Halttunen puts it, "by contact with the evil world outside the home." It is a play about the sanctity of private life, performed for a private audience. And the professional actress, Miss Cameron, who is included in the select group in attendance, enters into the illusion as thoroughly as the most naive theatergoer. Above all, it is a play of, and for, mothers. "I wanted to show that the mother was the heroine as soon as possible," explains the playwright, Aunt Jo. And yet, despite the play's excessive sentimentality, the performance aims unconsciously at a certain kind of realism.

In this chapter of the novel Alcott represents the sentimental drama through a quasi-naturalistic mode of acting. Actors are most successful when they just act natural. For example, "Josie's unaffected start when she sees her [mother, Meg, who also plays her stage mother], and the cry, 'Why there's mother!' was such a hearty little bit of nature, it hardly needed the impatient tripping over her train as she ran into the arms that seemed now to be her nearest refuge" (211). But, while Josie is theatrically unhistrionic, the play has no psychological content. It is, as a melodrama, entirely plot driven. Dramaturgically, the play at Plumfield is deeply conflicted. Dramatic realism begins in the home, in the family, among people with whom one is intimate and familiar, and the most perfect theatrical illusion is that which does not appear to be theater at all. But, at the same time, the play at Plumfield represents a retreat from issues that theater raises elsewhere in Alcott's work. As a whole, *Jo's Boys* clearly, even insistently, marks both the compelling force and the limitations of sentimental theater. "Having endeavored to suit everyone by many weddings, few deaths, and as much prosperity as the eternal fitness of things will allow," the narrator cynically remarks in the end, "let the music stop, the lights die out, and the curtain fall forever on the March family" (316).

In 1879 Ibsen wrote a radical new play called *A Doll House*. In it the female protagonist, a housewife named Nora, comes to realize that what she thought had been domestic felicity had been a fantasy, a performance. The epiphany that her entire life has been an act moves the play to a new kind of theater. In a conclusion that stunned Victorian audiences first in Europe and, fifteen years later, in America, Nora articulates her wish for a marriage that is "real"; then she slams the door, irrevocably, behind her. This single act moved the drama into a new kind of moral space. In this play Ibsen rejects complacency about the theatricality of social life, but he also eschews the sort of sentimental unmasking which aims, reductively, to distinguish the sincere from the depraved. This form of dramatic realism indicates a space of moral ambiguity in which the exuberantly theatrical meets the theatrically unhistrionic.

Although Alcott manifests no awareness at the end of her life of the domestic realism beginning to appear on European stages, she does show, in a variety of works and genres, that the theater of private life is full of contradictory demands. Despite the self-conscious theatricality of the private sphere in late-nineteenth-century America, Alcott's actresses ultimately fail to bridge the gap between domesticity and theater. Their attempts lead to death, insanity, or, at least, to the stigma of moral corruption. Alcott's own life and career, both somewhat constricted by domestic obligations, further contribute an element of pathos to the unresolvable tensions she represents in her oeuvre. Private theatricals in Alcott's work indicate, most significantly, the limits of old dramaturgical modes for representing a complete, morally complex domestic space. And yet, Alcott implies, theater of some kind is an inescapable aspect of existence. "It is impossible," she admits simply, in her last novel, "for the humble historian of the March family to write a story without theatricals in it" (203).

SIX

UNPACKING THE BOX

Form and Freedom in the Dramatic Writings of Henry James

It is a bad way of excusing an artist, to say that the content of his works is good and even excellent, though they want the right form. Real works of art are those where content and form exhibit a thorough identity.

G.W.F. HEGEL, *Science of Logic*

I scratched my head. "Is it something in the style or something in the thought? An element of form or an element of feeling?"

He indulgently shook my hand again, and I felt my question to be crude and my distinctions pitiful.

HENRY JAMES, "The Figure in the Carpet"

On Saturday, 5 January 1895, Henry James's play *Guy Domville* was performed at the Saint James Theatre in London. Although James had been writing dramas since boyhood and had already converted two novels into plays (*The American* and *Daisy Miller*), *Guy Domville* was his first full-length, original work to be performed on the professional stage, and his anxiety had been mounting for weeks. At 9:00 P.M. the stalls were packed with celebrities (including William Archer, H. G. Wells, John Singer Sergent, and Bernard Shaw), and the pit and gallery were filled with a public eager to see their favorite actor, the dashing George Alexander. As the curtain rose, however, James himself was not in the theater. Instead, the self-described "nervous, sensitive author" was across town watching Oscar Wilde's new drama, *An Ideal Husband.* Only at the evening's end did he leave the Haymarket Theatre and travel back across town to enter by the stage door, as his play was concluding. Then, in the midst of curtain calls, the bewildered James was thrust on stage. "I no sooner found myself in the presence of those yelling barbarians," James later wrote, "than the dream and delusion of my having made a successful appeal to the cosy, childlike, naif, domestic British imagination . . . dropped from me in the twinkling of an eye" (*Letters* 1:234). James gaped as "all the forces of civilization in the house waged a battle of the most gallant, prolonged and sustained applause with the hoots and jeers and catcalls of the roughs."

Years later, in his *Experiment in Autobiography* (1934), H. G. Wells, who had been "a raw young dramatic critic" for the *Pall Mall Gazette* on the fateful night, wrote that the scene at the Saint James only contributed to his own disinclination for any further adventure in the theater. That night had provided Wells with his first sight of Henry James, and it proved to be the beginning of a sincere yet troubled friendship between the two authors. Wells amusedly remembers James as "a sensitive man lost in an immensely abundant brain," the last person one might expect to be drawn to the professional theater. James was "formal, formally Æsthetic, conscientiously fastidious and delicate," Wells writes, "and yet he was consumed by a gnawing hunger for dramatic success" (451). The attraction of the fastidious Henry James to a contemporary theater of seemingly limited artistic value, however, Wells explains by reference to his friend's very formalism. James passionately believed in theater as "a finished and definite something demanding devotion":

> He could imagine this gathering of several hundred people for three hours' entertainment on a stage becoming something very fine and important and even primary in the general life. I had no such belief. I was forming a conception of a new sort of human community with an unprecedented way of life, and it seemed to me to be a minor detail whether this boxed-up performance of plays, would occur at all in that ampler existence I anticipated. (457)

Wells is but one of many, including James himself, to insist not only on James's formalism but also to notice his intense interest in dramatic form in particular and his attraction to the "formal" demands of the theater. I have singled out Wells's comments primarily because of his peculiar metaphor, "the boxed-up performance of plays," for not only is it indicative of an idiom prevalent in late nineteenth-century discussions of form, but it is also pervasive in James's own representations of theater in fiction and criticism.

Most famously, in a review of Tennyson's *Queen Mary* (1875), James describes the form of a "real drama" as a tightly and ingeniously packed box:

> The fine thing in a real drama, generally speaking is that, more than any other work of literary art, it needs a masterly structure. It needs to be shaped and fashioned and laid together, and this process makes a demand upon an artist's rarest gifts. He must combine and arrange, interpolate and eliminate, play the joiner with the most attentive skill; and yet at the end effectually bury his tools and sawdust, and invest his elaborate skeleton with the smoothest and most polished integument. The five-act drama—serious or humorous, poetic or prosaic—is like a box of fixed dimensions and inelastic material, into which a mass of precious things are to be packed away. It is a problem in ingenuity and a problem of the most interesting kind. The precious things in question seem out of all proportion to the compass of the receptacle; but the artist has an assurance that with patience and skill a place may be made for each, and that nothing need be clipped or crumpled, squeezed or damaged. The false dramatist either knocks out the sides of his box, or plays the deuce with its contents; the real one gets down on his knees . . . keeps his ideal, and at last rises in triumph, having packed his coffer in one way that is mathematically right.[1]

The strongest impression of this extraordinary passage is of the obvious and frustrating incongruity of the boxlike structure and the "precious things" that go into it. The young James's intensely material conception of the drama epitomizes a rhetoric of dramatic form which obtained at a particular moment of crisis in the modern theater. James and his contemporaries had inherited the rigid conventions of a neoclassical, or "closed," dramatic form, but they did not also inherit that drama's historically determined subjects. Thus, in this review James goes on to claim that, because the drama is the most highly crafted of literary forms, it requires the most beautiful of subjects: "In a play, certainly, the subject is of more importance than in any other work of art. Infelicity, vagueness of subject, may be outweighed in a poem, a novel, or a picture, by charm of manner, by ingenuity of execution; but in a drama the subject is of the essence of the work—it *is* the work." Here James articulates a deeply traditional, indeed classical, theory that form and content are fundamentally separate, and this passage has often been cited as evidence of his advocacy of the rigors of the well-made play.[2] The notion that the form is "ideal," imposing certain structural requirements on the author, leads to the conclusion that the author's freedom, as opposed to mechanical ingenuity, can be exercised only in the choice of subject. The content is historically contingent, but the form is transcendent.

The problem with generalizing about James's notion of dramatic form, however, is that, while his 1875 review seems categorical (and is, in fact, the product of much study and theatergoing), James claims to have learned something new about form after the theater debacle of 1895. Six months after his humiliating opening night, while plotting *The Spoils of Poynton,* he reflects that the one important lesson he learned from his passionate and disappointing engagement with the theater was the lesson of form: "When I ask myself what there may have been to show for my long tribulation, my wasted years and patiences and pangs, of theatrical experiment, the answer, as I have already noted here, comes up as just possibly *this:* what I have gathered from it will perhaps have been exactly some such mastery of fundamental statement—of the art and secret of it, of expression, of the sacred mystery of structure" (*Complete Notebooks* 127).

The sacred mystery that was not evident before, one may infer from reading James's notebooks, prefaces, and letters, is that structure, or the art of expression, is not mechanical but organic. In his 1908 preface to *The Tragic Muse* James remarks, "There is life and there is life, and as waste is only life sacrificed and thereby prevented from 'counting,' I delight in a deep-breathing economy and an organic form." In his 1908 preface to *The Awkward Age* the self-defined "form lover" describes how the scenic method "helps us ever so happily to see the grave distinction between substance and form in a really wrought work of art signally break down" (22). *The Awkward Age* is explicitly modeled as a play, constructed almost exclusively in dialogue: "dialogue organic and dramatic, speaking for itself, representing and embodying substance and form" (14). And the novel as a whole, James insists, unfolds in acts: "I realise—none too soon—that the *scenic* method is my absolute, my imperative, my *only* salvation." Not surprisingly, much criticism of the late James supports the notion that the theater years led to more "experimental" and "scenic" novels.[3]

None of the criticism, however, adequately contextualizes James's "experiments" in theater history or acknowledges contradictions in James's prolific discussions of form. And James's own writings, which deal directly and indirectly with the notion of dramatic form, are hardly consistent; his various statements about form are complex, and the discrepancies indicate different meanings in the notion of form. Like Wells, James comes to imagine an ampler existence than that of the boxed-up performance of plays. But, while Wells imagines a "new sort of human community," with "shows" not unlike Rousseau's republican festivals, for James that ampler existence is still imagined in terms of theater.[4] Significantly, James does not turn his back on the drama after 1895, as he is often imagined to have done. The inconsistencies in James's comments about the drama (for he does not totally abandon the notion of a rigid form) indicate not only an incompleteness in his theories of form but also a conflicted relation to different dramaturgies. These dramaturgies can be approached under the headings of realism and melodrama. James's career in drama and fiction manifests a deep allegiance to both dramaturgies in a way that complicates his "dramatic writings" and also renders them unique.

THE TIGHTLY PACKED BOX

"As children we have all played with the little man who springs out of his box [*le boîte*]," writes Henri Bergson in 1900. "You squeeze him flat, he jumps up again. Push him lower, and he shoots up still higher. Crush him down beneath the lid, and often he will send everything flying . . . It is a struggle between two stubborn elements, one of which, being simply mechanical, generally ends up by giving in to the other."[5] In "Laughter" Bergson articulates two opposing notions of form. The first is an idea of form which is static or mechanistic. Laughter is produced by an impression of automatism or rigidity imposed on human action from without, "like a ready-made frame." Describing a creative tension between the "illusion of life" and the impression of "mechanical arrangement," Bergson explains that the laughter produced by a jack-in-the-box [*le diable à ressort*] is a corrective response to the human being who acts like a machine. The stress of life against rigidity, he argues, is the source of the comic. In those momentary epiphanies, whether of accident or of art, when mechanical form appears to be conditioning some activity, we are provoked to laughter; our personhood asserts itself against "a kind of physical obstinacy." Laughter is a social gesture that counteracts automatism or a systematic absentmindedness. Thus, the comic element appeals not to the emotions but purely to the intelligence. There is no pity and fear in comedy, only a recognition of "something mechanical encrusted on the living." The jack-in-the-box reveals the obstinacy of matter resisting the force of life and, thus, shows "how comic fancy gradually converts a material mechanism into a moral one."

The ready-made frame, which is capable of making us comic, lends us its rigidity instead of borrowing our flexibility. In this contrast between rigidity and flexibility, Bergson argues, lies the essential difference between comedy and what he calls "drama." Drama implies a second notion of form. Unlike comedy, drama does not tend to simplify but to be complicated by its own subject: "What the dramatist unfolds before us is the life-history of a soul, a living tissue of feelings and events—something, in short, which has once happened and can never be repeated" (164). The notion of form implied here is not static or mechanical but organic, presenting itself to us "as evolution in time and complexity in space" (118). Drama is characterized by elasticity and tension, as opposed to the inelasticity that leads to the explosion in comedy: "It stirs something within us which luckily does not explode, but which makes us feel its inner tension. It offers nature her revenge upon society" (163).

The organic form of drama is most clearly suggested in Bergson's use of the word *gracefulness* [*la grâce*]. Gracefulness is not imposed from without but generated from within. It is "the immateriality which . . . passes into matter" (78). In this formulation the soul, or what Bergson elsewhere calls the *élan vital,* the life force, shapes the matter that contains it. The soul is not immobilized by matter, as it is in comedy, but remains infinitely supple and perpetually in motion. In drama we forget the soul's materiality and think only of its vitality. Thus, drama and gracefulness generate not laughter but seriousness, not rigidity but freedom: "All that is serious in life comes from our freedom. The feelings we have matured, the passions we have brooded over, the actions we have weighed, decided upon and carried through . . . these are the things that give life its ofttimes dramatic and generally grave aspect" (111–12). The argument for seriousness and gracefulness epitomizes Bergson's revolt against the abstractions of natural science and the mechanistic worldview. In a lecture given at the Sorbonne in 1895 Bergson describes the "inner energy of an intelligence which at each moment wins itself back to itself, eliminating ideas already formed to give place to those in the process of being formed."[6] This notion of self-formation is profoundly at variance with material civilization. We will return to Bergson in considering specific applications of these theories to representations of character and plot in Henry James. Here Bergson's notions of comedy and drama help to establish the importance of particular tropes, such as the too-tightly-packed box or the ready-made frame, and the use of contrasting vocabularies, which indicate different impressions of form.

The dualities of flexibility and form, freedom and rigidity, are central to the idiom of the nineteenth-century theater. As Joseph Roach has shown, the relationship between "organical and mechanical modes" was at the root of contemporary discussions of acting (1985, 182). For instance, George Henry Lewes, whose study *On Actors and the Art of Acting* (1875) James called an "entertaining little book" (SA 79), anticipates Bergson in praising gracefulness in acting as opposed to the abrupt "discharge" of passion which is merely "mechanical."[7] And in 1893 James himself praises the "spontaneity," "freedom," and "vitality" of Fanny Kemble. Throughout her career, James writes, Kemble managed to avoid "handy formulas" and "superficial symmetries" (*Temple Bar* 506).

In crucial ways, moreover, the language of freedom and form, applied here to performers and performances, also pervades discourse about dramatic literature. Dramatic theory in the nineteenth century had largely focused on the relationship between the rigid form of the well-made play (*pièce bien faite*) and the content of the drama, which included features such as theme, character, and notions of ethical value. Eugène Scribe, who produced 374 individual works for theater, including thirty-five full-length plays and libretti for twenty-eight grand operas, perfected the form that nearly every dramatist of the century wrote within or against. A useful "blueprint" of the Scribean "système du théâtre" is provided by Maurice Valency:

> Scribe employed a five-act structure, with the climax in the fourth act, the denouement in the fifth and a quick curtain. The first act was mainly expository; its tone was gay. Towards its end, the antagonists were engaged, and the conflict was initiated. For the next three acts, the action oscillated in an atmosphere of mounting tension. In the fourth act . . . the stage was generally filled with people, and there was an outburst—a scandal, a quarrel, a challenge. At this point things usually looked pretty black for the hero. But the last act arranged every-

> thing; in the final scene, the cast was assembled, there were reconciliations and an equitable distribution of prizes, and the audience came out of the theatre smiling. (66–67)[8]

This formula was endlessly reproduced, and is employed to this day, with variations only in character, situation, and the machinery of complication. The complications of the well-made play, moreover, may themselves be endlessly multiplied, depending on the skill of the author, for not only is the master structure of the play formulaic, but each individual scene replicates in microcosm the structure of the play as a whole: "Each scene had its initial situation, its progression, complication, climax, peripeteia, and conclusion, so that it formed an autonomous whole within the total arrangement" (67).

Scribe's influence on dramatists of the following generation was profound and complex. Alexandre Dumas *fils* gives Scribe the backhanded compliment of calling him "a prestidigitator of the first rank." He disparages Scribe's plays as "a worthless liqueur in a worthless jar" (preface, *Un père prodigue*).[9] But Dumas insists that he is not attacking Scribe but is merely illustrating the shortcomings of "a marvelous juggler." Form is crucial, he argues, but "no one ever perishes because of form; he lives or dies according to the matter." This argument, though somewhat nebulous, is recapitulated by Henry James, himself a devout admirer of Dumas. In James's view Dumas's "special gift" was his "mastery of the dramatic form," but, significantly, the gift also was animated by a "moral sense [which] . . . was of the liveliest" (SA 267). James praises the form of Dumas's plays more than once but calls his most famous play, *La Dame aux Camélias,* "astonishing" for its *combination* of "freshness and form" (262). Dumas's plays are not "well made" in the Scribean sense.

La Dame aux Camélias, in particular, is incompletely realized as a well-made play. The traditional form is effectively in place for the first three acts, though with less juggling than in Scribe's plays, but the final two acts become the vehicle for Marguerite Gautier, the abandoned and dying heroine. Character, in other words, comes to dominate plot, and this shift in emphasis was unquestionably the reason for the play's astonishing and lengthy popular success.[10] As a boy, James had heard from his young female cousins "how many times . . . they had seen Madame Doche in *La Dame aux Camélias* and what floods of tears she had made them weep" (SA 262). The emotional reaction is related not simply to events of the play but specifically to the performance of the leading actress, and for many actresses the role of Marguerite was a great chance. *La Dame aux Camélias* represents an uneasy but productive relationship between form and content, and the tension is engineered in a way that deeply resonated with nineteenth-century audiences.

Fundamental problems in structure become evident in the fourth and, especially, in the fifth acts, but they are inherent from the beginning. Most important, there is no full-fledged antagonist to engage the hero, Armand, in conflict. The real source of dramatic action, the obstacle the lovers must overcome, is the "character" of Marguerite, her personal history as a courtesan. All formal problems are contingent upon the choices and actions of this central character, and, consequently, the play is not simply ordered by a structure extrinsic to the individuals. In the *scène à faire,* a confrontation between rivals for Marguerite's love, the structural awkwardness is indicated especially by a remarkable example of metatheatricality. Armand actually calls his rival a "deus ex machina," a reference that instantly establishes the limits of the stage and implies a space outside of the drama. Such a notion cannot be accommodated by a well-made play, in which one action leads logically to the next and in which characters simply do not have power to affect action beyond what the plot logically requires.

La Dame aux Camélias also indicates fundamental problems in combining a well-made formula with a quasi-tragic outcome. The final act has none of the well-made structure, relying intrinsically on the pathos of Marguerite. An important secondary character, for example, decides to marry, but, instead of representing this change through dialogue, Dumas conveys the engagement through the subjectivity of Marguerite, who learns of it in a letter and then exclaims: "And so there is happiness for everyone in the world, it seems, except for me. But there! I am ungrateful." The outcome of Dumas's play is remarkable because it manages paradoxically both to reject and to affirm the conventional outcome of interpersonal union (a requirement of the well-made formula). Marguerite's newly married friends enter the space of her death scene. As she breaths her last, she cries: "I am dying, but I am happy too, and it is only my happiness that you can see . . . And so you are married!"

The structural inconsistencies of Dumas's play, the shift in emphasis from plot to character, and the dramatic power of the female protagonist, in particular, provide a useful context in which to understand two of James's novels of the 1880s. The ambition of a female protagonist to challenge constrictive forms is central to James's last novels before the theater years. And the duality of form and content is thematized, as the theater itself becomes a metaphor for form. In *The Bostonians* and *The Tragic Muse* liberation from the box has both aesthetic and ethical connotations. In each work a female performer is "boxed" or threatened with being boxed. James's women are amply realized as individuals, but they also signify the prevalent nineteenth-century view that women, unlike men, are essentially spiritual beings. These heroines represent the claims of the *élan vital* against the men and women who try to stifle them. Verena Tarrant, the beautiful orator for women's liberation, declaims: "We require simply freedom; we require the lid to be taken off the box in which we have been kept for centuries. You say it's a very comfortable, cozy, convenient box, with nice glass sides, so that we can see out, and that all that's wanted is to give another quiet turn to the key. That is very easily answered. Good gentlemen, you have never been in the box, and you haven't the least idea how it feels!" (232).

Verena insists that traditional social roles for women are like a stifling box, and her ability to perform her protest seems like a kind of liberation. But Basil Ransome, Verena's would-be lover, believes that it is her role as a public performer which is really boxing her. He is possessed by a passion to free her from that role and is determined to put an end to her public performances altogether: "He kept talking about the box; he seemed as if he wouldn't let go of that simile. He said that he had come to look at her through the glass sides, and if he wasn't afraid of hurting her he would smash them in. He was determined to find the key that would open it" (276). Ransome is, in fact, extremely excited by Verena's performance inside the box. So, though he does, figuratively, smash in the sides of this box, ironically, he does not liberate Verena. The final image of her being carried off into the night by Ransome is one of claustration: "beneath her hood, she was in tears."

The Bostonians privileges a melodramatic plot (the ingenue rescued by the hero from the witch) over the "gracefulness"[11] of its central character. If *The Bostonians* represents the frustration of freedom and the rigidity of form, however, *The Tragic Muse* is more satisfying as a bildungsroman.[12] In *The Tragic Muse* the heroine, Miriam Rooth, aspires to, and achieves, a great deal of personal freedom by cultivating her own talents within traditional forms of the theater. And yet in this novel, too, the theater is frequently and explicitly associated with a box. As in *The Bostonians,* the theatrical box is represented both as a site of liberation and as a space of claustration. For example, Gabriel Nash, the aesthete often taken to be the author's surrogate, discovers a little paneled box that has been converted into a "theatrical museum" in the apartment of the great actress Madame Carré. He gazes appreciatively at "the trophies and tributes and relics collected by Madame Carré during half a century of renown." And yet the museumlike quality of this theatrical box is also deeply disturbing to Nash, a connoisseur of the drama: "The profusion of this testimony was hardly more striking than the confession of something missed, something hushed, which seemed to rise from it all and make it melancholy" (91). The "something missed" is Madame Carré *in performance;* this theatrical box contains only relics of the past, not an embodied *presence.* But maintaining life, or presence, within the box, is a difficult trick, as Miriam Rooth, the aspirant to Madame Carré's place on the Parisian stage, discovers. Thus, Miriam lashes out at her admirer, Peter Sherringham, in the language of boxes: "You admire me as an artist and therefore you wish to put me into a box in which the artist will breathe her last," she exclaims. "You must let her live!" (542). Like Verena Tarrant, Miriam Rooth is placed in the deeply contradictory position of a modern women who seeks both freedom and form but is unable, fully, to have both. "I'm studying Juliet," says Miriam, "and I want awfully to do her, but really I'm mortally afraid lest, if I should succeed, I should find myself in such a box" (586).

The Tragic Muse (1890) was to be James's last novel for more than five years while he devoted himself to playwriting. But the rhetoric of form and freedom, the lively performer and the confining box, which is central to his last novels of the 1880s is developed in his dramas, his short stories, and his drama criticism of the next five years. In 1889, while still writing *The Tragic Muse,* James had taken advantage of a visit of the Théâtre Libre to London to meditate deeply on the problem of dramatic form. The meditation itself takes the "scenic" form of a short dialogue that clearly articulates two opposing theories of the theater. In "After the Play" four friends come home to tea, and the gathering leads to a heated discussion of the state of contemporary theater. Fresh from a matinee performance of *Duc d'Enghien,* the friends energetically debate the relation between life and form in the theater. Auberon, a rigid formalist, expresses a view much like that of the early James: "In life [things] happen clumsily, stupidly, meanly. One goes to the theatre just for the refreshment of seeing them happen in another way—in symmetrical, satisfactory form, with unmistakable effect and just at the right moment."[13] As Brenda Murphy remarks, it is tempting to see James in this role, but Auberon's position is eloquently contradicted by Dorriforth, clearly the more sophisticated playgoer (43). In fact, Dorriforth's opinions ultimately dominate the discussion. In the theater, he claims, "what we surrender ourselves to is the touch of nature, the sense of life."[14] Dorriforth favors the "delicacy of personal art" represented in great character acting, and, around this notion, he articulates a new definition of the "scenic," which requires not a "pictorial whole, [but] a dramatic one." Disparaging the "mechanical arts" of set design and stage carpentry for seeking to achieve physical effects at the expense of life and, specifically, of character, Dorriforth wants to "overlay the romantic with the literal," to juxtapose realistic setting and romantic imagination.

The juxtaposition of the romantic and the literal indicates a dramaturgical duality that has often been noticed in James as a peculiar tension. Peter Brooks, for example, has argued most eloquently that James's late novels in particular reveal an underlying melodramatic ambition. The confronted power of evil and goodness, the sense of hazard and clash, the intensification and heightening of experience corresponding to dream and desire, all, in Brooks's view, exert a melodramatic fullness of meaning against a fabric of otherwise unremarkable appearances in the late James: "This means in practice a pressure on the surface—the surface of social forms, manners; and the surface of literary forms, style—in order to make surface release the vision of the behind" (171). Brooks's essay is a compelling account of how James's work complicates the terms of melodrama, "their relation to individual character and their conflict, while at the same time preserving their underlying identity and nourishing the drama from their substratum." But the essay also privileges the French Romantic stage (conflating Scribe, Sardou, and Dumas) over other dramaturgies, assuming that James's notion of the dramatic, or scenic, derived almost entirely from that broadly defined theater. Moreover, the extrapolation of terms from the melodramatic stage to James's fiction necessarily omits significant dramaturgical features that Brooks emphasizes elsewhere, such as the highly gestural nature of melodramatic movement and the hyperbolic quality of melodramatic language. Consequently, the essay addresses, only tangentially, conflicts and contradictions in theater of the fin de siècle.

As the piece on the Théâtre Libre indicates, James was deeply interested in the avant-garde of dramatic realism. And, significantly, this interest was largely expressed in terms of the relation between form and character. In an appreciative article on Ibsen in 1891 James praises the Norwegian dramatist's "habit of dealing essentially with the individual caught in the fact." *Hedda Gabler,* for example, is distinguished by "the firm hand" with which Ibsen "weaves the web," but the play is equally successful because of the heroine herself: "She is various and sinuous and graceful, complicated and natural; she suffers, she struggles, she is human, and by that fact exposed to a dozen interpretations" (SA 252). *Hedda Gabler* represents a productive tension between character and plot, subject and structure. Ibsen's play realizes the central figure as an internally complex individual, but the masterful dramatic form also transforms an essentially private and inward experience into the appearance of an interpersonal action. And James specifically praises Ibsen's handling of the "ticklish" relation between life and form: "For those who care in general for the form that he has practiced he will always remain one of the talents that have understood it best and extracted most from it, have effected most neatly the ticklish transfusion of life" (SA 255).

Ibsen's work does consistently thematize a tension between life and form. But, most often (and this is certainly true in *Hedda Gabler*), the tension leads to death. Ibsen's life-loving characters die because social or artistic (or social and artistic) conventions are incompatible with personal freedom and a rich interior experience. Conventions prevent his characters from realizing their inmost selves, and the conflation of social form and aesthetic form is explicit from *Peer Gynt* to *When We Dead Awaken.* Peter Szondi trenchantly observes that this frustration is inevitable in attempting to represent a private, subjective experience through an interpersonal and thus "objective" form: "Because [Ibsen] tried to reveal this hidden life dramatically, to enact it through the dramatis personae themselves, he destroyed it. Ibsen's figures could survive only by burrowing into themselves and living off the 'life lie.' Because he did not enclose them in a novel, because he did not leave them within their life but instead forced them to publicly declare themselves, he killed them" (18). In Szondi's view it is Ibsen's mastery of dramatic construction which enables him to endow his material with the *appearance* of "presence and function," though, in fact, the subject of the plays is not the present but the past, and the "truth" Ibsen represents is that of interiority, not intersubjective or objective experience.

Brooks makes a similar argument regarding the strengths of James's fiction when he claims that James transmutes the melodrama of external action into an intensification of his characters' internal lives. "In later novels," writes Brooks, "the melodrama of external action will tend to be more and more superceded in favor of a stance, from the outset, within the melodrama of consciousness" (157). Unlike Szondi, however, Brooks is primarily interested in the capacity of the novel creatively to abstract aspects of dramatic form; the contingencies of contemporary theater, with their much heightened interest in the representation of character, are secondary. To enrich and complicate his argument, therefore, it is important to notice that for James the theater was necessarily a disconcertingly public venue. Representations of theater in James's novels, therefore, do not signify a convenient avoidance of the messiness of the public venue but, rather, suggest a deep questioning of the social experience of literature. As Dorriforth comments in "After the Play": "The theatre consists of two things, *que diable*—of the stage and the drama, and I don't see how you can have it unless you have both, or how you can have either unless you have the other. They are two blades of a pair of scissors" (237). James's notion of "literary form," which Brooks takes to be more or less the same, though increasingly nuanced, throughout his long career, is profoundly conditioned by the different demands of the public and the private. The modern drama's most significant contribution to the history of theater may be discovered in the wide range of innovation by dramatists who attempt to negotiate the competing demands of public and private experience. Ultimately, as we shall see, James's notion of form is most significant in its reconceptualization of the role of the audience.

THE DRAMAS OF THE 1890S

In the theater James's fundamental problem was to be that, unlike Dumas or Ibsen, he would be unable to combine effectively a private (inward) subject with a public (interpersonal) form. In the late 1880s James's work had already featured an increasing concern about both the vulnerability of private experience faced with the compelling power of public forms and the demands of public life. His novels of the late 1880s are almost symmetrically balanced by the demands of both the private and the public. For example, Nick Dormer, the politician-turned-artist in *The Tragic Muse* (1890), clearly expresses this duality when he says, "The difficulty is that I'm two men . . . I'm two quite distinct human beings, who have scarcely a point in common; not even the memory, on the part of one, of the achievements or the adventures of the other" (192). Significantly, between 1886 and 1892 theater assumes greater importance as an explicit trope in James's fiction than at any other time. And no single piece of fiction more clearly represents both James's thinking about the social experience of art, including the contrast between drama and the novel, than his deeply self-reflexive story "The Private Life" (1892).

Much of "The Private Life" is the story of a novelist, Clare Vawdrey, who wants to write for the theater. But in the view of the narrator, an author himself, Vawdrey is simply unsuited for the job. The famous actress who has begged Vawdrey to write for her, the narrator claims, "would never extract her modern comedy from the mature novelist [Vawdrey], who was as incapable of producing it as he was of threading a needle." Clare Vawdrey represents a peculiar duality. In all varieties of public appearance he is unexceptional, and yet his novels are brilliant. For some time Vawdrey has been at work on Mrs. Adney's play. One evening, while the actress and Vawdrey converse upon a balcony, the narrator goes to Vawdrey's room to obtain the manuscript for a promised reading. Peculiarly, however, he there stumbles on Vawdrey himself, sitting silently in the dark, writing at his desk. The next evening, with the actress, the narrator spills the extraordinary beans:

> "There are two of them."
>
> "What a delightful idea!"
>
> "One goes out, the other stays at home. One is the genius, the other's the bourgeois whom we personally know. He talks, he circulates, he's awfully popular, he flirts with you—." (210)

The actress develops "an insane desire to see the author." She has fallen in love with the elusive private man, oddly, it seems, because he is totally solipsistic. As an actress, Mrs. Adney reasons, she can express all the passion in a relationship; in fact, she *requires* that the passion be all on her side. Brilliant interpersonal relationships, in short, require a complementary arrangement between public and private, theatrical and intellectual. This same realization strikes the narrator near the end of the story, while waiting out a rainstorm with Vawdrey's public half: "The world was vulgar and stupid, and the real man would have been a fool to come out for it when he could gossip and dine by deputy."

The successful novelist is ultimately unable to produce the great dramatic work, despite being chosen personally by the actress. The logic that demands this anticlimax becomes evident in the story's symmetrical counterplot, the story of Lord Mellifont. Perfect in costume and manner on every occasion, Lord Mellifont is the consummate performer. Even in a concourse of two he behaves as if he is amusing an immense circle of spectators. Never surprised or taken unaware, "he was always as unperturbed as an actor with the right cue. He had never in his life needed the prompter—his very embarrassments had been rehearsed" (196). For Lord Mellifont to be perceived is to be. He is all form and no substance: "He was all public and had no corresponding private life, just as Clare Vawdrey was all private and had no corresponding public one" (212). The epitome of successful authorship, as Vawdrey's career attests, is the novel. The mixing of public and private concerns, the demand for a public form (a play) from a private man (Vawdrey, the novelist) leads inevitably to disappointment.

James's plays of the 1890s are deeply concerned with the dilemma of the individual who must choose either to act according to forms imposed from without or to abandon those forms completely in favor of his or her own personal development; there is rarely a middle ground. Hence, the most remarkable feature of James's plays is the theme of disengagement of the individual subject from the formal demands of his or her milieu. Constrained by the good manners of polite society, the burden of family tradition, or the requirements of the marriage plot, James's protagonists consistently, and insistently, seek to extricate themselves from the demands of their particular dramas. Like Verena Tarrant and Miriam Rooth, Henry James's dramas contradict the complacent notion that a vibrant and dramatic subject may be neatly packed into "a very comfortable, cozy, convenient box." But, also like Nick Dormer and Clare Vawdrey, James's plays are at odds with a life they seem to yearn for, a life of material success and public acclaim.

The aesthetic problem that James tried to address in the 1890s is visible in his earliest dramatic writing. *Still Waters* (1871), one of James's first dramas, is a one-act play that thematizes its characters' failure to communicate and, ultimately, the failure of love to be realized as an interpersonal union. In *Still Waters* monologue follows monologue, as each character reveals a frustrating incapacity for action. Each monologue fails to bring inward experience into a space of objective relations. Horace, a hero who anticipates Guy

Domville, is unable either to speak to the woman he loves or, for a time, to assist her in obtaining the object of her own desire, the happy but stupid Felix. Horace appears absolutely paralyzed: "If only I could speak to her—or speak for her! Now that her heart is wounded and tender, might I say a word for myself? It's hard lines to be able neither to console her nor to help her,—to see it and be powerless."

Ultimately, the only action—or, more precisely, the only movement—in the drama is the act of departure. One character must leave the space of the play so that, theoretically, the cycle of frustration may be converted into a consummation between two. *Still Waters,* as the title suggests, is fundamentally at variance not only with material civilization but with many of the social forms employed for basic human interaction:

> *Emma:* I don't play, I don't sing, I could have offered you no music. Besides it's Sunday. I don't mind croquet, but if people had heard our balls—
> *Felix:* We should have been lost! I would gladly have shared perdition with you. But in fact, my dear young lady, you were shooting quite beyond the mark. Croquet and music and a formal walk! I can be happy with less machinery. Your mere presence—

The clacking of croquet balls, with implications of material form and active sexuality, is rejected in favor of "mere presence." So, the play seems to privilege a kind of passive being at the expense of meaningful interaction in the sphere of the "in between." And yet the play represents an important contradiction. For the characters do not entirely reject the formal requirements of courtship; they reject certain forms, while, unwittingly, they are constrained by others. It is this unconsciousness of form which is essentially comic.

Despite their desire just to be, the inaction of all three characters is the result of an absentminded acceptance of highly rigid and restrictive social forms. Paradoxically, despite Felix's happy dismissal of games, the imperative of form is asserted again and again as, in fact, the very source of the lovers' frustrations. In short, dramatic form is figured as social form, which, in turn, is so overdetermined that it prohibits rather than engenders action. For example, Emma is prohibited by social forms from broaching the topic of her love to the object of it, Felix. She has, she tells Felix, "a passion for dignity" (an assertion that later also characterizes the comically rigid Mrs. Newsome in *The Ambassadors*). And Horace is scarcely allowed, by standards of propriety, to compliment the pretty Emma on her good looks without engendering mass confusion. In this play form is like a ready-made frame.

The remarkable notion that form is both a hindrance and a necessity, vital and ineffectual, assumes greater clarity when placed in the context of the important trope of packing. In this early play the only action that characters *have to do* is to prepare for departure, to pack their bags. Significantly, however, packing does not mean that departure will necessarily occur. Felix is the first to decide to leave. But, just at the moment that he decides to pack his bags, he notices Emma's beauty; thus, paradoxically, the machinery that will keep him from leaving is set in motion just as he prepares to pack:

> *Felix:* (*Looking at her while he hesitates.*) Her eyes are not light blue either—they are dark blue.—If you like, I'll bring down my valise and my duds and pack them up here. Pack them up I must!
> *Emma:* (*Turning away a moment, to herself.*) Does he wish to force me to ask him to stay? Is there, in men, such a thing as coquetry? . . . You insist on my formally inviting you. It's simpler to do while you're in sight and in mind; simpler, too, for you to stay than to go and come again.
> *Felix:* You have really a genius for simplification.

When the idea of packing is introduced, the conversation turns directly to a discussion of both form and simplification. And yet central to the play is the idea that human relations are not simple and that form is inadequate to convey real feeling. Thus, Felix's insistence on packing seems contrived, especially because he does not leave. In fact, Felix's packing becomes an explicit theme of absurdity. "You'll see what I *can* do!" he ends up declaring to Horace. "I've packed up my valise, but I shan't go."

The ridiculousness of packing when there is love to be made is, finally, suggested self-consciously by the characters themselves. Emma literally does not know if Felix is coming or going:

> *Emma:* (*Aside.*) What has happened?—Your valise . . . is standing packed at your door.
> *Felix:* (*Aside.*) I can't say I love her outright *à propos* of a valise. Dear young lady, I have been rending my heart.

Ultimately, it is the loverless Horace who is forced to act (he must depart) because his love is *un*requited: "I can't stand this. I shall pack up *my* valise." Horace's departure is the most important action of the play. He must renounce the world of love. Horace prizes his own subjectivity over the world of social forms, and, in his departure, he becomes the prototype of the Jamesian dramatic hero. His last words, "Farewell. Be happy—be very happy," are, as Leon Edel remarks, deeply similar to Guy Domville's last words, thirty years later: "Be kind to him. Be good to her. Be good to her" (CPJ 87).

Disengagement, the defining feature of James's dramatic oeuvre, is most explicitly realized in a Restoration-style comedy, *Disengaged* (1892–95), written during the heat of the author's theatrical tribulation. The fundamental action of this comedy is to disengage a poorly suited couple who have been trapped insidiously by social forms. This premise, which strikingly inverts the ordinary courtship-marriage plot, provokes a profound sense of the discrepancy between dramatic form and content. And, indeed, though James first described the drama as a "*comedy,* pure and simple," he admitted in a letter to Augustin Daly, who intended to produce the play in London but never did, "Its fault probably is fundamental and consists in the slenderness of the main motive—which I have tried to prop up with details that don't really support it."[15]

The first act introduces two strangely related tropes, photography and ruins, which appear simultaneously when Lady Brisket and Percy Trafford enter from nearby ruins with a conspicuously unwieldy camera. Photography and ruins both have a profound connection to sexual relations in this play, and this connection is made explicit even before the camera-laden, and putatively adulterous, characters enter. Sir Montagu Brisket and his sister Mrs. Wigmore consider a walk to the ruins themselves and then discuss the other couple's approach:

Sir Montagu: Well, then, come to the ruins.
Mrs. Wigmore: You needn't take me—the ruins are here.
Sir Montagu: (*Blank.*) Here?
Mrs. Wigmore: The ruins of your domestic security!

(*Enter from the left, from the ruins,* Lady Brisket *and* Percy Trafford, *he carrying a photographic camera and certain accessories, with which he is considerably encumbered and embarrassed, while she, very pretty and elegant, in light gloves, with her laced-fringed parasol up, nurses in its case a prepared plate, ready to be inserted into the instrument.*)

In relation to the workings of a machine (the camera) or the workings of history (embodied in the ruins), the human subject is not an agent but is merely passive. The characters are circumstantially contingent to a history that is completed or to a mechanical operation that requires only the impulse of setting the machine in motion. As Walter Benn Michaels suggests, "The action of making the picture is . . . not so much an action as an event, and the picture itself is best understood as the outcome of a series of mechanical interactions between the camera and nature" (218).[16]

Photography is the tool of the reductive and greedy intellect of Mrs. Wigmore, whose primary mission is to marry off her aptly named daughter, Blandina. A photograph serves to trap the "innocent" Captain Prime, who agrees, in an ill-conceived moment, to pose with Blandina for a photo.

Blandina: (*Smiling seductively.*) Captain Prime!
Prime: (*His face to the stone bench, with his newspaper, without turning round.*) Miss Wigmore?
Blandina: Have you ever been taken?
Prime: Taken? I've been pursued, but I've never been captured.
Trafford: (*Busy with the apparatus.*) Oh, we'll capture you now—I warn you we never miss! Miss Wigmore, keep extraordinarily still.
Blandina: (*Agitating herself.*) Then Captain Prime must keep still too!

Ultimately, Prime is forced physically into position. He and Blandina are molded like clay figures and then told to "keep perfectly still." The photograph manages to combine a notion of being "taken" sexually with that of being captured like a prisoner. A photograph of the two young people, "side by side," everyone agrees, will compel Prime to propose. The photograph thus simplifies a relationship to the point of falsifying it, depriving Prime of the freedom to choose, pursue, and win a bride. Prime himself acts with the kind of absentmindedness which Bergson describes as the target of laughter.

In the bondage of his unhappy engagement Prime becomes an utterly passive hero; he is defined not by an action (movement toward a goal) but by an event that has been concluded. Significantly, therefore, Mrs. Wigmore instructs Blandina that, as soon as the picture is taken, she is to lead Captain Prime to the ruins:

Mrs. Wigmore: You'll go to the ruins afterwards.
Blandina: Yes, mamma.
Mrs. Wigmore: Visit them thoroughly. Do you remember their history?
Blandina: No, mamma.
Mrs. Wigmore: One of the most celebrated sanctuaries of the Middle Ages; begun in the eleventh century, terminated in the fourteenth.
Blandina: Yes, mamma.
Mrs. Wigmore: Injured by fire under Henry the Seventh; despoiled of its treasures under Henry the Eighth.
Blandina: Yes, mamma.

Characters meet in dead space, alienated from one another, and their ostensible *presence* is entirely conditioned by the past and by death. In James's novels and stories the theme of historical decay represents features of a character's interior life (such as Isabel Archer's realization of her marital mistake as she sits among the ruins in Rome), but in the drama the subject of the past only mitigates against the potential for dramatic action, frustrating presence, which is the necessary condition of theater.

Ultimately, Prime's ability to marry as he chooses depends on a freedom that is represented by another character. Mrs. Jasper, for whom the play was earlier named, represents the foil for Prime's bondage and ultimately the vehicle of his redemption. While he is captured, she is free. "She's so enviable, in her freedom," Prime says of her. As in *Still Waters,* however, this play adopts deeply contradictory attitudes toward form. While *Disengaged* struggles to reassert the marriage plot of a well-made comedy, individual characters assert their desire for the kind of freedom which only comes with social disengagement. The form-freedom duality pervades the language of the play. On the one hand, Mrs. Jasper avoids being boxed in by other people. In her own estimation the one accomplishment she lacks is "the art of passing unperceived." She refuses to be photographed, just as she resists Sir Montagu's "propensity to draw me into corners."[17]

Yet, while it is invidious to be boxed in by someone else (to be "taken"), freedom assumes empirically the same form as captivity. The distinction between the freedom of life and the rigidity of form, which the play insists on thematically, collapses upon itself. Mrs. Jasper employs the same idiom to describe her ideal of personal freedom as she does to disparage unpleasantly constrictive relations. In act 2 she and Prime recognize their mutual attraction, and they describe freedom as a deep burrowing into self, which is only qualified by the notion that subjectivity can be expanded to accommodate two:

> *Mrs. Jasper:* (*Reflecting.*) Well, we must find something. Something very safe.
> *Prime:* There can be nothing so safe as a quiet corner and a box of water-colors.
> *Mrs. Jasper:* (*Thoughtful.*) Yes, they're a kind of burrow.
> *Prime:* A burrow is what I require.
> *Mrs. Jasper:* I see. (*Then after an instant.*) You must come down into mine!
> *Prime:* (*Earnest.*) Is there room in it for two?
> *Mrs. Jasper:* (*Smiling.*) With mutual accommodation! I'll give you lessons.

The impulse of the play is not toward the theatricality of disclosure but toward the antitheatricality of enclosure. And yet, unlike other dramas of the modern period for which claustration produces a generative tension and, indeed, in Ibsen and especially in Strindberg, genuine torment, *Disengaged* does not cultivate the tension.[18] Prime does not actively struggle; he is passive. He distinguishes himself from the "men of the world" who trapped him (Trafford and Coverly), being essentially, like Mrs. Jasper and the other feminine characters, a creature of the private sphere. His military costume is misleading, for it represents only form and does not indicate his "true" self. Prime needs Mrs. Jasper to "restore [him] to life"; he wants her to "lead [him] to a different altar, insisting, in what seems an unconscious contradiction, "I had to consent [to the marriage], but I also had to fly." No space of engagement (with all of its meanings) is established until the conclusion of the play, where it simply seems contrived. When Prime declares, "I must live in the moment," apparently asserting a desire for the active and the interpersonal," he immediately contradicts himself: "To be among your books, your sketches, your flowers—gives me a sense of strength." His comfort is only fortified by the world of objects. Prime seeks the security of a ready-made frame. He does not animate the world of objects but is shaped by them. Aestheticism, as so often in James's novels, represents a refusal of active engagement with other living beings.[19]

All of James's plays of the 1890s represent a struggle to accommodate dualities of performer and spectator, private and public, personal freedom and dramatic convention. In a lugubrious prefatory note to *Theatricals: Second Series* (1895), a publication of two relatively short plays, James articulates his two views of dramatic form. On the one hand, he stresses "cultivation" and "organic" form, noting that these plays represent an "anxious cultivation of limits," striving for a "brevity [that] is intelligible only when organic" (CPJ 347). But, on the other hand, form and content are understood to be essentially separate. The cultivation of limits may be damaging if transported "too much to the plane of subject." Unfortunately, James laments, "the hard meagerness of theatrical form [is] committed to think after all so much more of the clock than of the subject." An overly elaborate form may be damaging to the various and shifting subject that it contains. The drama must aim for small units of intelligibility. The solution to the demands of the theater, therefore, the need to cram his subject into the three hours between the evening trains, "seems to lie in the region of small receptacles" (350).

The Reprobate, the second of the two small receptacles in *Theatricals: Second Series,* outrageously thematizes the duality of freedom and form. The explicitness of this duality is largely due to the play's obvious genre limitations. The first half of the play is little more than farce in the spirit of Labiche, though the second half of the play represents the by now familiar assertion of the central character's subjectivity. Farce, derived from the Latin *farcire,* "to stuff," epitomizes Bergson's theory of comedy, the illusion of life bursting out of the rigidity of form. And *The Reprobate* is filled with Bergson's language of confinement and explosion. The action focuses on the bizarrely overexecuted repression of the thirty-year-old Paul Doubleday by the two guardians appointed by his late father's will, his stepmother, Mrs. Doubleday, and the family friend Mr. Bonsor. At the age of twenty Paul allegedly gave rein to the most vicious passions, traveling to Paris with a music hall comedienne (Nina Freshville, the epitome of freshness), an episode that has convinced his guardians, who in turn have managed to convince him, that he is utterly unable to control himself. As a result, Paul is literally kept under lock and key, deprived of money, cigars, women, books (especially one called *The Experience of Life*). His captors maintain their rigid system based upon the propriety of sacrifice. "You know our system," says Mr. Bonsor. "The more sacrifices you make, the easier it is to make 'em." Paul docilely agrees to regulate himself accordingly. "We've reduced it to a science," says Mrs. Doubleday. "We organize his hours; we regulate his thoughts; we control his imagination."

Set against the rhetoric of scientific control are metaphors of explosion. The puritanical Mrs. Doubleday's lover, Mr. Chanter, expresses a "passion, with all the ardour of a sentiment long repressed, bursting forth in a flood!" Paul's youthful indiscretions are explained as the result of inclinations that "burst forth" after being repressed until his twentieth year. Often the stage directions specify that Paul's speech is "explosive." Late in the play Mr. Bonsor reports that he has heard that Paul is "extinct," to which Paul replies: "Does he take me . . . for a volcano? In [that] case I'm in lively eruption!" The danger of Paul's "eruption" is exactly what characters in the first half of the play are working to prevent. Indeed, in the first act Paul himself is dreadfully afraid that he may unexpectedly erupt. On his first meeting with the desirable Blanche Amber, Mr. Bonsor's niece, Paul expresses "a visible mixture of impetuosity and caution, which gives him an odd air."

> *Paul:* . . . You're free—because you're good!
> *Blanche:* It's better to have passions and control them.
> *Paul:* That's just what I didn't do—when I came down here!
> *Blanche:* (*After an instant.*) Was it a passion that brought you?
> *Paul:* I don't know what to call it, Miss Amber. It was an emotion not to be controlled! See, I'm getting worse!

Blanche finds Paul interesting, however, because of his wild past. And she becomes immensely excited by rumors that the notorious Nina Freshville, the music hall comedienne, has returned to excite him. Such encounters, she exclaims, "make you feel you live!" Paul, on the other hand, indoctrinated in the most rigid form of social discipline, complains, "Yes, but in the tomb of my reputation."

Although the box metaphor recurs throughout the play, Paul is not simply the mechanical jack-in-the-box that his explosiveness implies. He is also a human being capable of living both freely and in conformity with social mores. Paul is neither as dangerous as he fears nor as expressionless as he desires. Thus, Blanche can say, perhaps expressing the hopes of the playwright, that the struggle to moderate his passions "makes your problem wonderfully interesting—your situation intensely dramatic." When Paul asks Blanche if she wants to keep him as a trophy, she replies: "Stuffed—in a glass case? No, I want you living; I want you fluttering." And that wish is eventually fulfilled. The drama of Paul's character is represented in a profound change midway through the play, when he recognizes that he will not simply explode when presented with the materials of vice. If, in the first half of the play, his character threatens an explosion from rigidity, in the second half he represents a healthier, "organic" tension. The climax of the play is a moment of self-revelation in act 2, when Paul is left alone with all of the objects that are supposed to be capable of setting him off: "I'm face to face with everything that, for years, I've been taught to dread—*have* dreaded. Tobacco, cards, wine, (*then taking up the French novel*) women! Here they are—all in a row! (*Looking round him.*) The real thing—and I'm alone with them! I'm therefore free, ain't I? free as I haven't been since—Ah, when *was* it? . . . It may be a trap of my funny fate. But if it's a trap, I ain't caught! I am resisting; I *have* resisted. (*Following up his induction.*) I ain't so bad, then, now; I must be getting better!" The rest of the play is filled not only with the language of Paul's liberation (He is "drunk" with the "sense of freedom") but also with a new language of captivity. He is, after all, not completely liberated; now he feels "bound" to Blanche. When Nina Freshville tries to seduce him to fly with her back to France he resists:

> *Mrs. Freshville:* You shrink—you desire some regular form?
> *Paul:* I've been taught in all these years that some regular form is proper.

Ultimately, we see, in Bergson's terms, drama replacing comedy. If the first act represents Paul as a virtually mindless dupe, absentmindedly submitting to a rigid confinement, the play shifts its emphasis, midway through the second act, to focus on the development of Paul's character and his dawning self-awareness and, in James's terms, cultivation of limits. By the end of the play Paul claims to have come of age, in a legal sense, to have grown into his maturity (his inheritance was to be withheld, ridiculously, until he was forty). "I've grown," he says. "Ten years in an hour!" Paul is the rare Jamesian hero who is completely and happily engaged at the play's end. He allows himself to be "taken" in the same sense that Captain Prime had been (photographically and, almost, nuptually) in *Disengaged,* but here the form is neither confining nor insidious. In fact, freedom comes through form. Blanche meets Paul in the final tableau "in happy freedom while he takes both her hands and respectfully kisses them."

Leo Levy has called *The Reprobate* "the most successful of James's plays," "a philosophical comedy, touching upon the true conditions of moral freedom in its insistence that the escape from evil is through the autonomous discoveries of the self" (85, 86). Levy overstates the obviousness of moral experience in the play (good triumphing over evil) in order to further his project of defining all of James's dramas as "versions of melodrama."[20] But his most problematic claim is that the value of *The Reprobate* resides in the "authority of Paul's release." For it is the very completeness and suddenness of Paul's transformation, or "release," that will most tax any audience's imagination. The fatal flaw of *The Reprobate* is the sudden shifting of gears as Paul comes into a sense of himself. After years of confinement he does not exactly erupt; he suddenly and inexplicably mutates. To grow ten years in a single hour is a radical and incredible example of *bildung.* The shift from farce to drama, which can be explained neither by reference to plot nor by intrinsic qualities of character, indicates the play's deep structural instability. And the play's structural flaws were especially evident in production. After seeing *The Reprobate* in 1919, Arnold Bennett tellingly dismissed James's well-known pretensions to mastery of dramatic form: "James asserts several times that he had mastered the whole technique of the drama. He never had. Not long since I saw *The Reprobate.* It contained some agreeable bits; but the spectacle it provided of an unusually able and gifted man trying to do something for which his talents were utterly unfitted was painful; it was humiliating. Half the time the author obviously had not the least idea what he was about."[21] In *The Reprobate* we see in Paul Doubleday the two radically incongruous men that his name suggests. Like Nick Dormer and Claire Vawdrey, Paul is "two quite distinct human beings."

The Jamesian dramatic hero cannot decide whether to be active or passive, whether to privilege his own subjectivity or the objective (from the character's perspective) workings of the plot. And this confusion, manifested in the theme of disengagement and the bizarre inversion of, or struggle against, the traditional marriage plot, may be said to climax on 5 January 1895, with the opening of *Guy Domville* at the Saint James Theatre. This play represents the culmination of James's theatrical career not only because he experienced a personal trauma on the stage but also because *Guy Domville* begins with what may have been the best act James ever wrote, exciting expectations in the audience which it egregiously frustrates.[22] The first act of the play takes place in the garden of an English country house in the 1780s, where Guy is in the process of disengaging himself as tutor for the son of a lovely widow, Mrs. Peverel. He is preparing to retreat from the world entirely and to assume Holy Orders. The beautifully written first act, well acted by George Alexander and Marion Terry on the opening night, created a delicate romantic mood. Soon, however, Lord Devenish, the wicked nobleman and emissary for Guy's cousin's wife, arrives to inform Guy that his cousin has been killed in a hunting accident, that he is now the last of the distinguished family line and heir to its wealth, and that his duty is to give up the church and to marry. Despite the fine acting and excellent dialogue, in this ending of the first act are the telltale signs of James's dramatic schizophrenia. Like Paul Doubleday, Guy changes abruptly and totally:

> *Guy:* . . . (*With a complete transformation and a passionate flourish.*) Long, long live the Domvilles!—Away, away for London! (*Exit the house.*)
> *Mrs. Peverel:* (*Surrendering herself to her joy.*) He's free—he's free!

Of course, Guy is not free, not only because he is now assuming familial and social duties but also because he is no longer true to himself. And it is precisely this confusion of freedom and form which leads the play to break down in the second act.

The second act takes place in Mrs. Domville's villa at Richmond. The play no longer features the highly crafted dialogue and subtly developed characters of the first act but, rather, the thick plot of melodrama and a hero who has been transformed from scholar to dandy. As Leon Edel remarks: "In forsaking the simplicity of his first act Henry James had yielded to the clap-trap of artificial drama, to the *ficelle* structure of Sardou and the other dramatists he had studied with such assiduity at the Théâtre Français . . . The mood created by the first act had been utterly destroyed" (1990, 473). The audience in the pit began to fidget, the actors to lose their cool. Writing for the magazine *Woman,* Arnold Bennett summarizes the second act in his review of the opening night, aptly capturing the exasperation of a spectator whose expectations have been undermined:

> The second act is tedious. We meet Guy gaily dressed, in the full enjoyment of life and betrothed to Mary Brasier . . . But Mary is in love with a young naval lieutenant, George Round . . . and when through plot and counterplot, and after much mock drunkenness between himself and Round, Guy gets to know of this, he assists the pair to make an entirely preposterous and impossible elopement, and sets off to return to Porches [Mrs. Peverel's home] with a heart full of hatred for Lord Devenish and his scheming paramour Mrs. Domville.[23]

As Bennett's disillusionment indicates, the play is couched in two contrasting dramaturgies. It begins and ends as a realist drama (Guy does, ultimately, become a priest). And the primary focus of the realist drama is, of course, the character of Guy Domville, the drama of how to win a subjective freedom when faced with demands imposed from without. The middle of the play, however, is dominated by melodramatic types, such as the evil lord, and the juggling of the highly intricate plot of a well-made play, including an elaborate drinking scene lifted from Emile Augier's *L'aventurière*.[24] Both the hero and the play are schizophrenic, and it is Guy's vacillation (not simply indecision but the assumption of radically contradictory roles) which provided the rowdies with fodder for their fire, whatever their various motivations for abusing the sensitive author.[25] Notoriously, when Alexander emotionally delivered his final speech, "I'm the last, my lord, of the Domvilles," a shout came up from the pit: "It's a bloody good thing y'are."

Fifteen years later James wrote to H. M. Walbrook, then drama critic of the *Pall Mall Gazette,* of reviving the play. Guy Domville's weakness, writes James, was "that he was the victim of my ideal of a certain supreme technical perfection—whereby I made a unity, for unity's sake, of what should have been two sequent steps in the drama, and so compressed my matter into an economy too drastic and of which no single sapient creature understood the beautiful, the compositional intention and interest" (CPJ 835). The subject-object opposition thematized in Guy's rejection of his public responsibilities had been brought home to the author most powerfully after the final curtain, as James stood trembling before the "yelling barbarians." His late comment to Walbrook is significant not only because it is a modest critique of his own previous ideal of formal perfection but also, and more important, because in the subtle phrasing of the second clause James implies the harm of excluding the audience from his tightly packed box. In this late comment on the play James involves the fourth wall in the compositional process. Instead of disdain for the roughs, the comment manifests a sensitivity to the spectators for whom the drama must compose an interest. In the place of the "cosy, childlike, naif, domestic British imagination," the "sapient creatures," whose understanding must be cultivated, represent the crucial move from the technical to the organic.

REIMAGINING THE AUDIENCE

James was deeply self-conscious about the basic problems in his dramas, and the stories he wrote in the early 1890s elucidate his recognition that total disengagement from social form or from dramatic form was not only unsatisfying but also ethically irresponsible. "Nona Vincent" (1892) explicitly represents this unsatisfactory detachment of a formalistic artist from the subject of his drama. In hindsight, however, the story also represents a revelation with great significance for James's later work. In the first half of this gently ironic and mildly self-mocking story an ambitious, young playwright, Allan Wayworth, spends his evenings with the "charming" and "beguiling" Mrs. Alsager, discussing his literary aspirations and disappointments. Wayworth is a formalist with a rigid conception of the scenic art. He is proud enough to imagine that he has achieved "some sort of mastery of the scenic idea."

> The scenic idea was magnificent once you embraced it—the dramatic form had a purity which made some others look ingloriously rough. It had the high dignity of the exact sciences, it was mathematical and architectural. It was full of the refreshment of calculation and construction, the incorruptibility of line and law . . . The more he tried the dramatic form the more he loved it, the more he looked at it the more he perceived in it. What he perceived in it indeed he now perceived everywhere; if he stopped, in the London dusk, before some flaring shop-window, the place immediately constituted itself behind the footlights, became a framed stage for his figures. He hammered at these figures in his lonely lodging, he shaped them and he shaped their tabernacle; he was like a goldsmith chiselling a casket, bent over with the passion for perfection. (5)

To Wayworth the actual acting of the play he has written is a secondary concern, but Mrs. Alsager insists that it must be produced. And she proves to be Wayworth's "good genius" in two ways. First, she is the inspiration for his conception of the heroine, Nona Vincent, and, second, she actively finds a theater that will stage the play.

The central problem of the story is represented through the performance itself. It is a familiar topic in James: a capable young actress struggling against a dramatist's rigid conception of form. Moreover, this problem is again framed in terms of the conflict between public demands and private fulfillment. Violet Grey, a "crude" yet "graceful" young actress, not unlike Verena Tarrant, does not immediately fulfill Wayworth's conception. And his tireless coaching does not make her a better actress, though she does fall in love with him. When Mrs. Alsager, who is deeply interested in the girl's "character, her private situation," points this out, however, she is rebuffed because Wayworth hates "talking about the passions he might have inspired." But, without realizing it, Wayworth is also falling in love with Violet, and this development leads to a profound conflict:

> [Violet] pleased him as a charming creature—by her sincerities and perversities, by her varieties and surprises of her character and by certain happy facts of her person. In private her eyes were sad to him and her voice was rare. He detested the idea that she would have a disappointment or an humiliation, and he wanted to rescue her altogether, to save and transplant her. One way to save her was to see to it, to the best of his ability, that the production of his play should be a triumph; and the other way—it was really too queer to express—was almost to wish that it shouldn't be. (19)

The opening performance is, indeed, a disappointment for the actress, who does not comprehend the role taught to her by the rigidly formalistic Wayworth. But then a miraculous event occurs. Both the actress and the author receive separate visitations that reveal the living spirit of the play. Wayworth, at home, having collapsed in his chair from exhaustion, is visited, an hour after dusk, by the spirit of Nona Vincent herself, the "living heroine of his play": "She was more familiar to him than the women he had known best, and she was ineffably beautiful and consoling. She filled the poor room with her presence, the effect of which was as soothing as some odour of incense . . . Nothing more real had ever befallen him . . . When she bent her deep eyes upon him they seemed to speak of safety and freedom and to make a green garden of the future. From time to time she smiled and said: 'I live—I live—I live' " (27). The next evening, as he watches the play, Wayworth discovers that Violet too has a totally new and accurate conception of the role. When he approaches her after the performance, bursting with congratulations, she tells him that she has had a revelation. She had been visited at the same hour as he, not by a ghost it seems but by Mrs. Alsager. Without trying to coach, the beautiful lady gave her a true sense of the role—"By letting me look at her. By letting me hear her speak. By letting me know her." The result of this theatrical success is a personal success, the marriage of author and actress, which also entails Violet's retirement from the stage.

If we take "Nona Vincent" to be, in part, an allegory of James's own relation to the dramatic subject, Allan Wayworth's revelation is significant. The climax and peripeteia of the story occurs not on the stage but in Wayworth's room, which Nona Vincent fills "with her presence." In the playwright's experience "nothing more real had ever befallen him." In this scene the subject-object opposition is obviated. The spectator and performer are no longer in a chiasmic relation, alienated across the footlights, but in an intimate space of "safety and freedom." It is no longer the subject that is isolated and packed into the box; rather, spectator and performer are in the same box together.

The notion of a box that encompasses spectators and performers alike also had been foreshadowed in *The Tragic Muse,* by Miriam Rooth, though in this earlier novel the metaphor expresses her disillusionment. Miriam explicitly conflates the popular stage, which she understands as a kind of box, with the boxes from which the spectators, including her lover, Peter Sherringham, sit and watch her: "If you should see some of the creatures who have the face to plant themselves there in the stalls, before one, for three mortal hours! I dare say it would be simpler to have no bodies, but we're all in the same box, and it would be a great injustice to the idea, and we're all showing ourselves all the while; only some of us are not worth paying" (553). Both *The Tragic Muse* and "Nona Vincent" anticipate a dramatic reconceptualization of the space of action in James's later fiction and drama. Miriam's cynical comment, for example, anticipates Lambert Strether's realization, early in *The Ambassadors,* that "the figures and faces in the stalls were interchangeable with those on stage" (92).

In James's later work the space of action is no longer the stage itself but the space of the spectator. In the absence of the audience the basic elements of theatrical production are strictly mechanical. The same text is played every night by the same actors on the same set beneath the same lights. Each night, however, brings a different audience, and it is in the relation *between* actors and audience, with each performance, that newness is realized. Hans-Georg Gadamer has discussed this relationship between actors and audience as the defining structural characteristic of any experience of art. Gadamer's notion of structure [*Gebilde*] is not mechanical, but, like the notion of structure implied by Bergson's "drama," this kind of structure achieves its full being only each time it is played. "Drama is a kind of playing that, by its nature, calls for an audience," Gadamer remarks. "Thus it is not really the absence of a fourth wall that turns the play into a show. Rather, openness toward the spectator is part of the closedness of the play. The audience only completes what the play as such is. This point shows the importance of defining play as a process that takes place 'in between' " (109). James's recognition of the importance of the audience is the crucial factor in his reimagining of the "scenic" art and "organic" form. Generally, in work after 1895 he imagines the stage not as a box gazed upon from without but, rather, as a space of inclusion in which the spectator too participates. Hence, James's novels of the 1890s are filled with references to an imagined, extradiegetic audience, as in "the acute observer we are constantly taking for granted" (*Awkward Age* 228).

Furthermore, in *The Art of the Novel* James defines his actors as spectators themselves. "The figures in any picture, the agents in any drama," he writes in his 1908 preface to *The Princess Casamassima,* "are interesting only in proportion as they feel their respective situations; since the consciousness, on their part, of the complication exhibited forms for us their link of connexion with it." In suggesting that the actor in the text is also a surrogate spectator for the reader, James implies that there is no longer an opposition between spectator and actor. Significantly, however, this subversion of the opposition means that it is not enough simply to watch; spectating must also entail a certain kind of involvement. Thus, James famously goes on, "there are degrees of feeling," and it is those who are "finely aware and richly responsible . . . who 'get most' out of all that happens to them and who in so doing enable us, as readers of their record, as *participators by fond attention,* also to get most" (62; my emph.). The spectator, like the actor, is a living being whose participation in the drama indicates an important responsibility. The role of the spectator in the performance implies a complex action of sympathy. In some of the most beautiful writing on James in recent years, Martha Nussbaum has strongly argued that "moral knowledge . . . is not simply intellectual grasp of propositions; it is not even simply intellectual grasp of particular facts; it is perception. It is seeing a complex, concrete reality in a highly lucid and richly responsive way; it is taking what is there, with imagination and feeling" (152). Nussbaum's thesis suggests a new notion of "objectivity" in interpersonal relations. The objectivity that she describes is " 'internal' and human. It does not even attempt to approach the world as it might be in itself, uninterpreted, unhumanized" (164).

None of James's novels more clearly represents the organic sense of spectatorship and, significantly, the relation of spectatorship to *bildung,* than *What Maisie Knew* (1897), published only two years after James's embarrassment on the London stage. Maisie's modus vivendi is the mode of spectatorship. "It was as if the whole performance had been given for her—a mite of a halfscared infant in a great dim theatre" (23). Maisie silently gazes upon but also literally grows up, and participates, in a world of conspicuously theatrical grown-ups. Her "little gravely-gazing soul" is like a "boundless receptacle" (27), while her parents act as loudly and predictably as the most melodramatic actors. Maisie, however, unlike spectators at conventional melodramas, is literally drawn into the action. One example among many of Maisie's explicitly theatrical acts of spectatorship occurs as she and her stepfather, Sir Claude, stroll in the park, only to see Maisie's mother strolling with another man: "What idea, as she now grandly came on, did mama fit? —unless that of an actress, in some tremendous situation, sweeping down to the footlights as if she would jump them. Maisie felt really so frightened that before she knew it she had passed her hand into Sir Claude's arm. Her pressure caused him to stop, and at the sight of this the other couple came equally to a stand and, beyond the diminished space, remained a moment more in talk" (121).

In this diminished space spectatorship constitutes for Maisie and, by extension, for the reader an important kind of action. James remarks in his preface to the novel that her "small expanding consciousness" provides the novel with an ironic center, which brings all of the other characters together. Maisie has "the wonderful importance of shedding a light far beyond any reach of her comprehension." Particularly important, James continues, is the ability of Maisie's "freshness" to transform appearances otherwise vulgar and empty: "[Appearances] become, as she deals with them, the stuff of poetry and tragedy and art" (11–12). Recalling the terms in which James lamented his theatrical failure in 1895, it is possible to recognize in Maisie precisely the "childlike, naif, domestic British imagination" (*Letters* 1:234) to which James had tried so desperately and unsuccessfully to appeal with *Guy Domville.*

What Maisie Knew imagines the spectator as an utterly innocent and inevitably expanding consciousness, but this representation is also limited by Maisie's lack of experience and her physical helplessness. The most brilliant example of the organic sense of the scenic in James is *The Ambassadors.* In James's favorite among his own novels the space of the spectator becomes the place of action. When Strether first sees Chad they are both literally in a theater box:

> The door of the box had opened, with the click of the *ouvreuse,* from the lobby, and a gentleman, a stranger to them, had come in with a quick step. The door closed behind him, and, though their faces showed him his mistake, his air, which was striking, was all good confidence. The curtain had just again arisen, and, in the hush of the general attention, Strether's challenge was tacit, as was also the greeting, with a quickly-deprecating hand and smile, of the unannounced visitor. He discreetly signed that he would wait, would stand, and these things and his face, one look from which she had caught, had suddenly worked on Miss Gostrey. She fitted to them all an answer to Strether's last question. The solid stranger was simply the answer—as she now, turning to her friend, indicated . . . They were in the presence of Chad himself. (152–53)

Nowhere is James more dramatic. Tension is achieved not on the stage but in the space of spectatorship. Strether's identification of Chad is "one of the sensations that count in life." And, unable to talk without disturbing the other spectators, he experiences "the life of high pressure . . . while he sat there, close to Chad, during the long tension of the act. He was in the presence of a fact that occupied his whole mind, that occupied for the half-hour his senses themselves all together" (153). As a purposeful spectator, Strether is most deeply engaged. But he also complicates the notion of being a participator by fond attention, for he is never fully absorbed, and, thus, he is never exactly a performer himself; he always retains an important detachment. Gadamer describes the special ability of the spectator both to participate and to remain independent of the action, when he writes, "The play itself is the whole, comprising players and spectators. In fact, it is experienced properly by . . . one who is not acting in the play but watching it. In him the game is raised, as it were, to its ideality" (109). Strether retains a detachment that is the most important qualification of the spectator's ethical importance in James's later work.

As the ideal spectator, Strether approaches experience with a radically open mind, often realized in "uncontrolled perceptions" that are characterized by "*fresh* backward, *fresh* forward, *fresh* lateral flights" (90; my emph.). Strether's openness to experience and freshness of perception are contrasted from the beginning with the rigidity of his employer. In *The Ambassadors* form is almost totally represented by the immensely dignified and rule-oriented Mrs. Newsome, Chad's mother. Significantly, in representing Mrs. Newsome's proscriptive nature, James returns to his metaphor of the tightly packed box: "She had, to her own mind, worked the whole thing out in advance, and worked it out for me as well as for herself. Whenever she has done that, you see, there's no room left; no margin, as it were, for any alteration. She's filled to the full, packed as tight, as she'll hold, and if you wish to get anything more or different either out or in—. . . You've got morally and intellectually to get rid of her" (447). Mrs. Newsome has the reductive vision of the melodramatist. Her son is intended to fit into the well-made play of which she is the author. As Nussbaum notes, Chad becomes in his mother's eyes "the youth" and Mme de Vionnet "the Person." The kind of well-made world which the lady from Woolett desires allows freedom neither to the performer nor to the spectator. Like Ibsen's Mrs. Alving or, for that matter, James's Mrs. Doubleday, Mrs. Newsome seeks unsuccessfully to restrain her child's desire for freedom (freedom realized in each case as life in Paris). But, also like those other mothers, Mrs. Newsome is constricted by her own sense of propriety. Significantly, it is Mrs. Newsome herself who is described as "tightly packed." Her most serious failing is that she refuses to participate by fond attention. She spectates only by deputy.

And yet Mrs. Newsome's deputizing of Strether returns us to the important notion that Strether's fond attention is qualified by the fact that he is not "related." Despite the freshness of his "uncontrolled perceptions," he is not by any means a totally liberated character. As the ideal spectator, he is included in the action, but also, as spectator, he can never experience action as deeply as the actor. As Nussbaum eloquently suggests, "The perceiver as perceiver cannot see it all; to get the whole he must at times stop being the sort of person who cares for wholeness." Strether cannot both immerse himself and retain his critical intelligence. This opposition between immersion and detachment represents a wonderful but also poignant transformation in James's later work of the earlier, more simplistic dichotomy of freedom and form. And, though brilliantly exampled in the late novels, this opposition, too, may be understood most clearly in James's writings about and for the theater.

In 1904 James returned to America after an absence of twenty years. In *The American Scene,* his account of that visit, theater is a crucial vehicle for expressing his relationship to his social and aesthetic surroundings. Visiting the Bowery Theatre to see a young actor in whom he has taken an interest, James is nearly overwhelmed by an "element of contrast with an image antediluvian, the memory of the conditions of a Bowery theatre, *the* Bowery Theatre in fact, contemporary with my more or less gaping youth" (194). Feeling beset on all sides by "Hebrew names" and "Hebrew faces," James makes his way to "a curtained corner of a private box." America has become stupid, smelly, noisy, and ethnic: "The old signs would have been those of some 'historic' community, so to speak, between the play and the public, between those opposed reciprocal quantities" (195). Although James's quiet reticence amid the confectionary-munching multitude is characteristic, more remarkable is his belief that the American theater was once characterized by a "community . . . between the play and the public." Thus, his retreat into the private box is a movement that dramatizes not just a fastidious revulsion from vulgarity and otherness but also disappointment with his own sense of detachment. This theater experience does not impel the sensitive spectator to participate, and the consequence is a striking example of nostalgia for an ideal of theater which the elderly James imagines to have existed in his "antediluvian" America.

When, at the age of seventy, however, with an introspective eye, James turns his attention more pointedly to the American theater of the 1850s, groping for his "earliest aesthetic seeds," he also attributes to his childhood self an important (though perhaps exaggerated) critical apparatus. In *A Small Boy and Others* (1913) he reflects on the complex excitements he experienced at Barnum's Museum in New York, where he watched an early production of *Uncle Tom's Cabin* in 1853. He recalls the richly populated theater, "the social scheme . . . in its careless charity, worthy of the golden age." The pleasant boyhood memories include the deep aromas of peppermint and orange-peel, the dim and crowded hall, the tensely anticipated rising of the curtain. There "flocked together the least of us and the greatest, with differences of appetite and of reach, doubtless, but not with differences of place and of proportionate share" (161). It is a nostalgic picture of what James perceives as a rare moment of social harmony in America. And yet James believes that, even as a boy, he had also a detached and more skeptical sense of his surroundings: "Uncanny though the remark perhaps, I am not sure that I wasn't . . . more interested in the pulse of our party, under my tiny recording thumb, than in the beat of the drama and the shock of its opposed forces." He attended the spectacle, he claims, in order *not* to be beguiled but to enjoy "with ironic detachment" both the play itself and, more important, the audience, himself included. In this comment are not the aesthetic seeds but the late reflections of an author with a deeply complex notion of the role of the spectator in the work of art: "I could know we had all intellectually condescended and that we had yet had the thrill of an aesthetic adventure; and this was a brave beginning for a consciousness that was to be nothing if not mixed and a curiosity that was to be nothing if not restless" (164).

James's late writings for the theater also manifest a fascinating tension between involvement and ironic detachment. Indeed, the prefaces of 1908 (collected in *The Art of the Novel*), which contain such rich critical discussions of organic form, are written during a period of intensely revived theatrical expectations. In 1907, thirteen years after his theatrical tribulation, James was again tempted by the professional stage. Of the half-dozen plays or sketches for plays which James wrote over the next two years, his one-act play *The Saloon,* a dramatic reworking of his 1892 story "Owen Wingrave," is most important for appreciating his changing conception of the drama. There are three fundamental reasons for the play's significance. First, Owen Wingrave is deeply similar to Guy Domville not only in terms of character traits but also in his basic dramatic problem—his antipathy to fulfilling his family obligations and his impulse to disengagement. Second, an interesting correspondence between James and Bernard Shaw centers on *The Saloon* and reveals crucial dramaturgical assumptions on the part of both authors. Third, *The Saloon* is James's only ghost play, an attempt to overlay the romantic with the literal in the strictest sense. And the relationship between the hero and the ghost, as James conceived it, has profound implications for the concept of audience.

The Saloon is the story of a young man who comes from a long line of military heroes. Owen Wingrave has been trained to be a soldier himself, and everyone expects him to fulfill his duty and to maintain the family honor. Owen, however, hates blood and violence and would rather read poetry. His view of honor, he insists, "is not to go in for the consecration of the brute but for the affirmation of the Man and the liberation of the Spirit." The ironic twist of the story is that Owen really is a soldier at heart. Ultimately, alone one night in the saloon, he defies the family ghost and dies a soldierly death while rejecting the military tradition. It is this fatal engagement with the ghost which makes Owen an important new type of hero.

The significance of Owen's death, however, is not immediately apparent, and Bernard Shaw, for one, was appalled by the ending. "In the name of human vitality," he writes, "WHERE is the charm in that useless, dispiriting, discouraging fatalism? . . . What is the use of writing plays?—what is the use of anything?—if there is not a Will that finally moulds chaos itself into a race of gods with heaven for its environment." The hero must be able to exorcize ghosts. "No man who doesn't believe in ghosts ever sees one. Families like these are smashed every day and their members delivered from bondage, not by heroic young men, but by one girl who goes out and earns her living or takes a degree somewhere." After the exchange of several wonderful letters, James fully addressed the crucial objection:

> I seem not to understand . . . what you mean by the greater representational interest of the "man's getting the better of the ghost" . . . There was only one question to me, that is, that of my hero's within my narrow compass, and on the lines of my very difficult scheme of compression and concentration, getting the *best of everything,* simply; which his death makes him do . . . by his creating for us, spectators and admirers, such an intensity of impression and emotion about him as must promote his romantic glory and edifying example for ever . . . Danger there must be therefore, and I had but one way to prove dramatically, strikingly, touchingly, that in the case before us there *had* been; which was to exhibit the peril incurred. It's exhibited by the young man's

> lying there gracefully dead—there could be absolutely no other exhibition of it scenically; and I emphasize "gracefully"!

James's letter indicates the workings of the organic form in this play. Owen must *free* the Spirits, including his own, by performing a dangerous act of spectatorship. He must, in a sense, invoke the Spirit of his family to appear before him, and his final act of watching is his most heroic. Significantly, this spirit is not intended to appear on stage. The action of the play must climax in the fundamentally dangerous, indeed fatal, act of spectatorship. Hence, James's dismay when, in Gertude Kingston's 1911 production in London, the ghost actually materialized on stage, "a pale, dimly-seen figure." The ghost's materiality immediately reduces, in Bergson's terms, the dramatic to the comic, drawing our attention from the spiritual to the physical. Instead, as James pointedly insists, the young man has to be consumed by the spectacle he provokes. The death consequent upon the intensity of his impression is exactly what renders the drama "graceful," but, significantly, death is also the end of the spectator. The heroic spectator cannot both be consumed and live. He cannot be fully absorbed in the spectacle and retain his critical detachment.

Shortly after the *Guy Domville* fiasco in 1895, William Archer had declared that, if James would "write solely for the ideal audience within his own breast, he will certainly produce works of art."[26] By writing for such an audience in his late fiction, James unquestionably produced works of art. And it is not only his novels that realize the complexities of audience and the importance of organic form. By positioning James in theater history, we can gain a new perspective on the importance of the audience during a crucial stage in the development of dramatic realism. James's own inconsistencies and contradictions indicate the difficult birth of the modern drama from the well-made play and the melodramatic theater. But, as Anne Margolis has commented, James already had excited much sympathy among the leading proponents of realism even after the opening night of *Guy Domville,* and their qualified defenses of both James and his play indicate their support for the theatrical avant-garde, "which considered James one of their own, whether rightly or wrongly."[27]

James himself, however, had a more complex and fluid understanding of the theater than he is generally allowed. Indeed, in his "Rough Statement for

The Chaperone" (1907) he seems to mock his own earnestness and simplicity of thirteen years earlier. The most completely imagined scene in this rough sketch involves a youth named Guy Manger, who has arrived at the birthday or coming-of-age party of Rose Tranmore with a highly conspicuous box: "[Guy] carries in his hand a small, or indeed a rather ridiculously large, box done up in white paper and pink ribbon, a tribute in the form of chocolate-creams, marrons glacés, or whatever he has brought in the form of a birthday offering to the young Rose; but that he has immediately become shy, self-conscious, and awkward about, on finding it a question of his sallying forth with it across the lawn and presenting it before a lot of people" (CPJ 614). In James's swift and subtle change of heart, not a small but an absurdly large box, one senses the self-consciousness of the parody as well as an aversion to presenting a host of people with a large and ridiculously contrived object. Unlike his youthful categorical pronouncements on the scenic art, James's more mature theories of the theater tend to be expressed indirectly. In *What Maisie Knew, The Ambassadors,* and even *The Saloon* the author represents an understanding of the fourth-wall illusion which surpassed the theories expressed by the most successful playwrights of his day. In his dramatic writings James was already imagining new and complicated ways of manipulating and subverting the box of dramatic illusion. It took a sensitive critic such as A. B. Walkley to imagine, after seeing *Guy Domville* on the opening night, that "Mr. James's play is a defeat out of which it is possible for many victories to spring; in gathering the enemy's spears into his heart he has made a gap through which his successors will be able to pour in triumph."[28]

Notes

PREFACE

1. In particular, the present study has been deeply influenced by David Grimsted's excellent history of American melodrama, *Melodrama Unveiled: American Theater and Culture, 1800–1850* (Berkeley: University of California Press, 1968); and Lawrence Levine's brilliant treatment of nineteenth-century American "public culture," *Highbrow/Lowbrow: The Emergence of Cultural Hierarchy in America* (Cambridge: Harvard University Press, 1988).

2. Smith wonders why, despite increasing interest in "marginal" texts, recent works in cultural studies continue to ignore texts for the theater. See Susan Harris Smith, *American Drama: The Bastard Art* (Cambridge: Cambridge University Press, 1997), 9–56. Indeed, theater has been curiously neglected by most American cultural and literary histories to date. In David S. Reynolds's massive study of popular cultural forms, for example, theater is conspicuously absent. See Reynolds, *Beneath the American Renaissance: The Subversive Imagination in the Age of Emerson and Melville* (Cambridge: Harvard University Press, 1989). Lawrence Buell does make some reference to theater in *New England Literary Culture: From Revolution through Renaissance* (Cambridge: Cambridge University Press, 1986), noting that by the early 1800s the Boston stage had influenced the lives of many New Englanders of literary bent, but he also emphasizes the eventual "revulsion against drama on both aesthetic and moral grounds once it became clear that the polite element in society was not going to control the behavior of the theatre" (385) and, therefore, implies that theater's significance for literature becomes negligible. Stephen Railton's study *Authorship and Audience: Literary Performance and the American Renaissance* (Princeton: Princeton University Press, 1991) focuses on what he calls the "literary performances" of major American authors, by which he means in particular how they relate to a public through the book, an important topic that I also hope to explore, but Railton is not particularly interested in how an actual historical theater might play a role in such a transaction. There have been some exceptions, however, to this antitheatrical bias in American literary and cultural studies. Constance Rourke shows profound connections between American theater and literature in *American Humor: A Study of the National Character* (New York: Harcourt, Brace and Co., 1931). More recently, Randall Knoper's excellent study *Acting Naturally: Mark Twain in the Culture of Performance* (Berkeley: University of California Press, 1995)

shows that "Twain's interests in performance and expression are consistently associated in his thinking and writing with the theater" (8).

3. Significantly, while the copious tradition of American antitheatricalism expresses much that is continuous with a tradition of antitheatricalism which goes back to Plato, the accusation of excessive truthfulness is one of the most important deviations from standard antitheatrical positions. As early as 1765, John Witherspoon, in *A Serious Enquiry into the Nature and Effects of the Stage: And a Letter Respecting Play Actors* (Glasgow: n.p., 1757), indicts the drama for being *too truthful* and, therefore, an "improper method of instruction" (qtd. in Barish 297). See Jonas Barish, *The Antitheatrical Prejudice* (Berkeley: University of California Press, 1981). I will discuss this notion of theater's truth value (a notion of being more real than real life) at greater length in chapter 2, "Character on Stage: Walt Whitman and American Theater," and chapter 3, "Another Version of the Whale-Ship Globe: Narrative and Drama in *Moby-Dick*."

4. Quoted in Grimsted, *Melodrama Unveiled,* 48. Conway was, in fact, Emerson's first emissary to Whitman and Whitman's "first official literary visitor." See Justin Kaplan, *Walt Whitman: A Life* (New York: Simon and Schuster, 1980), 203, 213.

5. Regarding these energetically theatrical spaces, one might think of Joseph Roach's "vortices of behavior": places "where the gravitational pull of social necessity brings audiences together and produces performers . . . from their midst." Such a vortex, Roach claims, is a "center of cultural self-invention." See Roach, *Cities of the Dead: Circum-Atlantic Performance* (New York: Columbia University Press, 1996), 28.

6. Although the literature in this area is extensive, Judith Butler's provocative work in gender and cultural studies may be considered exemplary. Butler argues that the self is constituted in performance and that gender, in particular, is "performative," a "doing": "Identity is performatively constituted by the very 'expressions' that are said to be its results." See Butler, *Gender Trouble: Feminism and the Subversion of Identity* (New York: Routledge, 1990), 25. In *Bodies That Matter: On the Discursive Limits of "Sex"* (London: Routledge, 1993) Butler writes that "performativity must be understood not as a singular or deliberate 'act,' but, rather, as the reiterative and citational practice by which discourse produces the effects that it names" (2). Also see *Excitable Speech: A Politics of the Performative* (New York: Routledge, 1997), in which Butler positions herself in relation to theorists of the "performative" in language from Austin to Derrida.

7. Of Evreinoff's many projects perhaps most significant historically was his organization of mass spectacles celebrating the Russian Revolution.

CHAPTER 1. SETTING THE STAGE

1. As Michael Slater indicates, *Nicholas Nickleby* was itself a novel that was dramatized faster than it had come out. The real "literary gentleman" who is the object of Dickens's wit here was W. T. Moncrief, a hack playwright whose *Nicholas Nickelby and Poor Smike; Or, The Victim of the Yorkshire School* was produced at the Strand Theatre on 20 May 1839. Dickens's novel was published in monthly installments between 31 March 1838 and 30 September 1839. Also of significance *in* the novel is the fact that Mr. Crummles's acting company, which plays a central role in the life of Nicholas, departs for America, where Crummles, who has a rapidly expanding family, expects to find a great demand for juvenile tragedy and a "tolerably good engagement." See Charles Dickens, *Nicholas Nickleby,* ed. Michael Slater (London: Penguin Books, 1978), 723.

2. See Garff B. Wilson, *Three Hundred Years of American Drama and Theatre from* Ye Bear and Ye Cubb *to* Hair (Englewood Cliffs, N.J.: Prentice-Hall, 1973), 49.

3. The Kembles were touring and performing in America to full houses in 1832 and 1833, when the young Fanny Kemble penned these remarks. Yet, as Eleanor Ransome remarks in her textual notes to Kemble's writings, Kemble was, in fact, helping to form American poetry, as the thirteen-year-old Walt Whitman crossed again and again by ferry from Brooklyn to see Kemble and her father act. Whitman later recalls the experience of those "mimic scenes" in *Specimen Days,* in which he describes Fanny as, in those days, "just matured" (P&P 704). See *The Terrific Kemble: A Victorian Self-Portrait from the Writings of Fanny Kemble,* ed. Eleanor Ransome (London: Hamish Hamilton, 1978), 79. Also, for vivid descriptions of the "crammed" houses ("They collect in crowds for upwards of an hour before the doors open, and when the bolts are withdrawn, there is yelling and shouting as though the town were on fire"), see *Fanny Kemble: The American Journals* (93). Of course, the long-lived Fanny Kemble also had an influential and extensive relationship with Henry James many years later.

4. Edgar Allan Poe, "The American Drama" (1845), in *Selections from the Critical Writings of Edgar Allan Poe,* ed. F. C. Prescott (New York: Gordian Press, 1981), 107–48.

5. Judith Butler's recent treatment of "hate speech" may be suggestively applied to the nominative power of utterances in melodrama. "If hate speech acts in an illocutionary way," writes Butler, "injuring in and through the moment of speech, and constituting the subject through that injury, then hate speech has an interpellative function" (24). In short, the speech act brings the subject into existence and is conditioned by its "conventional, that is, 'ritual' or 'ceremonial' dimension" (25). In a similar sense the melodramas rely on a set of linguistic conventions or

rituals, by which language has an explicit power to constitute its subjects. And, inversely, hate speech has a "melodramatic" quality. See Judith Butler, *Excitable Speech: A Politics of the Performative* (New York: Routledge, 1997).

6. John Augustus Stone, *Metamora; or, The Last of the Wampanoags* (1829), in *American Drama: Colonial to Contemporary,* ed. Stephen Watt and Gary A. Richardson (New York: Harcourt, Brace and Co., 1995); George Henry Boker, *Francesca da Rimini,* in *Representative American Plays from 1767 to the Present Day,* ed. Arthur Hobson Quinn (New York: D. Appleton-Century Co., 1917).

7. After being rejected by theaters in Stockholm and Copenhagen, *Ghosts* was performed in the original language in Chicago at the Aurora Turner Hall before an audience of Scandinavian immigrants. This production is the first on record of any Ibsen play in America, and after the Chicago debut the production toured Minneapolis and other cities of the Midwest with large Scandinavian populations. See Michael Meyer, *Ibsen* (1967; rpt., London: Penguin Books, 1985), 512.

8. William Dean Howells, "Life and Letters," *Harper's Weekly* 39, 11 May 1895, 436.

9. Significantly, Whitman never developed a taste for the work of dramatic realists. For example, in conversations with Whitman in Camden in 1888, Horace Traubel repeatedly pressed for a verdict on Ibsen. "You don't seem to take any great shine to Ibsen," Traubel says. "No," Whitman responds, "it seems that way" (*With Walt Whitman in Camden* [1907; rpt., New York: Rowman and Littlefield, 1961], 2:483). Later Whitman remarks, "My impression of the work was that it was light: that may have come from the loss by translation, but I doubt it" (2:490).

10. Michael Fried's remark that "the success, even the survival, of the arts has come increasingly to depend on their ability to defeat the theatre" is closely related to the theories of dramatic realists, though, in fact, Fried suggests an affinity between his view and the theories of Artaud, a connection that I do not believe to be entirely valid. Still, Fried notes that the importance of rejecting theatricality is "nowhere more evident than within the theatre itself, where the need to defeat . . . theatre has chiefly made itself felt as the need to establish a drastically different relation to its audience." See Michael Fried, "Art and Objecthood," in *Minimal Art,* ed. Gregory Battock (New York: Dutton), 139. As Marvin Carlson suggests, Fried attempts to exclude the audience "precisely because it introduced into the art experience a sense of contingency, time, and situation" (*Performance: A Critical Introduction* [London: Routledge, 1996], 139). The tension between reading and being a member of an audience is also explicitly discussed in Fried's great work detailing the crucial artistic dichotomy between "theatricality" and "absorption" in *Absorption and Theatricality: Painting and the Beholder in the Age of Diderot* (Berkeley: University of California Press, 1980).

11. The epistemological importance of the voice is also made explicit in *The Bos-*

tonians when we are told, "It was impossible to have any idea of Verena Tarrant unless one had heard her" ([1886; rpt., London: Penguin Books, 1982], 48).

12. *The Scarlet Letter* was, in fact, performed in New York as an opera during Hawthorne's lifetime, though Hawthorne had remarked, "I think it might possibly succeed as an opera, though it would certainly fail as a play" (qtd. in Rourke, *American Humor: A Study of the National Character* [New York: Harcourt, Brace and Co., 1931], 188). Clearly, the author thought of his novel in terms of the stage.

13. Levine traces the declining popular interest in both oratory and Shakespeare to demographic changes in America (such as massive immigration by non-English speakers), changes in public life, and changes in forms of communication (*Highbrow/Lowbrow,* 46).

14. Joseph Roach describes extensively the close ties between rhetoric and acting, beginning with Quintilian. See Roach, *The Player's Passion: Studies in the Science of Acting* (Newark: University of Delaware Press, 1985), 23–57.

15. Brockden Brown, incidentally, was a close friend of William Dunlap, one of America's most prominent early playwrights and men of the theater. Dunlap was known as "the father of American drama," as mentioned earlier. And he later wrote Brockden Brown's biography, when his own income from the theater began to dwindle. Dunlap had hoped to transform the theater into an institution for social good, a project that he realized was doomed by, for example, "a man who could whirl around on his head with crackers and other fireworks attached to his heels." See Grimsted, *Melodrama Unveiled,* 19.

16. The German-born Mansfield (1854–1907), an arrogant and controversial figure, was the first American manager to produce Shaw and one of the first to stage regular productions of Ibsen. He was, however, like Irving, first and foremost a Shakespearean actor. Both Irving and Mansfield consciously aimed to inspire a cult of personality, described by Garff B. Wilson as "the substitution of the performer's personality for the dramatic character, or the portrayal of dramatic characters which fit the performer's personality so exactly that the performer and character are practically identical." See Wilson, *Three Hundred Years of American Drama and Theatre* (Englewood Cliffs, N.J.: Prentice-Hall, 1973), 269. Also see Murphy, *American Realism and American Drama,* 18–19.

17. William Winter, *Life and Art of Edwin Booth* (New York: Macmillan, 1894), 250.

18. George C. D. Odell, *Annals of the New York Stage* (New York: Columbia University Press, 1928), 3:225. Also see Wilson, *Three Hundred Years of American Drama and Theatre,* 137.

19. In fact, Forrest was only five feet ten inches tall, though, still, substantially taller than Booth. See Richard Moody, *Edwin Forrest, First Star of the American Stage* (New York: Alfred A. Knopf, 1960), 76–77.

20. *The Columbian Orator,* a grammar school classic, was one of the most popular books of its kind and went through many editions. It was also a favorite of Frederick Douglass, who was particularly attracted to a dramatic dialogue between master and slave. Douglass writes that at the age of twelve, he "got hold of a book entitled 'The Columbian Orator.' Every opportunity I got, I used to read this book. Among much other interesting matter, I found in it a dialogue between a master and his slave . . . In this dialogue, the whole argument in behalf of slavery was brought forward by the master, all of which was disposed of by the slave." See *Narrative of the Life of Frederick Douglass, an American Slave,* ed. Houston A. Baker (1845; rpt., New York: Penguin Books, 1986), 83.

21. "In the Bowery Theatre's earlier days," writes Laurence Senelick, "a row of iron spikes had extended across the stage before the footlights and halfway up the proscenium arch to prevent . . . audience participation. A policeman was stationed at the front of the pit with a rattan cane to stifle shouts of 'Hi! hi!' or any extraordinary rumpus, but some thought he more than contributed to the general uproar" (*The Age and Stage of George L. Fox, 1825–1877* [Hanover, N.H.: University Press of New England, 1988], 87).

22. Peter Brooks writes that in melodrama emotion "was held to be susceptible of complete externalization in legible integral postures. Acting style was predicated on the plastic figurability of emotion, its shaping as a visible and almost tactile entity" (*The Melodramatic Imagination: Balzac, Henry James, Melodrama, and the Mode of Excess* [New Haven: Yale University Press, 1976], 47).

23. Laurence Senelick, whose study of Fox is my principal source, comments that Fox seemed, remarkably, always to be at the crux of major changes in American life. When the Civil War erupted, he was among the first to enlist, becoming a hero to his fans. Upon his return Fox exploited his wartime experiences for theatrical ends, staging, for example, a drama called *Bull Run.* Furthermore, he quickly staged parodies of other, more "serious" productions in New York, such as Booth's *Hamlet* in 1870. While Fox's lasting influence has not generally been acknowledged, it is from his brand of physical humor that vaudeville originates. And his physical humor can even be seen in silent films. Indeed, one of the most remarkable features of the few photographs of Fox's mobile face is his amazing resemblance to Stan Laurel (of Laurel and Hardy). See Senelick, *Age and Stage of George L. Fox.*

24. Notably, Curtis had made fun of Edwin Forrest's kind of acting, describing it as "the muscular school; the brawny art; the biceps aesthetics; the tragic calves; the bovine drama; rant, roar, and rigamarole" ("Editor's Easy Chair," *Harper's New Monthly Magazine* 28 [December 1863]: 131–33). For an extensive treatment of Booth's Hamlet, see Charles H. Shattuck, *The Hamlet of Edwin Booth* (Urbana: Uni-

versity of Illinois Press, 1969). And for further discussion of Curtis's theatergoing and the significance of his dramaturgical tastes, especially regarding Forrest and Booth, see Levine, *Highbrow/Lowbrow,* 57–58.

25. See Charles Shattuck, "The Feminization of Shakespeare," *Shakespeare on the American Stage: From Booth and Barrett to Sothern and Marlowe* (Washington, D.C.: Folger Books, 1987), 2:93–141.

26. Sarah Bernhardt, *The Art of the Theatre* (London: Dial Press, 1925), 137.

27. It should be noted that James found this realist style of acting inappropriate in certain dramas, and especially in Shakespeare. "Realism is a very good thing," he writes, "but it is like baking pudding in a porcelain dish; your pudding may be excellent but your dish gets cracked. An actor who attempts to play Shakespeare must establish for himself a certain Shakespearean tradition; he must make sacrifices. We are afraid that as things are going, most actors find it easier to sacrifice Shakespeare than to sacrifice to him" (SA 34).

28. See Brenda Murphy, *American Realism and American Drama,* 18, 30. Also see Howells's article "Good Acting, Poor Plays," in *A Realist in the American Theatre,* 63–66. For more of Jefferson's views on acting, see *The Autobiography of Joseph Jefferson,* ed. Alan S. Downer (Cambridge: Harvard University Press, 1964).

29. Of course, Artaud is speaking of more than the visual, but for purposes of clarity we may consider mise-en-scène to refer primarily to the set or what we might call "the look of the stage," including elements of spectacle. Literally, it means the way the stage is dressed.

30. George Washington Parke Custis, *Pocahontas; or, The Settlers of Virginia,* in *Representative American Plays from 1767 to the Present Day,* ed. Arthur Hobson Quinn (New York: D. Appleton-Century Co., 1917).

31. See "A Full and Reliable Account of the Extraordinary Meteoric Shower of Last Saturday Night," in *The Californian: Sketches of the Sixties* (San Francisco: John Howell, 1926), 153. Twain's own novel *Roughing It!* was staged by Augustin Daly as one of Daly's "original spectacles" and was advertised as presenting "a dramatic kaleidoscope in four acts and ten tableaux."

32. See William Dunlap, *History of the American Theatre and Anecdotes of the Principal Actors* (1832; rpt., New York: Burt Franklin, 1963), 280.

33. Arthur Hobson Quinn suggests that the stunt is not even original to Daly, who may have derived the idea from Randall Matthews's play *The Engineer,* a copy of which was found among Daly's manuscripts. Quinn goes on to suggest that the circumstances are different in Matthews's play and less dramatic, but the idea's lack of clear origin gives a sense of mid-century American drama's intertextuality. See Quinn, *A History of the American Drama* (New York: Appleton-Century-Crofts, 1923), 2:11–12; Marvin Felheim, *The Theater of Augustin Daly: An Account of the Late*

Nineteenth Century American Stage (Cambridge: Harvard University Press, 1956), 47–66; Richard Fawkes, *Dion Boucicault: A Biography* (London: Quartet Books, 1979), 172–74; Senelick, *Age and Stage of George L. Fox,* 151.

34. *The Poor of New York,* incidentally, became *The Poor of Liverpool, The Poor of Leeds, The Poor of Manchester, The Streets of Islington,* and *The Streets of London.* As Boucicault put it: "I localize each town, and hit the public between the eyes; so they see nothing but fire. Eh voila! I can spin out these rough-and-tumble dramas as a hen lays eggs. It's a degrading occupation, but more money has been made out of guano than out of poetry" (qtd. in Fawkes, *Dion Boucicault,* 148).

35. This kind of theater epitomizes what Victor Turner describes as "liminoid" phenomena. Turner stresses that liminoid genres, unlike liminal genres, are not conceived as "anti-structure" but as "play," which involves experimentation (*Process, Performance, and Pilgrimage: A Study in Comparative Symbology* [New Delhi: Concept, 1979], 45–54).

36. For a more extensive production history of *Margaret Fleming* and of the play's significance, see Quinn, *A History of the American Drama,* 2:140–46. Also, for a treatment both of *Margaret Fleming* and of Herne's relation to Ibsen, see John Perry, *James A. Herne: The American Ibsen* (Chicago: Nelson-Hall, 1978), 181–96.

37. See *Margaret Fleming,* in Quinn, *Representative American Plays.*

38. Grimsted tells how crowds met Jenny Lind on her arrival in each town: "in Baltimore people even insisted on unhitching her horses and drawing her carriage themselves into the city" (*Melodrama Unveiled,* 58).

39. See Bruce McConachie for a brief description of the Kean riots in 1825, in *Melodramatic Formations: American Theatre and Society, 1820–1870* (Iowa City: University of Iowa Press, 1992). Discussions of the Astor Place Riot can be found in McConachie as well as in Joel Porte, *In Respect to Egotism: Studies in American Romantic Writing* (Cambridge: Cambridge University Press, 1991); and Levine, *Highbrow/Lowbrow.* Also see Wilson, *Three Hundred Years of American Drama and Theatre,* 85–87. I discuss the Astor Place Riot in chapter 3, "Another Version of the Whale-Ship Globe." Furthermore, the alcoholic or inebriate side of theater can be seen in the variety houses that sprang up in the 1860s and 1870s. Douglas Gilbert notes, "Variety halls with wine rooms and bars red-lighted every thriving town in America." And, he says, "New York was well supplied with variety houses, all of them beer halls" (*American Vaudeville: Its Life and Times* [New York: Dover Publications, 1940], 11, 14).

40. Porte (*In Respect to Egotism*) discusses, in particular, the relevance of the Astor Place Riot for understanding the work of Herman Melville.

41. Grimsted notes that "perfect order usually provoked perfect surprise" (*Melodrama Unveiled,* 60).

42. See Jean-Cristophe Agnew, whose terms I employ here *(Worlds Apart: The*

Market and the Theater in Anglo-American Thought, 1550–1750 [Cambridge: Cambridge University Press, 1986], 196). As another example of the pervasiveness of theater in American social thought, even Thoreau uses theater to describe "our behavior to all new men and women," though not specifically in an economic context. In *A Week on the Concord and Merrimack Rivers* Thoreau writes, "We are continually acting a part in a more interesting drama than any written" (*A Week on the Concord and Merrimack Rivers* [1849; rpt., Orleans, Mass.: Parnassus Imprints, 1987], 331).

43. E. Irenaeus Stevenson, "Music and Manners," *Harper's Weekly* 41, 5 June 1897, 570. Lawrence Levine's research, in establishing and documenting the contrast between earlier and later American audiences, has been especially groundbreaking. See Levine, *Highbrow/Lowbrow.*

44. Robert Brustein, "Eugene O'Neill," *The Theatre of Revolt: An Approach to the Modern Drama* (Chicago: Elephant Paperbacks, 1991), 319–60.

45. Poe's mother, Eliza, was one of the most popular American actresses of her day when she died, at the age of twenty-four. She had played nearly three hundred roles, acting, singing, and dancing in major theaters around the country. Poe was a small child when his mother died, and yet, as Kenneth Silverman remarks, "however dim Poe's recollection of her and her life, it stirred actively enough to fill his works with allusions to the stage and to singing and dancing" (*Edgar Allan Poe: A Mournful and Never-Ending Remembrance* [New York: HarperCollins, 1991], 136).

46. Stowe was also actively interested in the theater, and, when the actor Joseph Jefferson was performing *Rip Van Winkle* in Boston, Stowe sent him a note through her publisher requesting a meeting. In the course of a long and pleasant "chat" Stowe discussed her interest in the play, focusing particularly on how she was struck by the scene in which Rip meets his daughter. See *The Autobiography of Joseph Jefferson* (1890; rpt., Cambridge: Harvard University Press, 1964), 335.

CHAPTER 2. CHARACTER ON STAGE

1. The dramatic quality of some aspect of Whitman's work is noted in the titles of several prominent scholarly works. I am thinking, for example, of Kerry C. Larson, *Whitman's Drama of Consensus* (Chicago: University of Chicago Press, 1988); E. Fred Carlisle, *Uncertain Self: Whitman's Drama of Identity* (East Lansing: Michigan State University Press, 1973); and Howard J. Waskow's chapter on "Monodrama," in *Whitman: Explorations in Form* (Chicago: University of Chicago Press, 1966), to name only a few.

2. Quotations from Whitman's poems are generally taken from the 1891–92 "deathbed" edition, since it is the most complete collection of his poetry. Furthermore, Whitman insists that his impressions of the theater of his youth pervade even his latest work. Quotations from the 1855 edition are indicated as such.

3. *The Stage; or, Theatrical Inquisitor* (London: G. Creed) was published throughout the nineteenth century, beginning in 1828.

4. See David Reynolds, *Beneath the American Renaissance: The Subversive Imagination in the Age of Emerson and Melville* (Cambridge: Harvard University Press, 1989), 15–54. An excellent discussion of the transference of religious energies into secular activities in nineteenth-century American culture may also be found in Ann Douglas, *The Feminization of American Culture* (New York: Anchor Books, 1988).

5. An example of this tendency can be seen in Richard Penn Smith, *The Disowned; Or, The Prodigals* (1829), a translation of Jouslin de la Salle's play *Le Caissier* (1826). Smith noted of his adaptation of the original: "The termination was without a climax, for Amelia is still alive, and the man to whom she is devotedly attached is given in marriage to another. Besides, a blemish is unnecessarily thrown upon the character of Amelia, which diminishes the interest awakened by her situation. The result proved the alterations to be judicious, and the powerful acting of Mr. Rowbotham never failed to rivet the attention, and elicit the unqualified applause of the audience." See Arthur Hobson Quinn, *A History of the American Drama* (New York: Appleton-Century-Crofts, 1923), 1:209–10.

6. Hegel's "modes of presentation" include the objective character of *epic,* the subjective nature of *lyric,* and the expressive potential, the ability to give external shape to the inner side of objectivity, of the *dramatic.* In the modern age, however, the form of art has ceased to be the highest need of the spirit; art transcends itself, and the artist "receives his content from himself; he is the true spirit of man, determining his own destiny, observing the infinite variety of his own feelings and situations, contemplating and expressing them. To him, nothing is alien which can come to life in the heart of man" (qtd. in Karl Löwith, *From Hegel to Nietzsche: The Revolution in Nineteenth-Century Thought* [New York: Columbia University Press, 1964], 37).

7. David Reynolds also argues for the "fluid exchange between different cultural idioms" in what he calls the "performance culture" of Whitman's day. Reynolds, however, discusses theater, oratory, and opera as essentially separate categories with dissolving boundaries, whereas I intend to stress a homologous relationship between the various cultural forms and the pervasiveness of the theatrical idiom. Still, *Walt Whitman's America* represents a significant revision of the Matthiessen approach (*Walt Whitman's America: A Cultural Biography* [New York: Alfred A. Knopf, 1995]). Also see Betsy Erkkila, *Whitman the Political Poet* (New York: Oxford University Press, 1989), for a strong critique of Matthiessen's brand of historicism.

8. In *November Boughs* Whitman describes Father Taylor as the only "essentially perfect orator" he has ever heard (P&P 1143).

9. A fascinating and bizarre example of the relationship between body and spirit is found in S. Weir Mitchell's story "The Case of George Dedlow," pub-

lished in the *Atlantic Monthly* in July 1866. In the story Dedlow, who has lost all of his limbs through amputation during the Civil War, finds that he becomes "less conscious of myself, of my own existence, than used to be the case" (qtd. in Walter Benn Michaels, *The Gold Standard and the Logic of Naturalism: American Literature at the Turn of the Century* [Berkeley: University of California Press, 1987], 25). The story ends with a weird séance in which, unlike the other participants who call up dead relatives, Dedlow summons his legs, which, though invisible, actually support him for a short wobble. Walter Benn Michaels observes: "The séance both confirms and disconfirms the identification of self with body. On the one hand the whole point of the story is to insist that the self does not essentially consist in anything like pure spirit . . . On the other hand, as the ending also makes clear, no body can exist as body alone . . . Body parts have spirits too" (24–25).

10. This dichotomy in acting theory is ancient. Joseph Roach traces the "double-bladed axe for the historical, continuing, and apparently inexhaustible combat between technique and inspiration in performance theory" to Quintilian's *Institutio Oratoria* (*Player's Passion,* 26). In our own century we can see versions of such theories, conditioned by specific historical factors, in the differences, for example, between Stanislavski and Brecht. Stanislavski advocates identification of the actor with the role: "Closeness to your part we call perception of yourself in the part and of the part in you . . . The actions are based on inner feelings . . . Inside of you, parallel to the line of physical actions, you have an unbroken line of emotions verging on the subconscious . . . Moreover you can speak for your character in your own person" (12). Brecht, on the other hand, advocates a self-consciousness about technique in acting which results in what he calls an "alienation effect" for both actor and spectator. See Constantin Stanislavkski, *An Actor's Handbook,* ed. and trans. Elizabeth Reynolds Hapgood (New York: Theatre Arts Books, 1963); and Bertolt Brecht, *Brecht on Theatre: The Development of an Aesthetic,* ed. and trans. John Willett (New York: Hill and Wang, 1964).

11. Roach's brilliant account of "vitalism" demonstrates connections between Garrick's "Electrical fire" and the discovery of electricity as an "unplumbed and all-pervading force" through the work of Franklin and Priestly. Roach also notes another metaphor that appears prominently in Whitman, namely, the acoustical metaphor of "vibration," a term that appears commonly in acting and physiological theory from the mid-eighteenth to the mid-nineteenth centuries. See Joseph Roach, *The Player's Passion: Studies in the Science of Acting* (Newark: University of Delaware Press, 1985), 93–115.

12. The "ordinary actor struts and rants" without assuming *into his own identity* the character he represents. The difference between the "true actor" and the "ordinary actor" is a difference "as between mind and body" (GF 322).

13. T. S. Eliot's notion of the "objective correlative"—"a set of objects, a situa-

tion, a chain of events which shall be the formula of that *particular* emotion; such that when the external facts, which must terminate in sensory experience, are given, the emotion is immediately evoked" ("Hamlet," *Selected Prose of T. S. Eliot,* ed. Frank Kermode [New York: Harcourt Brace Jovanovich, 1956], 45–49)—is, according to J. A. Cuddon, derived from the American painter Washington Allston, who first used it about 1840. See Cuddon, *The Penguin Dictionary of Literary Terms and Literary Theory* (London: Penguin Books, 1976).

14. David Reynolds has remarked that Whitman was later to understand Lincoln's assassination as a tragic drama. "He had been prepared to interpret the event," Reynolds claims, "by his immersion in the emotional acting style of John Wilkes Booth's father" (*Walt Whitman's America,* 160).

15. In her excellent article "Reification and American Literature" Carolyn Porter argues that American writers were responding to a particular social reality "breeding an extreme form of alienation." This world, where one's own activity becomes a commodity, generates people who assume a passive or "contemplative" stance. Therefore, Porter suggests, "only when the apparently stable and given world is understood as already mediated can it be understood as the realm of change, of what Marx called 'sensuous human activity.' " See Porter, "Reification and American Literature," in *Ideology and Classic American Literature,* ed. Sacvan Bercovitch and Myra Jehlen (Cambridge: Cambridge University Press, 1986), 188–217.

16. *Franklin Evans* has been republished in *The Uncollected Poetry and Prose of Walt Whitman,* vol. 2, ed. Emory Holloway (Gloucester, Mass.: Peter Smith, 1972). All citations of Whitman's novel are from this volume.

17. "Whitman Reviews Himself," *Brooklyn Daily Times,* 29 September 1855; reprinted in *Critical Essays on Walt Whitman,* ed. James Woodress (Boston: G. K. Hall, 1983), 23–25. The stress on varieties of postures in *The Columbian Orator* ("There ought to be no appearance of stiffness, but a certain ease and pliableness, naturally suiting itself to every expression") conjures up images of the many photographs of the insouciant Whitman, especially the most famous photograph inserted in the first edition of *Leaves of Grass.*

18. See Harold Aspiz, "The Whitman Persona and Whitman's Physical Self," *Walt Whitman and the Body Beautiful* (Urbana: University of Illinois Press, 1980), 3–33.

19. Although Fisher describes not an aesthetics of assimilation (such as that described by Lawrence or Anderson), he does describe an "aesthetics of identity." And in "Democratic Social Space: Whitman, Melville, and the Promise of American Transparency" theater is an important model for the kind of oppositional structure that, Fisher argues, Whitman generally seeks to dissolve (*Representations* 24 [Fall 1988]: 60–101).

20. Also see Donald Pease, "Blake, Crane, Whitman, and Modernism: A Poetics of Pure Possibility," *PMLA* 96 (1981): 64–85; Allen Grossman, "The Poetics

of Union in Lincoln and Whitman: An Inquiry toward the Relationship of Art and Policy," in *The American Renaissance Reconsidered,* ed. Walter Benn Michaels and Donald E. Pease (Baltimore: Johns Hopkins University Press, 1985), 183–208; and Betsy Erkkla, *Whitman the Political Poet* (New York: Oxford University Press, 1989).

21. The city itself represented the ultimate spectacle that absorbed its spectators. For example, Whitman writes of hiking up the stairs in the American Museum, placing a chair by one of the front windows, and staring out, from his roomy niche, upon "the busiest spectacle this busy city may present. One mighty rush of men, business, carts, carriages, and clang" ("An Hour in a Balcony," in *Walt Whitman of the New York* Aurora: *Editor at Twenty-two,* ed. Joseph Jay Rubin and Charles H. Brown [State College, Pa.: Bald Eagle Press, 1950], 26).

22. Significantly, John M. Robertson uses exactly the same language, though with a different agenda, to describe two plays of this decade by William Dean Howells, *Out of the Question* (1877) and *A Counterfeit Presentment* (1877). Robertson writes that, "though they have a species of delicacy that raises them above contemporary drama, [they] can only be classed as specimens of dainty confectionery." Still, "despite this confectionery quality, it is impossible not to perceive the delicacy and ingenuity with which our palates are titillated." See Robertson, *Essays toward a Critical Method* (London: T. F. Unwin, 1889), 173, 197.

23. A sense of the tension between individualism and union is manifested in Allen Grossman's fine article "The Poetics of Union in Whitman and Lincoln: An Inquiry toward the Relationship of Art and Policy," in *The American Renaissance Reconsidered,* ed. Walter Benn Michaels and Donald E. Pease (Baltimore: Johns Hopkins University Press, 1985), 183–208. Whitman, argues Grossman, is the "literary master of union," and the poetic line is the theater of presence, across time, which unifies the world. Yet, while Whitman's "song" reconciles (or attempts to reconcile) variety and order, the logic of presence has "its own violence." In the end, Grossman concludes, Whitman's project of union (like Lincoln's) remains "virtual and paradoxical." Thus, a "faithful response to Whitman's originality will be a continual critique, in view of a policy toward institutions, of the structures of representation."

24. Larson stresses a reading of the poems *as drama* and notes that in Whitman's poetry "the relationship between author and reader is not something Whitman works *from* but works *toward.* Precisely what most poetry takes for granted Whitman takes as his explicit subject" (*Whitman's Drama of Consensus,* 8). Here the notion of "working toward" consensus can be understood more deeply if Whitman's interest in theater and the performative culture, as well as the nature of audiences in that culture, are considered. Much critical attention has been paid to the prominent role of the audience in nineteenth-century American literature in

general. See, for example, Stephen Railton, *Authorship and Audience: Literary Performance and the American Renaissance* (Princeton: Princeton University Press, 1991). Railton's study does not specifically examine Whitman but treats the proposition that writing in mid-nineteenth-century America should be conceptualized as a public gesture, not as a private act.

CHAPTER 3. "ANOTHER VERSION OF THE WHALE-SHIP GLOBE"

1. Olson's first published articulation of his view that Shakespeare's plays "became a great metaphor by which Melville objectified his own original vision" may be found in "Lear and Moby-Dick," *Twice a Year: A Semi-Annual Journal of Literature, The Arts, and Civil Liberties,* no. 1 (Fall–Winter 1938): 165–89. The quotation is taken from Olson, *Call Me Ishmael* (New York: Grove Press, 1947). Subsequent references are to the latter work. For a more recent study of Melville's interest in Shakespeare and, particularly, the relationship between *King Lear* and *Moby-Dick,* see Julian Markels, *Melville and the Politics of Identity: From* King Lear *to* Moby-Dick (Urbana: University of Illinois Press, 1993).

2. Lawrence Buell, "Observer-Hero Narrative," *Texas Studies in Literature and Language: A Journal of the Humanities* 21, no. 1 (1979): 93–111. For related studies, see Walter L. Reed, *Meditations on the Hero: A Study of the Romantic Hero in Nineteenth-Century American Fiction* (New Haven: Yale University Press, 1974); and Kenneth A. Bruffee, *Elegaic Romance: Cultural Change and Loss of the Hero in Modern Fiction* (Ithaca: Cornell University Press, 1983).

3. I take this term from Hannah Arendt: "The space of appearance comes into being wherever men are together in the manner of speech and action, and therefore predates and precedes all formal constitution of the public realm." See Arendt, *The Human Condition* (Chicago: University of Chicago Press, 1958), 199.

4. The Greek root of *theater, theatron,* is literally the space of viewing, seeing, looking. In "The Castaway" (chap. 93) Pip, the cabin boy, who speaks both madness and heaven's sense, conveys the overpowering quality of a physical presence and the immensity of space that language manifestly cannot represent: "I look, you look, he looks; we look, ye look, they look." Anthony Kubiak comments that this passage indicates a sense in which "theatricality seems to define reality." See Kubiak, "Modern Theatre and *Moby-Dick:* Writing and Sounding the Whale," *Modern Drama* 34 (March 1991): 115. The specular experience, significantly, occurs only in the present tense. Moreover, most deadly encounters with the white whale occur, time and time again, in the same "tragic spot." And Ishmael frequently remarks that experience literally expands beyond representability in narrative: "The intense concentration of self in the middle of such a heartless immensity [the sea], my God! who can tell it?" (347).

5. See Joel Porte, *In Respect to Egotism: Studies in American Romantic Writing* (Cambridge: Cambridge University Press, 1991).

6. This notice is reprinted in T. Alston Brown, *A History of the New York Stage: From the First Performance in 1732 to 1901* (New York: Dodd, Mead and Co., 1903), 1:415.

7. For an example of Forrest's patriotic rhetoric, see his "Oration Delivered at the Democratic Republican Celebration," on the Fourth of July, 1838, in New York City. I am grateful to Ted Widmer for a copy of this speech.

8. In addition to Jack Chase's resemblance to both avatars of Jack Cade, there is another clue in chapter 68 that Melville had *2 Henry VI* on his mind at the time of writing *White-Jacket.* There he suggests that the "king-commodores" of men-of-war "enact on the ocean the proud part of mighty Richard Nevil, the king-making earl of the land." As Richard Nevil was entrenched in the man-of-war castle of Warwick, so is the commodore housed in the ship. Warwick, of course, like Jack Cade, ends up on the side of York in *2 Henry VI* and literally has the last word of the play. The commodore, therefore, plays this part, and Jack Chase is on his side. The master-at-arms who guards the commodore is likewise compared to Warwick's heroic sentries. Melville, however, characteristically goes on to deflate the very comparison he has announced so boldly: "But, unwittingly, I have ennobled, by grand historical comparison, this prying, pettifogging, Irish informer of a master-at-arms" (289). In a sentence the heroic lies in ruins.

9. Jack's flair for the symbolism of public life and the overt theatricality of his reincorporation into the crew may also be fruitfully understood as manifestations of what Victor Turner calls "social drama." The concept of the social drama, Turner explains, is "a device for describing and analyzing episodes that manifest social conflict . . . The drama consists of a four stage model, proceeding from breach of some relationship regarded as crucial in the relevant social group . . . to the application of legal or ritual redress or reconciliation between the conflicting parties . . . The final stage is either the public and symbolic expression of reconciliation or else of irremediable schism" (*Dramas, Fields, and Metaphors: Symbolic Action in Human Society* [Ithaca: Cornell University Press, 1974], 78–79). In particular, Turner's study of the conflict between Henry II and Thomas Becket, a conflict between a monarch and a "commoner" in which both actors seem complicitous in the staging and progression of events, supplies a highly significant framework against which to understand the scene between Captain Claret and Jack (60–98). For a fine discussion of the theory of subversion and containment, see Jonathan Dollimore, "Introduction: Shakespeare, Cultural Materialism and the New Historicism," in *Political Shakespeare: New Essays in Cultural Materialism,* ed. Jonathan Dollimore and Alan Sinfield (Manchester: Manchester University Press, 1985), 10–15. D. H. Lawrence articulates the contradictions by which power achieves its ends

from the other side, the point of view of the people in America: "Do away with masters, exalt the will of the people. The will of the people being nothing but a figment, the exalting doesn't count for much . . . When you have got rid of masters, you are left with this mere phrase of the will of the people. Then you pause and bethink yourself, and try to recover your wholeness" (*Studies in Classic American Literature* [London: Penguin Books, 1923], 14).

10. "The diary," comments Grimsted, "reeking of self-doubt and condemnation as well as exaggerated scorn for others, was Macready. And the public cards, full of paranoia and complete self-righteousness, were Forrest" (*Melodrama Unveiled: American Theater and Culture, 1800–1850* [Berkeley: University of California Press, 1968], 69).

11. Buntline, inventor of "Buffalo Bill" and numerous racy exposé-novels, was also a popularizer of the American figure known as the "B'hoy" (street slang for *boy*). The b'hoy was always raring for a fight and spouting slang, but he was also smart and often a cultural poser. As David Reynolds writes, "Because union activity declined during a decade of extreme economic instability, workers were forced to mythmaking and jingoistic nationalism, and the b'hoy persona embodied both deep hostilities and jingoistic nationalism. With his combined hyperbolic Americanism and jaunty defiance, he became the ideal mixed hero of radical-democrat humor. As a fully indigenous, complex character, he was destined to have a marked effect on American literature." One literary character who manifests certain features of the b'hoy, Reynolds notes, is Ishmael. See Reynolds, *Beneath the American Renaissance* (463–65).

12. See Grimsted, *Melodrama Unveiled,* 67.

13. Robert Caserio argues that Ishmael, who keeps from the hustings, is, implicitly, a representative of the Divine Inert; it is Ishmael who is one of the "true princes." Melville, Caserio believes, favors quiescence and passivity over the imposition of form, or "plot," on events, and this chapter, in his view, provides a key to understanding a "new moral as well as intellectual relation to action" in both *White-Jacket* and *Moby-Dick.* Caserio's argument is provocative, but it claims too much. First of all, Caserio employs *narrative* as too broad a term. We have seen how the limits of "narrative" may come into view if aspects of Melville's texts are viewed as "drama." Second, Caserio is highly selective in his use of evidence. Ishmael is, by no means, always a priest of the Divine Inert; from the opening chapter alternate modes of representation are posited. And Ahab is, by no means, entirely opposed to the Divine Inert, for his action is often said to be fated, or "predestinated." Caserio's chapter provides important insights into the paradox of inertia as an active, and politically resistant, force, but the attempt to extend this idea too broadly is reductive. See Caserio, *Plot, Story and the Novel: From Dickens and Poe to the Modern Period* (Princeton: Princeton University Press, 1979).

14. I am indebted to Scott Stevens for this insight.

15. This story comes from a newspaper article for which, unfortunately, there is no archival record. I discovered the story as a scrap, pasted in an edition of James Rees's reminiscences. There is some reason to suspect it comes from the *New York Times* (14 July 1879) because another article from that issue is pasted next to it.

16. For Aristotle plot is the imitation of an action or, as he writes later, "the arrangement of the incidents." See *Aristotle's Poetics,* trans. S. H. Butcher (New York: Hill and Wang, 1961), 62.

17. For challenges to the Romance hypothesis, see John McWilliams, "The Rationale for 'The American Romance,'" *Boundary 2: An International Journal of Literature and Culture* 17, no. 1 (Spring 1990): 71–82; and Nina Baym, "Melodramas of Beset Manhood: How Theories of American Fiction Exclude Women Authors," *American Quarterly* 33, no. 2 (Summer 1981): 123–39.

18. Significantly, while the copious tradition of American antitheatricalism expresses much that is continuous with a tradition of antitheatricalism which goes back to Plato, the accusation of excessive truthfulness is one of the most important deviations from standard antitheatrical positions. As early as 1765, John Witherspoon, in *A Serious Enquiry into the Nature and Effects of the Stage,* indicts the drama for being *too truthful* and, therefore, an "improper method of instruction" (qtd. in Barish, *Antitheatrical Prejudice,* 297).

19. In 1993, when Michael Jackson said that he wished to be regarded as a person and not as a personality, he raised an issue, explicitly if unconsciously, which developed in the 1840s. Of course, the reason that the American public of the 1990s feels cheated or betrayed by what it perceives to be Michael Jackson's inauthenticity is rooted in the blurring of public and private. (Does Michael really love Lisa Marie or does he molest children? Are his peccadillos a part of his act or of his private life?) Personality is created on the stage, and it is only as a personality that Michael Jackson can be *known.*

20. Interestingly, the original version of the story, which comes from Dante's description of the lovers Francesca and Paolo in the fifth canto of the *Inferno,* contains no mention of Lanciotto, Francesca's husband.

21. Ibsen's first great play, the romantic verse drama *Brand,* was published in 1866. Brand is a priest, whose unrelenting commitment to truth leads ultimately to a form of apocalypse symbolized by a great avalanche at the end of the play.

22. If narrative progresses syntagmatically, along a horizontal axis, and the (melo)drama, which purports to represent cosmic truth (e.g., good versus evil), is paradigmatic/vertical, then at moments of intersection we may find what Bezanson calls the "constitution of meanings."

23. On the differences between tragic and melodramatic soliloquy, see Peter Brooks, *The Melodramatic Imagination* (New Haven: Yale University Press, 1976), 38.

24. See Marvin Carlson, *Theories of the Theatre* (Ithaca: Cornell University Press, 1984), 17–19; and Roland Barthes, *The Responsibility of Forms* (Berkeley: University of California Press, 1991), 72–73. Another, less conventional view of catharsis is suggested by Robert Heilman, who coins the phrase *melodramatic catharsis.* This term, he suggests, has the sense of "working off" or "working out" or simply "working": " 'Working out' is a useful term because it suggests both 'working out of the system' and 'workout' in the sense of 'exercise.' My own emphasis would be more on the 'workout,' the 'exercising' of certain impulses, and less on the 'elimination' that it may be argued is a by-product of the 'exercise.' " The Aristotelian term, Heilman says, is a liability unless it is used simply as a general metaphor for the not-easily-definable psychic aspect of aesthetic experience. Heilman's position is significant for our discussion because, first, as we shall see, the dramaturgy of melodrama is essential to an understanding of the dramatic in *Moby-Dick* and, second, because of the obvious importance of work in Ishmael's experience on the *Pequod.* See Robert Heilman, *Tragedy and Melodrama* (Seattle: University of Washington Press, 1968), 84.

25. My argument is intended, in part, to challenge a set of readings provoked by George R. Stewart's "Two *Moby-Dick*s" thesis, which claims that Melville rewrote *Moby-Dick* from chapter 23 on, in the summer of 1850. Franz Stanzel, for example, points to chapter 29, a scene between Ahab and Stubb, as the first moment when experiencing and narrating selves are divorced in *Moby-Dick.* Stanzel argues that the dematerialization of the experiencing self is directly connected with "the crucial reconception and reworking of the novel." He also believes that the epilogue, with its anticlimactic realism, should have been left out. See George R. Stewart, "The Two *Moby-Dicks,*" *American Literature* 25 (January 1954): 417–48; and Franz Stanzel, *Narrative Situations in the Novel:* Tom Jones, Moby-Dick, The Ambassadors, Ulysses (Bloomington: Indiana University Press, 1971), 59–91.

26. The world—as stage—as ship recurs throughout Melville's writing, of course. For example, in *White-Jacket* the man-of-war is presented both as a "world" and as a "continual theater." In *The Confidence-Man* Melville directly quotes Jacques's speech from *As You Like It,* twisting Shakespeare's notion of role-playing to reflect his own sense of the radical uncertainties of socioeconomic life.

27. Ishmael's dreaminess as a lookout seems to be echoed in Eugene O'Neill's *Long Day's Journey into Night.* In the fourth act Edmund, the younger son, recalls his days at sea, "on the American Line, when I was lookout on the crow's nest in the dawn watch. A calm sea that time. Only a lazy ground swell and a slow drowsy roll of the ship . . . Dreaming, not keeping lookout . . . Then the moment of ecstatic freedom came. The peace, the end of the quest, the last harbor, the joy of belonging to a fulfillment beyond men's lousy, pitiful, greedy fears and hopes and

dreams!" (Eugene O'Neill, *Long Day's Journey into Night* [1955; rpt., New Haven, Conn.: Yale University Press, 1984], 153).

28. Whitman's description of Junius Booth in the role of Richard III has remarkable parallels to this description of Ahab. In particular, both Whitman and Melville note that the power of the actor is conveyed not through verbal language but through a self-conscious manipulation of space and a knowledge of the eyes upon them. "With head bent," Whitman vividly recalls, Booth "slowly and in silence . . . walks down the stage to the footlights, musingly kicking his sword . . . I can hear the clank, and feel the perfect following hush of perhaps three thousand people waiting. (I never saw an actor who could make more of the said hush or wait, and hold the audience in an indescribable, half-delicious, half-irritating suspense)" (P&P 1191).

29. Artaud himself never exactly pins down what he means. "The word 'cruelty' must be taken in a broad sense, and not in the rapacious physical sense that it is customarily given . . . From the point of view of the mind, cruelty signifies rigor, implacable intention and decision, irreversible and absolute determination" (T&D 101). Elsewhere he suggests that cruelty is the "living whirlwind that devours the darkness." One of the best and, remarkably, one of the most clear discussions of Artaud's ideas is Jacques Derrida's essay "The Theatre of Cruelty and the Closure of Representation" (*Writing and Difference,* trans. Alan Bass [Chicago: University of Chicago Press, 1978], 232–50).

CHAPTER 4. THE RIGHT TO PRIVACY

Epigraphs: William Dean Howells, "Some New American Plays," collected in *A Realist in the American Theatre: Selected Drama Criticism of William Dean Howells,* ed. Brenda Murphy (Athens: Ohio University Press, 1992), 127; George William Curtis, "The Editor's Easy Chair," *Harper's New Monthly Magazine* 30 (April 1865): 675.

1. "The Old Apple Dealer," in *Mosses from an Old Manse* (1846), in *The Centenary Edition of the Works of Nathaniel Hawthorne* (Columbus: Ohio State University Press, 1974), 10:445. Leo Marx comments that Hawthorne "required the image of the railroad to convey that sense of loneliness in the crowd he thought characteristic of the new America" (*The Pilot and the Passenger: Essays on Literature, Technology, and Culture in the United States* [Oxford: Oxford University Press, 1988], 117).

2. Howells's early novel *Their Wedding Journey* may serve as a prototype for the railroad dramas, though in chapter 4, "A Day's Railroading," the characters actually reject the drawing-room car for the common-passenger car because of the latter's more "varied prospect of humanity." The passenger car, then, provides the

narrator with an opportunity to describe the basic tenets of realism: "It was in all respects an ordinary carful of human beings, and it was perhaps more worthy to be studied on that account" (W[illiam] D[ean] Howells, *Their Wedding Journey* [Boston: Houghton Mifflin, 1871], 86).

3. The modern American family, argues Carl Degler, emerged during the years between the American Revolution and 1830. Fundamental to the modern American conception of the family was the notion that the wife, "as mistress of the home, was perceived by society and herself as the moral superior of the husband, though his legal and social inferior. The organizational basis for this relationship was that woman's life was physically spent within the home and with the family, while the man's was largely outside the home, at work. The ideological justification of this division of labor and activity [is known as] 'the doctrine of the two spheres,' or 'separate spheres.' " See Degler, "The Emergence of the Modern American Family," in *The American Family in Social-Historical Perspective,* ed. Michael Gordon (New York: St. Martin's Press, 1983), 65.

4. Richard Sennett discusses the growing sense of "isolation in the midst of visibility" in nineteenth-century experience. The most direct literary representation of this phenomenon, one might argue, is Edgar Allan Poe's short story "The Man of the Crowd." Intimacy is one way of counteracting the sense of isolation in public places. "Intimacy," writes Sennett, "is an attempt to solve the public problem by denying that the public exists" (*The Fall of Public Man* [New York: W. W. Norton, 1974], 27).

5. Higham draws from a broad range of evidence to demonstrate the transformation he describes. He is also sensitive, however, to contradictions in American culture which indicate that this transformation is not final but is instead a dialectical process that, he feels, is a "major hallmark of contemporary culture." Moreover, the changes that mark the emergence of a pattern of consolidation are notable not only in the United States in the two decades following 1848 but also in Europe. The years following 1848 contain the seed of a change in American relations with Europe politically and culturally. See John Higham, *From Boundlessness to Consolidation: The Transformation of American Culture, 1848–1860* (Ann Arbor: William L. Clements Library, 1969).

6. Edwin Booth was said to be "the first Hamlet for many a day who, in the closet scene, does not consider it necessary to rave and rant at the Queen like a drunken pot-boy—he is the first Hamlet for many a day whose conduct in the same scene would not justify the interference of third parties, on the supposition that he intended to commit assault and battery upon his mother—he is the first Prince of Denmark for many a year who has dared, in this same scene, to conduct himself like a gentleman, and not a blackguard" (Charles H. Shattuck, *The Hamlet*

of Edwin Booth [Chicago: University of Illinois Press, 1969], 42). For a comprehensive history of Booth's Hamlet, see Shattuck's book.

7. There are twelve Roberts-Campbell comedies, mostly written in the 1880s. These satirical sketches are deservedly considered Howells's best work in drama. Walter J. Meserve, for example, calls them Howells's "most humorous and stage-worthy plays" ("Introduction," *The Complete Plays of William Dean Howells* [New York: New York University Press, 1960], xx).

8. Although women are designated by first names and men by last names in both *Out of the Question* and *A Counterfeit Presentment,* this is not true of all of Howells's comedies. In *The Parlor Car,* for example, Allen Richards is Mr. Richards, and Lucy Galbraith is Miss Galbraith.

9. Edwin Harrison Cady remarks that, for Howells, anyone could be a gentleman, "given the natural powers, energy, intellect, and sensitivity." For an extensive treatment of the "gentleman" in Howells and others, see Cady, *The Gentleman in America* (Syracuse: Syracuse University Press, 1949), 191.

10. The privileging of literature and reading as a means to civilization is clearly articulated in *The Rise of Silas Lapham.* In the novel Mr. Corey instructs his son, Tom, that "all civilization comes through literature now, especially in our country . . . We must read or we must barbarize . . . I doubt if the theatre is a factor of civilization among us. I dare say it doesn't deprave a great deal, but from what I've seen of it I should say that it was intellectually degrading" (Howells, *The Rise of Silas Lapham* [1885; rpt., London: Penguin Books, 1983], 118).

11. See Howells, *Life in Letters,* 1:230.

12. First printed in the *Atlantic Monthly* of 1875, when Howells was still editor, *Private Theatricals* was republished by his daughter in 1921 as *Mrs. Farrell: A Novel* (New York: Harper and Brothers, 1921).

13. For treatment of Howells's influence in the history of American theater, Arthur Hobson Quinn's study *The American Drama from the Civil War to the Present Day* (New York: Appleton-Century-Crofts, 1927) remains among the best. Also see Brenda Murphy, *American Realism and American Drama, 1880–1940* (Cambridge: Cambridge University Press, 1987).

14. As Mary Bess Whidden and Gary Scharnhorst comment, Howells and Barrett deeply shared an ambition to bring the stage and literature together, though each placed their emphasis differently. For the correspondence between the author and the actor, see *Staging Howells: Plays and Correspondence with Lawrence Barrett,* ed. George Arms, Mary Bess Whidden, and Gary Scharnhorst (Albuquerque: University of New Mexico Press, 1994).

CHAPTER 5. THE THEATER OF PRIVATE LIFE

1. See William Dean Howells, "A Question of Propriety," *A Realist in the American Theatre* (Athens: Ohio University Press, 1992). Ibsen's career, not unlike Alcott's in some respects, is characterized by a shift from writing "blood-and-thunder" poetic dramas such as *Brand* (1866) to intimate, prosaic scenes of domestic life such as those in *A Doll House* (1879). With the title of *A Doll House* I follow Rolf Fjelde's translation, since there is no possessive in the Norwegian, and this translation more accurately captures the play's concern with domestic space.

2. Notably, Herne's first appearance as an actor on stage was as George Shelby in *Uncle Tom's Cabin* in Troy, New York, in 1859.

3. Nina Auerbach has commented, "The world of the March girls is rich enough to complete itself, and in this richness lies the tension of *Little Women* and its two sequels" (*Communities of Women: An Idea in Fiction* [Cambridge: Harvard University Press, 1978], 55).

4. See, for example, Alcott's novel *Work: A Story of Experience* (1873), in which protagonist and short-term actress Christie Devon asks herself, "If three years of this life have made me thus, what shall I be in ten? A fine actress perhaps, but how good a woman?" (ed. Joy S. Kasson [New York: Penguin Books, 1994], 43). In "La Jeune; or, Actress and Woman" Mademoiselle Nairne appears in performance "not as most actresses take the stage, but as a pretty woman would enter her room." The same basic problem recurs in works as diverse as *Behind a Mask* and *Jo's Boys.*

5. Rachel (1820–58), the greatest French tragic actress of the nineteenth century, performed with her own troupe in New York between August 1855 and January 1856. Her greatest roles were in the classical repertoire, but Rachel was also known for being an inspired natural performer. See *The Cambridge Guide to World Theatre,* ed. Martin Banham (New York: Cambridge University Press, 1988).

6. Unlike Whitman, who preferred the elder Booth, Alcott found Edwin more appealing than his father: "Saw young Booth in Brutus, and liked him better than his father" (*Louisa May Alcott: Her Life, Letters, and Journals,* ed. Ednah D. Cheney [Boston: Roberts Brothers, 1890], 91). This preference, as much as any other evidence, indicates the changing nature of American theater.

7. Charles Shattuck's study *The Hamlet of Edwin Booth* (Chicago: University of Illinois Press, 1969) is the primary source for my discussion of Booth's *Hamlet.* The most extraordinary document in Shattuck's book is a massive recording, by a twenty-one-year-old fan named Charles Clarke, of Booth's performance of Hamlet in 1870 in Booth's Theatre in New York. Clarke attempted to capture every movement, gesture, and vocal effect and, as a result, has left an invaluable record.

Clarke was so overwhelmed by Booth's *Hamlet* that he not only went to see Booth eight times in 1870, but he also memorized the entire play in order to comprehend the experience as fully as possible. Booth's production at his own theater with his own company, and recorded in exhaustive detail by a young fan, all mark his cultural authority in 1870, at the height of his career. Shattuck has published Clarke's record along with the history of Booth's *Hamlet,* photographs, and copious citations from contemporary critics. From these materials I have constructed my argument. All further references to Booth's *Hamlet* are taken from documents cited in Shattuck's extensive work.

8. See James Robinson Planché, *The Jacobite: A Comic Drama in Two Acts* (New York: Douglas, 1848). It is important to remember that Alcott was playing the Widow at the age of twenty-six, while her older sister was still playing ingenues.

9. In Richard Brinsley Sheridan's play *The Rivals* (1775) Mrs. Malaprop incompetently defends the institution of the family in which, as she sees it, conjugal love plays very little part. Of her own departed husband she tells her niece, "I am sure I hated your poor dear uncle before marriage as if he'd been a blackamoor—and yet, miss, you are sensible what a wife I made!" (*The School for Scandal and Other Plays* [London: Penguin Books, 1988]).

10. I am indebted to Christine R. Bailey of the Pennsylvania State University Libraries rare books collection for a copy of the microfilm of Alcott's story from the *New York Atlas,* 12 September 1858. I became aware of this recently discovered story through Madeleine Stern's article "An Early Alcott Sensation Story: Marion Earle; or, Only an Actress!" *Nineteenth-Century Literature* 40, no. 1 (June 1992): 91–98.

11. Michelle Perrot describes these "natural characteristics" with particular reference to Hegel's *Principles of the Philosophy of Right* (1821), in *A History of Private Life,* vol. 4: *From the Fires of Revolution to the Great War,* ed. Michelle Perrot, trans. Arthur Goldhammer (Cambridge: Harvard University Press, 1990), 100.

12. Ann Douglas has commented on the "alike-yet-different" twinship of Jean Muir and Jo March. Not only do the two share initials, Douglas remarks, but both are extraordinarily theatrical. The difference is that Jean utilizes all her resources, while Jo, respecting the harmony of the March household, seldom explores her arsenal ("Introduction," *Little Women,* by Louisa May Alcott [New York: Signet Classics, 1983], xviii).

13. Fanny Kemble (1809–93) was an English actress who first came to America in 1832. In 1834, in Philadelphia, Kemble married Pierce Butler, whom she later learned to be a slave owner. This issue, among others, induced Kemble to leave her husband in 1845. They were divorced in 1848. Later that year she played Lady Macbeth to Macready's Macbeth. Kemble was also the niece of Sarah Siddons (argu-

ably the greatest tragic actress of the English stage), whose portrait Miss Cameron has upon her wall. For the last twenty-six years of her life Kemble gave "public" drawing-room readings of Shakespeare, which were famous throughout America. Significantly, Miss Cameron's principal piece of advice for Josie is to study Shakespeare.

14. Fanny Kemble, Alcott's model for Miss Cameron, had played Lady Macbeth opposite William Charles Macready, the other actor at the center of the Astor Place Riot. For more on the Astor Place Riot, see Lawrence Levine, *Highbrow/Lowbrow: The Emergence of Cultural Hierarchy in America* (Cambridge: Harvard University Press, 1988), 64–68; Bruce A. McConachie, *Melodramatic Formations: American Theatre and Society, 1820–1870* (Iowa City: University of Iowa Press, 1992), 147–52; and David Grimsted, *Melodrama Unveiled: American Theatre and Culture, 1800–1850* (Berkeley: University of California Press, 1968), 68–75.

CHAPTER 6. UNPACKING THE BOX

Epigraphs: G.W.F. Hegel, *Science of Logic,* trans. William Wallace (Oxford: Oxford University Press, 1975), 190; Henry James, "The Figure in the Carpet," in *Eight Tales from the Major Phase:* In the Cage *and Others,* ed. Morton Dauwen Zabel (New York: W. W. Norton, 1969).

1. Henry James, "Mr. Tennyson's Drama," *Galaxy* 20, no. 3 (September 1875): 398.

2. See Leon Edel, "Henry James: The Dramatic Years," in *The Complete Plays of Henry James* (1949; rpt., Oxford: Oxford University Press, 1990); F. W. Duppee, "Henry James and the Play," *Nation* 171, 8 June 1950: 41; Henry Popkin, "Pretender to the Drama," *Theatre Arts* 33 (December 1949): 32; Edwin Clark, "Henry James and the Actress," *Pacific Spectator* 3 (Winter 1949): 90; and August W. Staub, "The Well-Made Failures of Henry James," *Southern Speech Journal* 27 (Winter 1961): 91–101.

3. See Leon Edel, *Henry James, The Treacherous Years* (New York: J. P. Lippincott, 1969), 108–15; Walter Isle, *Experiments in Form: Henry James's Novels, 1896–1901* (Cambridge: Harvard University Press, 1968), 1–18; Leo B. Levy, *Versions of Melodrama: A Study of the Fiction and Drama of Henry James, 1865–1897* (Berkeley: University of California Press, 1957), 90–119; and Francis Fergusson, "James's Idea of Dramatic Form," *Kenyon Review* 5 (Autumn 1943): 498.

4. In his famous, antitheatrical letter to M. D'Alembert, Rousseau writes, "There ought to be many [entertainments in a republic]. It is in republics that they were born, it is in their bosom that they are seen to flourish with a truly festive air . . . We already have many of these public festivals; let us have even more . . . But let us not adopt these exclusive entertainments which close up a small number

of people in melancholy fashion in a gloomy cavern." See Jean-Jacques Rousseau, *Politics and the Arts: Letter to M. D'Alembert on the Theatre,* trans. Allan Bloom (Ithaca: Cornell University Press, 1960), 125.

5. "Nous avons tous joué autrefois le diable qui sort de sa boîte. On l'aplatit, il se redresse. On le repousse plus bas, il rebondit plus haut. On l'écrase sous son convercle, et souvent il fait tout sautet . . . C'est le conflict de deux obstinations, dont l'une, purement mécanique, finit poutant d'ordinaire par cédar à l'autre" (*Le rire: essai sur la signification du comique* [Paris: Librairie Félix Alcan, 1928], 69–70). The original text reveals that Bergson too uses the language of boxes (*les boîtes*).

6. Henri Bergson, *Écrits et paroles,* ed. R.- M. Mosse-Bastide (Paris: Presses Universitaires de France, 1957), 1:84–94.

7. See G. E. Lewes, *On Actors and the Art of Acting* (London: Smith, Elder, and Co., 1875), 113. Lewes, an immensely learned man, who wrote on a wide range of subjects, including philosophy, psychology, and literature, produced a theory of the mind that is deeply relevant to this theory of acting. For Lewes's scientific writings about organism and mechanism, see G. E. Lewes, *The Physical Basis of the Mind* (1877; rpt., London: Kegan Paul, Trench, Truber, and Co., 1893). Also see Joseph Roach, "Second Nature: Mechanism and Organicism from Goethe to Lewes," in *The Player's Passion: Studies in the Science of Acting* (Newark: University of Delaware Press, 1985), 160–93.

8. For an even more intricate description of the well-made play, see Stephen S. Stanton, "Introduction," Camille *and Other Plays* (New York: Hill and Wang, 1957), xii–xx. "It is to be noted," writes Stanton, "that the will of the characters in this type of drama is always subordinate to the exigencies of the plot and to the artifices employed by the author" (xv).

9. The same metaphor reappears in Strindberg's preface to *Miss Julie* (1888), in which he writes, "Some countries, it is true, have attempted to create a new drama by using the old forms with up to date contents, but . . . as no new form has been devised for these new contents, the new wine has burst the old bottles."

10. Clayton Hamilton argues that the play's long-term popular success was largely due to the ambition of high-powered actresses to pass the "test." See "The Career of Camille," *The Theory of the Theatre* (New York, 1939), 369–71. After a Broadway production in 1956, however, Brooks Atkinson complains that when Marguerite "totters and staggers and gasps in the last act one does not suffer as one should." See "Why Camille?" *New York Times,* 19 September 1956. The importance of the role of Marguerite for defining a transition from melodrama to realism is also clearly implied in the 1890s, in Chekhov's play *The Seagull,* for Arkadina had made a great name playing the role on the stage and then, in a sense, plays it "for real" in a private scene with Trigorin.

11. The way *grace* is defined in *The Bostonians* has much in common with the way Bergson uses the term. For example, Ransome is particularly impressed with the grace of Verena in performance:

> He had read, of old, of the *improvisatrice* of Italy, and this was a chastened, modern, American version of the type, a New England Corinna, with a mission instead of a lyre. The most graceful part of her was her earnestness, the way her delightful eyes, wandering over the "fashionable audience" (before which she was so perfectly unabashed), as if she wished to resolve it into a single sentient personality, seemed to say that the only thing in life she cared for was to put the truth into a form that would render conviction irresistible . . . There was not a glance or a motion that did not seem part of the pure, still-burning passion that animated her. (228)

12. The German critic and philosopher Wilhelm Dilthey, an almost exact contemporary of James, describes the relationship of bildungsroman to "self-development" and "inner culture" in his 1910 essay on Hölderlin. See Dilthey, *Selected Works,* ed. Rudolf A Maakkreel and Frithjof Rodi (Princeton: Princeton University Press, 1985), 5:335. Hans-Georg Gadamer defines the nineteenth-century notion of *bildung* as a process of self-formation which "is not achieved in the manner of a technical construction, but grows out of an inner process of formation and cultivation." See *Truth and Method,* 2d ed., trans. Joel Weinsheimer and Donald G. Marshall (New York: Continuum, 1995), 11. W. H. Bruford translates *bildung* as "self-cultivation" in *The German Tradition of Self-Cultivation: "Bildung" from Humboldt to Thomas Mann* (London: Cambridge University Press, 1975). The usual translation, *self-formation,* as David Sorkin remarks, points to the central idea of bildung, "a notion of the integral development of personality through form." See David Sorkin, *The Transformation of German Jewry, 1780–1840* (Oxford: Oxford University Press, 1987), 15.

13. Henry James, "After the Play," in *The Scenic Art: Notes on Acting and the Drama: 1872–1901,* ed. Allan Wade (New Brunswick: Rutgers University Press, 1948), 226–42.

14. In this argument, as well as in the form of the sketch itself, James's dialogue is reminiscent of Dryden's *Essay in Defense of Dramatic Poesy.* Dryden's mouthpiece, Neander, argues that French drama is inferior to English because it is not "animated with the soul of poesy," meaning "imitation of humour and passions." The new English dramas are praised for being "fuller of spirit": "The lively imitation of nature being in the definition of a play, those which best fulfill that law ought to be esteemed superior to the others" (*John Dryden,* ed. Keith Walker [Oxford: Oxford University Press, 1987]), 102.

15. Henry James's letters to Augustin Daly, including this exchange over the planned production of *Disengaged,* are in the Theatre Collection of the Harvard University Library, Houghton Library.

16. Michaels's discussion focuses on the disempowerment of the photographer rather than the person photographed, and yet it seems suitable to understand photography in *Disengaged* as metaphor for the mechanical oppression of free will in general. Michaels also touches on the popularity of automatic writing in the late nineteenth century, a trend with similarly provocative connotations. See Walter Benn Michaels, "Action and Accident: Photography and Writing," *The Gold Standard and the Logic of Naturalism: American Literature at the Turn of the Century* (Berkeley: University of California Press, 1987), 215–44.

17. "Every corner of a house," writes Gaston Bachelard, "is a symbol of solitude for the imagination." Bachelard comments that representations of corners in literature are rare because "this purely physical contraction into oneself already bears the mark of a certain negativism." Thinking perhaps of the child compelled to stand in a corner, he notes that "the corner becomes a negation of the Universe." And yet the corner is also a sort of haven of immobility which as a "half-box" may illustrate "the dialectics of inside and outside." See Bachelard, *The Poetics of Space,* trans. Maria Jolas (Boston: Beacon Press, 1969), 136–37.

18. Ibsen's plays, as noted in the text, are pervaded by the tension between entrapment and freedom. In *The Wild Duck* Hedvig Ekdal sacrifices her life to Gregers Werle's rigid "demand of the ideal." But the Ekdal home itself, like the Helmer "Doll House," is a claustrophobic and suffocating space. Gregers indicates the boxlike nature of the home when he demands of Hjalmar Ekdal, "How can a man like you, who were always accustomed to be in the open, live in a stuffy town, boxed in by four walls like this?" (act 2). In Strindberg one might think of the straitjacketed Captain at the end of *The Father,* as well as images of claustration and the struggle for liberation in the dream plays, such as the imprisoned mummy in *The Ghost Sonata* or the suffocation and eventual release of Indra's Daughter from the Lawyer's House in *A Dream Play.* Strindberg's plays are full of such examples.

19. See Millicent Bell, "The Disengagement from 'Things': The Spoils of Poynton," *Meaning in Henry James* (Cambridge: Harvard University Press, 1991), 204–22. Walter Benjamin makes a relevant comment on the collector who lives in his objects and whose property thus becomes like a "tactical sphere." Benjamin humorously remarks in "Unpacking My Library," "The smallest antique shop can be a fortress, the most remote stationery store a key position" ("Unpacking My Library," *Illuminations,* ed. Hannah Arendt, trans. Harry Zohn [New York: Schocken Books, 1968], 59–68).

20. Jacques Barzun makes a similar claim about *The Reprobate* and about James's

oeuvre as a whole in "James the Melodramatist," *Kenyon Review* 5 (Autumn 1943): 509–21.

21. Arnold Bennett, *Things That Have Interested Me* (London: Chatto and Windus, 1921), 315.

22. See H. G. Wells, *Pall Mall Gazette;* William Archer, *World;* A. B. Walkley, *Star;* Arnold Bennett, *Woman;* Bernard Shaw, *Saturday Review.*

23. See Arnold Bennett, *Woman,* 19 January 1895.

24. In his essay "The Théâtre Français" James writes that the drinking scene in Augier's romantic comedy "always remained in my mind as one of the most perfect things that I have seen on the stage." See "The Théâtre Français," *The Scenic Art: Notes on Acting and the Drama, 1872–1901,* ed. Allan Wade (New Brunswick: Rutgers University Press, 1948), 81.

25. It must be noted that a variety of factors may have contributed to the play's tumultuous reception on its opening night, including a conspiracy of some members of the audience against the actor-manager George Alexander. Notably, there was no trouble on subsequent nights of the play's five-week run. In fact, it was, in general, warmly received. Nonetheless, whatever the causes of the reaction of the first night, it was not a random response but a response directed at specific and peculiar features of the play.

26. William Archer, *Daily Chronicle,* 8 January 1895.

27. See Anne T. Margolis, *Henry James and the Problem of Audience: An International Act* (Ann Arbor: UMI Research Press, 1981), 91–96.

28. A. B. Walkley, *Star,* 8 January 1895.

Works Cited

Adelman, Janet. "'Born of Woman': Fantasies of Maternal Power in *Macbeth*." In *Cannibals, Witches, and Divorce: Estranging the Renaissance* (English Institute Essays), ed. Marjorie Garber, 90–121. Baltimore: Johns Hopkins University Press, 1987.

Agnew, Jean-Cristophe. *Worlds Apart: The Market and the Theater in Anglo-American Thought, 1550–1750*. Cambridge: Cambridge University Press, 1986.

Aiken, George L. *Uncle Tom's Cabin. The Longman Anthology of American Drama*. Ed. Lee A. Jacobus. New York: Longman, 1982.

Alcott, Louisa May. *Behind a Mask*. In *Alternative Alcott*. Ed. Elaine Showalter, 95–202. New Brunswick: Rutgers University Press, 1988.

———. *Comic Tragedies Written by "Jo" and "Meg" and Acted by the "Little Women."* Boston: Roberts Brothers, 1893.

———. *Jo's Boys and How They Turned Out*. Boston: Little, Brown, 1886.

———. "La Jeune; or, Actress and Woman." In *Freaks of Genius: Unknown Thrillers of Louisa May Alcott*, ed. Daniel Shealy. New York: Greenwood Press, 1991.

———. *Little Women*. New York: Signet Classic, 1983.

———. *Louisa May Alcott: Her Life, Letters, and Journals*. Ed. Ednah D. Cheney. Boston: Roberts Brothers, 1890.

———. "Marion Earle; or, Only an Actress!" *New York Atlas*, 12 September 1858.

———. "The Rival Prima Donnas." *Louisa May Alcott: Selected Fiction*. Ed. Madeleine Stern, Daniel Shealy, and Joel Myerson. Boston: Little, Brown, 1990.

———. *Work: A Story of Experience*. Ed. Joy S. Kasson. New York: Penguin Books, 1994.

Alcott, William A. *The Young Man's Guide*. Boston: T. R. Marvin, 1845.

Allen, Gay Wilson. *The Solitary Singer: A Critical Biography of Walt Whitman*. Chicago: University of Chicago Press, 1855.

Arendt, Hannah. *The Human Condition*. Chicago: University of Chicago Press, 1958.

Artaud, Antonin. *Selected Writings*. Ed. Susan Sontag, trans. Helen Weaver. Berkeley: University of California Press, 1976.

———. *The Theater and Its Double*. Trans. Mary Caroline Richards. New York: Grove Weidenfeld, 1958.

Aspiz, Harold. *Walt Whitman and the Body Beautiful*. Urbana: University of Illinois Press, 1980.

Atkinson, Brooks. "Why Camille?" *New York Times*, 19 September 1956.

Auerbach, Erich. *Mimesis: The Representation of Reality in Western Literature.* Trans. Willard R. Trask. Princeton: Princeton University Press, 1953.

Auerbach, Nina. *Communities of Women: An Idea in Fiction.* Cambridge: Harvard University Press, 1978.

———. *Private Theatricals: The Lives of the Victorians.* Cambridge: Harvard University Press, 1990.

Austen, Jane. *Mansfield Park.* Ed. Tony Tanner. New York: Penguin Books, 1966.

Bachelard, Gaston. *The Poetics of Space.* Trans. Maria Jolas. Boston: Beacon Press, 1969.

Banham, Martin, ed. *The Cambridge Guide to World Theatre.* New York: Cambridge University Press, 1988.

Bank, Rosemarie K. *Theatre Culture in America, 1825–1860.* Cambridge: Cambridge University Press, 1997.

Barish, Jonas. *The Antitheatrical Prejudice.* Berkeley: University of California Press, 1981.

Barnum, P. T. *Struggles and Triumphs, Or, Forty Years' Recollections.* Ed. Carl Bode. New York: Viking Penguin, 1981.

Barthes, Roland. *The Responsibility of Forms: Critical Essays on Music, Art, and Representation.* Trans. Richard Howard. Berkeley: University of California Press, 1991.

Baym, Nina. "Melodramas of Beset Manhood: How Theories of American Fiction Exclude Women Authors." *American Quarterly* 33, no. 2 (Summer 1981): 123–39.

Bell, Millicent. *Meaning in Henry James.* Cambridge: Harvard University Press, 1991.

Benjamin, Walter. *Illuminations.* Ed. Hannah Arendt. New York: Schocken Books, 1968.

———. *The Origin of the German Tragic Drama.* Trans. John Osborne. London: Verso, 1977.

Bennett, Arnold. *Things That Have Interested Me.* London: Chatto and Windus, 1921.

Bergson, Henri. *Écrits et paroles.* Ed. R.- M. Mosse-Bastide, 1:84–94. Paris: Presses Universitaires de France, 1957.

———. "Laughter." *Comedy.* Ed. Wylie Sypher, 61–190. Baltimore: Johns Hopkins University Press, 1956.

———. *Le rire: essai sur la signification du comique.* Paris: Librairie Félix Alcan, 1928.

Bernhardt, Sarah. *The Art of the Theatre.* Trans. H. J. Stenning. New York: Dial Press, 1925.

Berthoff, Warner. *The Example of Melville.* Princeton: Princeton University Press, 1962.

Bezanson, Walter E. "*Moby-Dick:* Document, Drama, Dream." In *A Companion to Melville Studies,* ed. John Bryant, 169–210. New York: Greenwood Press, 1986.

Bingham, Caleb. *The Columbian Orator.* Boston: J. H. A. Frost, Lincoln and Edmands, Stimpson and Clapp, Marsh, Capen and Lyon, 1832.

Bird, Robert Montgomery. *The Gladiator.* In *American Plays,* ed. Allan Gates Halline, 153–98. New York: American Book Co., 1935.

Boker, George Henry. *Francesca da Rimini.* In *Representative American Plays: From 1767 to the Present Day,* ed. Arthur Hobson Quinn. New York: Appleton-Century-Crofts, 1957.

Boorstin, Daniel J. *The Americans: The Democratic Experience.* New York: Vintage Books, 1974.

Boucicault, Dion. *Rip Van Winkle.* In *Representative American Plays: From 1767 to the Present Day,* ed. Arthur Hobson Quinn, pp. 339–432. New York: Appleton-Century-Crofts, Inc., 1957.

Brooks, Peter. *The Melodramatic Imagination: Balzac, Henry James, Melodrama, and the Mode of Excess.* New Haven: Yale University Press, 1976.

Brown, Charles Brockden. *Wieland; Or, The Transformation: An American Tale.* Garden City, N.Y.: Anchor Press, 1973.

Brown, T. Allston. *A History of the New York Stage: From the First Performance in 1732 to 1901,* vol. 1. New York: Dodd, Mead, 1903.

Bruffee, Kenneth A. *Elegaic Romance: Cultural Change and Loss of the Hero in Modern Fiction.* Ithaca: Cornell University Press, 1983.

Bruford, W. H. *The German Tradition of Self-Cultivation: "Bildung" from Humboldt to Thomas Mann.* London: Cambridge University Press, 1975.

Brustein, Robert. *The Theatre of Revolt: An Approach to the Modern Drama.* Chicago: Elephant Paperbacks, 1991.

Buell, Lawrence. *Literary Transcendentalism: Style and Vision in the American Renaissance.* Ithaca: Cornell University Press, 1973.

———. *New England Literary Culture: From Revolution through Renaissance.* Cambridge: Cambridge University Press, 1986.

———. "Observer-Hero Narrative." *Texas Studies in Literature and Language: A Journal of the Humanities* 21, no.1 (Spring 1979): 93–111.

Burke, Kenneth. *A Grammar of Motives.* 1945. Reprint. Berkeley: University of California Press, 1969.

Butler, Judith. *Bodies That Matter: On the Discursive Limits of "Sex."* London: Routledge, 1993.

———. *Excitable Speech: A Politics of the Performative.* New York: Routledge, 1997.

———. *Gender Trouble: Feminism and the Subversion of Identity.* New York: Routledge, 1990.

Carlisle, E. Fred. *Uncertain Self: Whitman's Drama of Identity.* E. Lansing: Michigan State University Press, 1973.

Carlson, Marvin. *Performance: A Critical Introduction.* London: Routledge, 1996.

———. *Theories of the Theatre: A Historical and Critical Survey, from the Greeks to the Present.* Ithaca: Cornell University Press, 1984.

Caserio, Robert L. *Plot, Story and the Novel: From Dickens and Poe to the Modern Period.* Princeton: Princeton University Press, 1979.

Chase, Richard. *The American Novel and Its Tradition.* New York: Anchor Books, 1957.

Clark, Edwin. "Henry James and the Actress." *Pacific Spectator* 3 (Winter 1949).

Clarke, Asia Booth. *The Elder and the Younger Booth.* Boston: James R. Osgood and Company, 1882.

Cohn, Dorrit. *Transparent Minds: Narrative Modes for Presenting Consciousness in Fiction.* Princeton: Princeton University Press, 1978.

Covares, Francis G. "The Plebeian Moment: Theatre and Working-Class Life In Late Nineteenth-Century Pittsburgh." In *Theatre for Working-Class Audiences in the United States, 1830–1980,* ed. Bruce A. McConachie and Daniel Friedman, 47–60. Westport, Conn.: Greenwood Press, 1985.

Cuddon, J. A. *The Penguin Dictionary of Literary Terms and Literary Theory.* London: Penguin Books, 1976.

Curtis, George William. "Editor's Easy Chair." *Harper's New Monthly Magazine* 28 (December 1863): 131–33; and 30 (April 1865): 673–75.

Custis, George Washington Parke. *Pocahontas; Or, The Settlers of Virginia* (1830), in *Representative American Plays from 1765 to the Present Day,* ed. Arthur Hobson Quinn. New York: Appleton-Century-Crofts, 1957.

Degler, Carl N. "The Emergence of the Modern American Family." In *The American Family in Social-Historical Perspective,* 3d ed., ed. Michael Gordon, 61–79. New York: St. Martin's Press, 1983.

Denier, Tony. *The Amateur's Hand-Book and Guide to Home or Drawing Room Theatricals: How to Get Them Up and How to Act in Them.* New York: Samuel French, 1866.

Derrida, Jacques. *Writing and Difference.* Trans. Alan Bass. Chicago: University of Chicago Press, 1978.

Dickens, Charles. *Nicholas Nickleby.* Ed. Michael Slater. London: Penguin Books, 1978.

Dilthey, Wilhelm. *Selected Works,* vol. 5. Ed. Rudolf A. Maakkreel and Frithjof Rodi. Princeton: Princeton University Press, 1985.

Dollimore, Jonathan, and Alan Sinfield, eds. *Political Shakespeare: New Essays in Cultural Materialism.* Manchester: Manchester University Press, 1985.

Dougherty, James. *Walt Whitman and the Citizen's Eye.* Baton Rouge: Louisiana State University Press, 1993.

Douglas, Ann. "Introduction." *Little Women.* New York: Signet Classic, 1983.

Douglass, Frederick. *Narrative of the Life of Frederick Douglass, an American Slave.* Ed. Houston A. Baker. 1845. Reprint. New York: Penguin Books, 1986.

Downer, Alan S. *The Eminent Tragedian: William Charles Macready.* Cambridge: Harvard University Press, 1966.

Dryden, John. *An Essay of Dramatic Poesy. John Dryden.* Ed. Keith Walker. Oxford: Oxford University Press, 1987.

Dumas, Alexandre, fils. *Camille (La Dame aux Camélias).* Camille *and Other Plays.* Ed. Stephen S. Stanton, trans. Edith Reynolds and Nigel Playfair. New York: Hill and Wang, 1957.

———. "Preface" (1868), *Un Père Prodigue* (1859). In *European Theories of the Drama.* Ed. Barrett H. Clark, 383–88. New York: Crown Publishers, 1947.

Dunlap, William. *History of the American Theatre and Anecdotes of the Principal Actors.* 1832. Reprint. New York: Burt Franklin, 1963.

———. *A Trip to Niagara; or, Travellers in America. A Farce in Three Acts.* (New York: E. B. Clayton, 1830).

Duppee, F. W. "Henry James and the Play." *Nation* 171, 8 June 1950: 19–69.

Durivage, F. A. "Delsarte." *Atlantic Monthly* 27, no. 163 (May 1871).

Edel, Leon. "Henry James: The Dramatic Years." In *The Complete Plays of Henry James.* Ed. Leon Edel, 19–69. 1949. Reprint. Oxford: Oxford University Press, 1990.

———. *Henry James: The Treacherous Years.* New York: J. P. Lippincott, 1969.

Elam, Keir. *The Semiotics of Theatre and Drama.* London: Routledge, 1980.

Eliot, T. S. "Hamlet." In Selected Prose of T. S. Eliot. Ed. Frank Kermode (New York: Harcourt Brace Jovanovich, 1956), 45–49.

Emerson, Ralph Waldo. *Essays and Lectures.* New York: Library of America, 1983.

Erkkila, Betsy. *Whitman the Political Poet.* New York: Oxford University Press, 1989.

Evreinoff, Nicolas. *The Theatre in Life.* Ed. and trans. Alexander I. Nazaroff. New York: Brentano's, 1927.

Faner, Robert D. *Walt Whitman and Opera.* Philadelphia: University of Pennsylvania Press, 1951.

Fawkes, Richard. *Dion Boucicault: A Biography.* London: Quartet Books, 1979.

Felheim, Marvin. *The Theater of Augustin Daly: An Account of the Late Nineteenth Century American Stage.* Cambridge: Harvard University Press, 1956.

Fergusson, Francis. "James's Idea of Dramatic Form." *Kenyon Review* 5 (Autumn 1943): 495–507.

Fetterly, Judith. "Impersonating 'Little Women': The Radicalism of Alcott's *Behind a Mask.*" *Women's Studies* 10 (1983): 1–14.

Fisher, Philip. "Democratic Social Space: Whitman, Melville, and the Promise of American Transparency." *Representations* 24 (Fall 1988): 60–101.

———. *Hard Facts: Setting and Form in the American Novel.* New York: Oxford University Press, 1987.

Forrest, Edwin. *Oration Delivered at the Democratic Republican Celebration of the Sixty-Second Anniversary of the Independence of the United States, in the City of New York, Fourth July, 1838.* New York: J. W. Bell, 1838.

Fried, Michael. *Absorption and Theatricality: Painting and the Beholder in the Age of Diderot.* Berkeley: University of California Press, 1980.

———. "Art and Objecthood." *Minimal Art.* Ed. Gregory Battock. New York: Dutton.

Frost, S. A. *Mr. John Smith, Amateur Theatricals and Fairy-Tale Dramas. A Collection of Original Plays, Expressly Designed for Drawing-Room Performance.* New York: Dick and Fitzgerald, 1868.

Gadamer, Hans-Georg. *Truth and Method,* 2d ed. Trans. Joel Weinsheimer and Donald G. Marshall. New York: Continuum, 1995.

Garrick, David. *Letters.* Ed. David M. Little and George M. Kahrl. 3 vols. Cambridge, Mass.: Harvard University Press, 1963.

Gilbert, Douglas. *American Vaudeville: Its Life and Times.* New York: Dover Publications, 1940.

Goffman, Erving. *The Presentation of Self in Everyday Life.* New York: Doubleday, 1959.

de Goncourt, Edmond, and Jules. "Preface de la Premiére Édition" (1864). Reprinted in *Germinie Lacerteux.* Paris: G. Charpentier and Co., 1889.

Greenblatt, Stephen. *Renaissance Self-Fashioning: From More to Shakespeare.* Chicago: University of Chicago Press, 1980.

Grimsted, David. *Melodrama Unveiled: American Theater and Culture, 1800–1850.* Berkeley: University of California Press, 1968.

Grossman, Allen. "The Poetics of Union in Whitman and Lincoln: An Inquiry toward the Relationship of Art and Policy." In *The American Renaissance Reconsidered,* ed. Walter Benn Michaels and Donald E. Pease, 183–208. Baltimore: Johns Hopkins University Press, 1985.

Halttunen, Karen. *Confidence Men and Painted Women: A Study of Middle-Class Culture in America, 1830–1870.* New Haven: Yale University Press, 1982.

———. "The Domestic Drama of Louisa May Alcott." *Feminist Studies* 10, no. 2 (September 1984): 232–54.

Hamilton, Clayton. "The Career of Camille." *The Theory of the Theatre.* 369–71. New York: Henry Holt, 1939.

Hanners, John. *"It Was Play or Starve": Acting in the Nineteenth-Century Popular Theatre.* Bowling Green, Ohio: Bowling Green State University Popular Press, 1993.

Hawthorne, Nathaniel. *The Scarlet Letter.* In *Great Short Works of Nathaniel Hawthorne,* ed. Frederick C. Crews. New York: Harper and Row, 1967.

———. "The Old Apple Dealer," in *Mosses from an Old Manse* (1846). In *The Centenary Edition of the Works of Nathaniel Hawthorne,* vol. 10, p. 445. Columbus, Ohio: Ohio State University Press, 1974.

Hegel, Georg Wilhelm Friedrich. *Aesthetics: Lectures on Fine Arts,* vol. 2. Trans. T. M. Knox. Oxford: Clarendon Press, 1975.

———. *Hegel's Logic.* Trans. William Wallace. Oxford: Oxford University Press, 1975.

Heilman, Robert Bechtold. *Tragedy and Melodrama: Versions of Experience.* Seattle: University of Washington Press, 1968.

Higham, John. *From Boundlessness to Consolidation: The Transformation of American Culture, 1848–1860.* Ann Arbor: William L. Clements Library, 1969.

Hone, Philip. *The Diary of Philip Hone: 1828–1851.* Ed. Bayard Tuckerman. New York: Dodd, Mead and Company, 1889.

Howard, Bronson. *The Autobiography of a Play.* New York: Dramatic Museum of Columbia University, 1914.

Howells, William Dean. *The Complete Plays of William Dean Howells.* Ed. Walter J. Meserve. New York: New York University Press, 1960.

———. "Life and Letters." *Harper's Weekly* 39, 11 May 1895.

———. *A Modern Instance.* New York: Penguin Books, 1984.

———. *Mrs. Farrell: A Novel* (aka *Private Theatricals*). New York: Harper and Brothers, 1921.

———. *A Realist in the American Theatre: Selected Drama Criticism of William Dean Howells.* Ed. Brenda Murphy. Athens: Ohio University Press, 1992.

———. *The Rise of Silas Lapham.* 1885. Reprint. London: Penguin Books, 1983.

———. *Staging Howells: Plays and Correspondence with Lawrence Barrett.* Ed. George Arms, Mary Bess Whidden, and Gary Scharnhorst. Albuquerque: University of New Mexico Press, 1994.

———. *The Story of a Play: A Novel.* Boston: Harper and Brothers, 1989.

———. *Their Wedding Journey.* Boston: Houghton Mifflin, 1871.

Ibsen, Henrik. *The Wild Duck.* Ed. William Archer, trans. Mrs. F. E. Archer. 1890. Reprint. London: Walter Scott, 1905.

Irving, Henry. "Address to the Students of Harvard University." MSS, 30 March 1885.

Isle, Walter. *Experiments in Form: Henry James's Novels, 1896–1901.* Cambridge: Harvard University Press, 1968.

James, Henry. *The Ambassadors.* 1908. Reprint. London: Penguin Books, 1986.

———. *The American Scene.* Ed. Leon Edel. 1907. Reprint. Bloomington: Indiana University Press, 1968.

———. *The Art of the Novel: Critical Prefaces.* 1908. Reprint. New York: Charles Scribner's Sons, 1950.

———. *The Awkward Age.* 1908. Reprint. London: Penguin Books, 1979.

———. *The Bostonians.* 1886. Reprint. London: Penguin Books, 1982.

———. *The Complete Notebooks of Henry James.* Ed. Leon Edel and Lyall H. Powers. New York: Oxford University Press, 1987.

———. *The Complete Plays of Henry James.* Ed. Leon Edel. New York: Oxford University Press, 1990.

———. "Frances Anne Kemble." *Temple Bar: A London Magazine for Town and Country Readers* 97 (April 1893): 503–25.

———. "The Figure in the Carpet." *Complete Stories: 1892–1898.* New York: Library of America, 1996.

———. *The Letters of Henry James,* vol. 1. Ed. Percy Lubbock. New York: Octagon Books, 1970.

———. "Mr. Tennyson's Drama." *Galaxy* 20, no. 3 (September 1875): 393–402 .

———. "Nona Vincent." *Complete Stories: 1892–1898.* New York: Library of America, 1996.

———. *The Notebooks of Henry James.* Ed. F. O. Matthiessen and Kenneth B. Murdock. Chicago: University of Chicago Press, 1947.

———. "The Private Life." *Complete Stories: 1892–1898.* New York: Library of America, 1996.

———. *The Scenic Art: Notes on Acting and the Drama: 1872–1901.* Ed. Allan Wade. New Brunswick: Rutgers University Press, 1948.

———. *A Small Boy and Others.* New York: Charles Scribner's Sons, 1913.

———. *The Tragic Muse.* 1890. Reprint. New York: Harper and Brothers, 1960.

———. *What Maisie Knew.* 1908. Reprint. New York: Anchor Books, 1954.

Kaplan, Fred. *Henry James: The Imagination of Genius: A Biography.* New York: William Morrow, 1992.

Kaplan, Justin. *Walt Whitman: A Life.* New York: Simon and Schuster, 1980.

Kemble, Fanny. *Fanny Kemble: The American Journals.* Ed. Elizabeth Mavor. London: Weidenfeld and Nicolson, 1990.

———. *The Terrific Kemble: A Victorian Self-Portrait from the Writings of Fanny Kemble.* Ed. Eleanor Ransome. London: Hamish Hamilton, 1978.

Kerman, Joseph. *Opera as Drama.* New York: Vintage Press, 1959.

Knight, G. Wilson. *Symbol of Man: On Body-Soul for Stage and Studio.* London: Regency Press, 1979.

Knoper, Randall. *Acting Naturally: Mark Twain in the Culture of Performance.* Berkeley: University of California Press, 1995.

Kubiak, Anthony. "Modern Theatre and Melville's *Moby-Dick:* Writing and Sounding the Whale." *Modern Drama* 34 (March 1991): 107–17.

Larson, Kerry C. *Whitman's Drama of Consensus.* Chicago: University of Chicago Press, 1988.

Lawrence, D. H. *Studies in Classic American Literature.* London: Penguin Books, 1923.

Lessing, G. E. *Hamburg Dramaturgy.* Trans. Helen Zimmerman. New York: Dover Publications, 1962.

Levine, Lawrence W. *Highbrow/Lowbrow: The Emergence of Cultural Hierarchy in America.* Cambridge: Harvard University Press, 1988.

Levy, Leo B. *Versions of Melodrama: A Study of the Fiction and Drama of Henry James, 1865–1897.* Berkeley: University of California Press, 1957.

Lewes, George Henry. *The Life of Goethe.* 1855. Reprint. New York: Frederick Ungar, 1965.

———. *On Actors and the Art of Acting.* London: Smith, Elder, and Company, 1875.

———. *The Physical Basis of the Mind.* 1877. Reprint. London: Kegan Paul, Trench, Trubner, and Company, 1983.

Leyda, Jay. *The Melville Log: A Documentary Life of Herman Melville, 1819–1891.* New York: Gordian Press, 1969.

Löwith, Karl. *From Hegel to Nietzsche: The Revolution in Nineteenth-Century Thought.* Trans. David E. Green. New York: Columbia University Press, 1964.

Macready, William Charles. *The Journal of William Charles Macready: 1832–1851.* Ed. J. C. Trewin. Carbondale: Southern Illinois University Press, 1967.

Margolis, Anne T. *Henry James and the Problem of Audience: An International Act.* Ann Arbor: UMI Research Press, 1981.

Markels, Julian. *Melville and the Politics of Identity: From* King Lear *to* Moby-Dick. Urbana: University of Illinois Press, 1993.

Marx, Leo. *The Pilot and the Passenger: Essays on Literature, Technology, and Culture in the United States.* Oxford: Oxford University Press, 1988.

Matthiessen, F. O. *American Renaissance: Art and Expression in the Age of Emerson and Whitman.* London: Oxford University Press, 1941.

McConachie, Bruce A. *Melodramatic Formations: American Theatre and Society, 1820–1870.* Iowa City: University of Iowa Press, 1992.

McConachie, Bruce A., and Daniel Friedman. *Theatre for Working-Class Audiences in the United States, 1830–1980.* Westport, Conn.: Greenwood Press, 1985.

McWilliams, John. "The Rationale for 'The American Romance.'" *Boundary 2: An International Journal of Literature and Culture* 17, no. 1 (Spring 1990): 71–82.

Melville, Herman. *The Confidence-Man: His Masquerade.* Oxford: Oxford University Press, 1989.

———. *Great Short Works of Herman Melville.* Ed. Warner Berthoff. New York: Harper and Row, 1969.

———. *Journal of a Visit to London and the Continent by Herman Melville: 1849–1850.* Ed. Eleanor Melville Metcalf. Cambridge: Harvard University Press, 1948.

———. *Moby-Dick.* Ed. Harrison Hayford and Hershel Parker. New York: W. W. Norton, 1967.

———. *Omoo: A Narrative of Adventures in the South Seas.* New York: Library of America, 1982.

———. *White-Jacket, or The World in a Man-of-War.* Oxford: Oxford University Press, 1990.

Meyer, Michael. *Ibsen.* 1967. Reprint. London: Penguin Books, 1985.

Michaels, Walter Benn. *The Gold Standard and the Logic of Naturalism: American Literature at the Turn of the Century.* Berkeley: University of California Press, 1987.

Montrose, Moses. *Representative American Plays by American Dramatists from 1765 to the Present Day,* vol. 2: *1815–1858.* New York: Benjamin Blom, 1925.

Moody, Richard. *Edwin Forrest: First Star of the American Stage.* New York: Alfred A. Knopf, 1960.

Moore, George. *The Use of the Body in Relation to the Mind.* New York: Harper and Brothers, 1847.

Murphy, Brenda. *American Realism and American Drama, 1880–1940.* Cambridge: Cambridge University Press, 1987.

Nathanson, Tenney. *Body, Voice, and Writing in* Leaves of Grass. New York: New York University Press, 1992.

Nettels, Elsa. *Language, Race, and Social Class in Howells's America.* Lexington: University Press of Kentucky, 1988.

Nussbaum, Martha C. *Love's Knowledge: Essays on Philosophy and Literature.* New York: Oxford University Press, 1990.

O'Connor, William Douglas. *The Good Gray Poet: A Vindication.* New York: Bunce and Huntington, 1866.

Odell, George C. D. *Annals of the New York Stage,* vols. 3 and 5. New York: Columbia University Press, 1931.

Olson, Charles. *Call Me Ishmael.* New York: Grove Press, 1947.

———. "Lear and Moby-Dick." *Twice a Year: A Semi-Annual Journal of Literature, the Arts, and Civil Liberties,* no. 1 (Fall–Winter 1938): 165–89.

O'Neill, Eugene. *Long Day's Journey into Night.* 1955. Reprint. New Haven: Yale University Press, 1984.

Ong, Walter J. *Orality and Literacy: The Technologizing of the Word.* London: Routledge, 1982.

Pease, Donald. "Melville and Cultural Persuasion." In *Ideology and Classic American Literature,* ed. Sacvan Bercovitch and Myra Jehlen, 384–417. Cambridge: Cambridge University Press, 1986.

Perrot, Michelle, ed. *A History of Private Life IV: From the Fires of Revolution to the Great War.* Trans. Arthur Goldhammer. Cambridge: Harvard University Press, 1990.

Perry, John. *James A. Herne: The American Ibsen.* Chicago: Nelson-Hall, 1978.

Planché, James Robinson. *The Jacobite: A Comic Drama in Two Acts.* New York: Douglas, 1848.

Poe, Edgar Allan. "The American Drama." In *Selections from the Critical Writings of Edgar Allan Poe,* ed. F. C. Prescott, 107–48. New York: Gordion Press, 1981.

———. "The Man of the Crowd." *The Works of Edgar Allan Poe,* 3:49–63. New York: P. F. Collier and Son, 1904.

———. "The Philosophy of Composition." In *Great Short Works of Edgar Allan Poe,* ed. G. R. Thomson, 528–41. New York: Harper and Row, 1970.

———. "The Spectacles." *The Works of Edgar Allan Poe,* vol. 3: *Tales of the Grotesque and Arabesque,* 315–56. 1894. Reprint. Freeport, N.Y.: Books for Libraries Press, 1971.

Popkin, Henry. "Pretender to the Drama." *Theatre Arts* 33 (December 1949): 32–35.

Porte, Joel. *In Respect to Egotism: Studies in American Romantic Writing.* Cambridge: Cambridge University Press, 1991.

Porter, Carolyn. "Call Me Ishmael, or How to Make Double-Talk Speak." In *New Essays on Moby-Dick,* ed. Richard Brodhead, 73–108. Cambridge: Cambridge University Press, 1986a.

———. "Reification and American Literature." In *Ideology and Classic American Literature,* ed. Sacvan Bercovitch and Myra Jehlen, 188–220. Cambridge: Cambridge University Press, 1986b.

A Practical Guide to Private Theatricals. New York: O. A. Roorbach, 1881.

Quinn, Arthur Hobson. *A History of the American Drama,* vols. 1–2. New York: Appleton-Century-Crofts, 1923, 1927.

———, ed. *Representative American Plays from 1767 to the Present Day.* 5th ed. New York: D. Appleton-Century, 1917.

Railton, Stephen. *Authorship and Audience: Literary Performance and the American Renaissance.* Princeton: Princeton University Press, 1991.

Rede, Leman T. *The Guide to the Stage: Containing Clear and Ample Instructions for Obtaining Theatrical Engagements.* Ed. Francis C. Wemyss. New York: Samuel French, 1861.

Reed, Walter L. *Meditations on the Hero: A Study of the Romantic Hero in Nineteenth-Century American Fiction.* New Haven: Yale University Press, 1974.

Rees, James. *The Life of Edwin Forrest with Reminiscences and Personal Recollections.* Philadephia: T. B. Peterson and Brothers, 1874.

Reynolds, David S. *Beneath the American Renaissance: The Subversive Imagination in the Age of Emerson and Melville.* Cambridge: Harvard University Press, 1989.

———. *Walt Whitman's America: A Cultural Biography.* New York: Alfred A. Knopf, 1995.

Roach, Joseph R. *Cities of the Dead: Circum-Atlantic Performance.* New York: Columbia University Press, 1996.

———. *The Player's Passion: Studies in the Science of Acting.* Newark: University of Delaware Press, 1985.

Robertson, John M. *Essays toward a Critical Method.* London: T. F. Unwin, 1889.

Robertson, Patricia. "*The Lesser Crew as Chorus in* Moby-Dick." *Publications of the Arkansas Philological Association* 7, no. 2 (Fall 1981): 61–82.

Rogin, Michael Paul. *Subversive Genealogy: The Politics and Art of Herman Melville.* New York: Alfred A. Knopf, 1983.

Rourke, Constance. *American Humor: A Study of the National Character.* New York: Harcourt, Brace, and Company, 1931.

Rousseau, Jean-Jacques. *Politics and the Arts: Letter to M. D'Alembert on the Theatre.* Trans. Allan Bloom. Ithaca: Cornell University Press, 1960.

Ryan, Mary. "The American Parade: Representations of the Nineteenth-Century Social Order." In *The New Cultural History,* ed. Lynn Hunt, 131–53. Berkeley: University of California Press, 1989.

Schechner, Richard. *Performance Theory.* New York: Routledge, 1988.

Schopenhauer, Arthur. "On Women." *Essays and Aphorisms,* 80–88. Trans. R. J. Hollingdale. London: Penguin Books, 1970.

Senelick, Laurence. *The Age and Stage of George L. Fox, 1825–1877.* Hanover, N.H.: University Press of New England, 1988.

Sennett, Richard. *The Fall of Public Man.* New York: W. W. Norton, 1974.

Shattuck, Charles H. *Shakespeare on the American Stage: From the Hallams to Edwin Booth.* Washington, D.C.: Folger Shakespeare Library, 1976.

———. *The Hamlet of Edwin Booth.* Urbana: University of Illinois Press, 1969.

Shawn, Ted. *Every little movement: a book about François Delsarte, the man and his philosophy, his science and applied aesthetics, the application of this science to the art of the dance, the influence of Delsarte on American dance.* Pittsfield, Mass.: Eagle Printing and Binding, 1954.

Sheridan, Richard Brinsley. *The School for Scandal and Other Plays.* Ed. Eric Rump. New York: Penguin Books, 1988.

Silverman, Kenneth. *Edgar A. Poe: A Mournful and Never-Ending Remembrance.* New York: HarperCollins, 1991.

Smith, Susan Harris. *American Drama: The Bastard Art.* Cambridge: Cambridge University Press, 1997.

Sorkin, David. *The Transformation of German Jewry, 1780–1840.* Oxford: Oxford University Press, 1987.

Stanton, Stephen S. "Introduction." Camille *and Other Plays.* New York: Hill and Wang, 1957.

Stanzel, Franz. *Narrative Situations in the Novel:* Tom Jones, Moby-Dick, The Ambassadors, Ulysses. Trans. James P. Pasack. Bloomington: Indiana University Press, 1971.

Staub, August W. "The Well-Made Failures of Henry James." *Southern Speech Journal* 27 (Winter 1961): 91–101.

Stern, Madeleine B. "An Early Alcott Sensation Story: *Marion Earle; or, Only an Actress!*" *Nineteenth-Century Literature* 40, no. 1 (June 1992): 91–98.

Stevenson, E. Irenaeus. "Music and Manners." *Harper's Weekly* 41, 5 June 1897, 570.

Stovall, Floyd. *The Foreground of* Leaves of Grass. Charlottesville: University Press of Virginia, 1974.

Strindberg, August. Preface to *Miss Julie*. Trans. Michael Meyer. London: Methuen, 1964.

Szondi, Peter. *Theory of the Modern Drama*. Ed. and trans. Michael Hays. Minneapolis: University of Minnesota Press, 1987.

Thoreau, Henry David. *The Writings of Henry David Thoreau: Journal,* vol. 1 (1837–46). Ed. Branford Torrey. New York: AMS Press, 1968.

Tocqueville, Alexis, de. *Democracy in America*. New York: Vintage Classics, 1990.

Traubel, Horace. *With Walt Whitman in Camden,* vols. 1, 2, 3, and 5. Boston: Small, Maynard and Company, 1906.

Turner, Victor. *Dramas, Fields, and Metaphors: Symbolic Action in Human Society*. Ithaca: Cornell University Press, 1974.

———. *Process, Performance, and Pilgrimage: A Study in Comparative Symbology*. New Delhi: Concept, 1979.

Twain, Mark. *The Adventures of Huckleberry Finn*. Ed. John Seelye. London: Penguin Books, 1985.

———. *Contributions to the Galaxy, 1868–1871*. Ed. Bruce R. McElderry Jr. Gainesville, Florida: Scholars' Facsimiles and Reprints, 1961.

Twain, Mark, and Bret Harte. *The Californian: Sketches of the Sixties*. San Francisco: John Howell, 1926.

Valency, Maurice. *The Flower and the Castle: An Introduction to Modern Drama*. New York: Schocken Books, 1982.

Waskow, Howard J. *Whitman's Explorations in Form*. Chicago: University of Chicago Press, 1966.

Watt, Ian. *The Rise of the Novel: Studies in Defoe, Richardson and Fielding*. Berkeley: University of California Press, 1957.

Wells, H. G. *Experiment in Autobiography*. New York: Macmillan, 1934.

Whitman, Walt. *Complete Poetry and Collected Prose*. New York: Library of America, 1982.

———. *The Complete Prose Works of Walt Whitman,* vol. 2. New York: G. P. Putnam's Sons, 1902.

———. *The Complete Writings of Walt Whitman,* vols. 2 and 7. New York: Knickerbocker Press, 1902.

———. *The Gathering of the Forces: Editorials, Essays, Literary and Dramatic Reviews and other material written by Walt Whitman as Editor of* The Brooklyn Daily Eagle *in*

1846 and 1847, vol. 2. Ed. Cleveland Rogers and John Black. New York: Knickerbocker Press, 1920.

———. *The Uncollected Poetry and Prose of Walt Whitman,* vols. 1–2. Ed. Emory Holloway. Gloucester, Mass.: Peter Smith, 1972.

———. *Walt Whitman and the Civil War: A Collection of Original Articles and Manuscripts.* Ed. Charles I. Glicksberg. New York: A. S. Barnes and Company, 1963.

———. *Walt Whitman of the New York* Aurora: *Editor at Twenty-Two.* Ed. Joseph Jay Rubin and Charles H. Brown. State College, Pa.: Bald Eagle Press, 1950.

———. *Walt Whitman's Workshop: A Collection of Unpublished Manuscripts.* Ed. Clifton Joseph Furness. Cambridge: Harvard University Press, 1928.

Wills, Garry. *Lincoln at Gettysburg: The Words That Remade America.* New York: Simon and Schuster, 1992.

Wilson, Garff B. *Three Hundred Years of American Drama and Theatre: From* Ye Bear and Ye Cubb *to* Hair. Englewood Cliffs, N.J.: Prentice-Hall, 1973.

Winter, William. *Life and Art of Edwin Booth.* 1893. Reprint. New York: Macmillan, 1894.

Witherspoon, John. *A Serious Enquiry into the Nature and Effects of the Stage: And a Letter Respecting Play Actors.* Glasgow: n.p., 1757.

Woodress, James, ed. *Critical Essays on Walt Whitman.* Boston: G. K. Hall, 1983.

Zweig, Paul. *Walt Whitman: The Making of the Poet.* New York: Basic Books, 1984.

Index

Library of Congress Cataloging-in-Publication Data

Ackerman, Alan L. (Alan Louis)

The portable theater : American literature & the nineteenth-century stage / Alan L. Ackerman, Jr.

p. cm.

Includes bibliographical references and index.

ISBN 0-8018-6161-6 (acid-free paper)

1. American literature—19th century—History and criticism. 2. Theater—United States—History—19th century. I. Title.

PS201.A28 1999

810.9′357—dc21

99-19382

CIP